PENGUIN BOOKS

Fighting with the Enemy

Susan Jacobs was born in Auckland, New Zealand. She has strong ties with Italy where she spent nine years studying Italian and teaching English in rural Umbria and Tuscany during the 1970s and 80s. Susan has a PhD in Italian from the University of Auckland, where she tutored part-time for many years. Currently she is Research Manager at the Auckland Institute of Studies at St Helens, and lives in Auckland with her partner and four daughters. This is her first book.

Fighting
WITH THE ENEMY

New Zealand POWs and the Italian Resistance

Susan Jacobs

PENGUIN BOOKS

PENGUIN BOOKS
Published by the Penguin Group
Penguin Books (NZ) Ltd, cnr Airborne and Rosedale Roads, Albany,
Auckland 1310, New Zealand
Penguin Books Ltd, 80 Strand, London, WC2R 0RL, England
Penguin Group (USA) Inc., 375 Hudson Street, New York, NY 10014, United States
Penguin Books Australia Ltd, 250 Camberwell Road, Camberwell,
Victoria 3124, Australia
Penguin Books Canada Ltd, 10 Alcorn Avenue, Toronto, Ontario,
Canada M4V 3B2
Penguin Books (South Africa) (Pty) Ltd, 24 Sturdee Avenue, Rosebank,
Johannesburg 2196, South Africa
Penguin Books India (P) Ltd, 11, Community Centre, Panchsheel Park,
New Delhi 110 017, India
Penguin Books Ltd, Registered Offices: 80 Strand, London, WC2R 0RL, England

First published by Penguin Books (NZ) Ltd, 2003
1 3 5 7 9 10 8 6 4 2

Designed by Mary Egan
Typeset by Egan-Reid Ltd, Auckland
Editorial services by Michael Gifkins & Associates
Printed in Australia by McPherson's Printing Group

ISBN 0 14 301862 0

A catalogue record for this book is available from the
National Library of New Zealand.
www.penguin.co.nz

Contents

*For all the New Zealand escapers
and the Italians who helped them*

*And per i nonni – grandfathers, the late Major Mario Diana,
Italian Royal Army, and Bombardier Brian Jacobs,
Second New Zealand Division*

Was it their background of long, wind-swept beaches, tumbling summer surf, great humped hills, pohutukawa-fringed bays, and plenty of breathing space even in the cities? Was it a generation of Plunket-raised babies? Was it the love of sport, with its widespread participation in rough and tumble games? What made all these commonplace types, for the most part stocky, unimaginative fellows, behave in this uncommon way?

Geoffrey Webster, 'Victory in Europe',
Auckland Star, May 9 1945, p. 9.

Introduction

May 2001. As I inched my way round the mossy cliff side clutching on to clumps of tough tussock and trying not to look down, I wondered how on earth I had found myself in this predicament. I was afraid of heights, had never abseiled in my life and was so scared my heart was nearly jumping out of my chest. I cursed Jack, who was the reason for my being there, but even as I did so, I chuckled at the thought of telling him how I had risked life and limb on his behalf.

I was on a precarious journey to a cave tucked into the face of a mountainous cliff about 800 metres above the Po Valley in the Friuli region of north-eastern Italy, close to the Yugoslav border. It was here that Jack Lang, together with fellow New Zealander Bob Smith and an American airman, Colonel Ross Greening, had lived for three months during the bitterly cold winter of early 1944. They were escaped prisoners-of-war who, assisted by Italian civilians and partisans, had been evading recapture by the Germans and had been directed to the cave by locals from the surrounding villages of Reant, Valle and Masarolis.

Jack had said the 'path' to the cave was 'a bit steep' and needed to be arrived at 'on foot', so I was prepared for some scrambling and climbing. But when my Italian collaborator produced several pairs of mountain boots, gloves, a rope and a pickaxe, the extent of Jack's laconic Kiwi understatement hit home. Cheerfully telling me to find a pair of boots I could fit, Franco started searching for a tree strong enough to tie the rope to.

I suggested that he go alone or that my 15-year-old daughter take my place, but Franco was adamant. 'How could you go back to New Zealand and tell Jack you didn't get to see his cave?'

So leaving my daughter with 82-year-old Anselmo, who had guided us to the spot by the side of the dusty road, I apprehensively set out down and then around the steep incline. I was harnessed to the rope which Franco, a 62-year-old retired architect and skilled mountaineer, would tie to successive trees. Flitting back and forth with the dexterity of a mountain goat, he tested slender saplings, which sprouted out at right angles, and assured me of their reliability. As I slid and crawled and grabbed, I wondered how Jack, admittedly much younger than me at the time, had managed to do this several times a day.

When I had lived in villages in the Umbrian and Tuscan countryside during the 1970s and 80s, there had been few acknowledged connections between Italy and New Zealand. Yet thousands of men of my father's generation had fought in the Italian campaign from September 1943 until May 1945. I knew too that my uncle, like many others, had been a prisoner-of-war for four years, some of that time spent in camps in Italy. But I could not equate my own experience of living in ancient stone cottages with few amenities, speaking only Italian, and reinventing my Kiwi self-image with the faded photos of young New Zealand men in battledress against an Italian rural backdrop.

Most New Zealand returned servicemen never talked much about their experiences anyway, and nothing was said to question the common perception that the Italian war effort was pitiful, and the Italian soldier or 'Eyetie' worthless in battle. Italy, fighting on the side of Germany from 1940 to 1943, was perceived to have changed sides when it looked as if they were losing. It was a surprise, therefore, to arrive in Italy in the summer of 1974 to find that the 'Resistance' was a constant point of reference and an icon of national identity and pride. I had heard of the French Resistance, but the existence, let alone the exalted status, of an Italian Resistance was completely ignored. This invisibility puzzled me. I soon heard of the *partigiani*, the partisan bands fighting the Germans in mountains and forests the length and breadth of the country and paving the way for Allied troops in their arduous push up the peninsula. I learned too of the bitter battles fought between Italian Fascists loyal to Mussolini and anti-Fascist partisans, which had left lacerating wounds, still unhealed today, on the Italian psyche.

But it was years later before I realised that thousands of escaped Allied prisoners-of-war, among whom were approximately 450 New

Zealanders, had been at large in the Italian countryside sharing the same vicissitudes, deprivations and tragedies as the Italian people. Some of them joined partisan brigades carrying out dangerous and under-resourced operations against the Germans. Hunted, fearful, often hungry and desperate to remain free, these men lived on their wits and determination, adapting to an unfamiliar terrain and the language and culture of a people who, until very recently, had been 'the enemy'.

Without the assistance of huge numbers of rural Italians who fed, sheltered and clothed them at the risk of their own lives, these men would not have survived. Through this shared experience, friendships were formed between New Zealanders and members of Italian families that have continued among their descendants to this day.

I set out to track down the veterans who had lived alongside the civilians and partisans in those dramatic months, inspired to bring together individual experiences played out against one of the most brutal and desperate periods in Italy's chequered history. I wanted to find out why so many people concealed and helped the escapers when food was scarce and their own lives were at risk. And I wanted to discover how these young, rugged colonial boys saw the Italian people and the tumultuous political events they were caught up in.

I didn't have far to look. A swathe of books and unpublished manuscripts exist bearing witness to the incredible, often heart-rending adventures of these young men from a country 20,000 kilometres away that most Italians at the time had never heard of. Although many veterans are no longer alive, sons and daughters have been eager for their stories to be known. With those men still living and now in their eighties, I shared many absorbing hours as we recalled Italian phrases and rhymes and compared notes on everything from harvesting the grapes to eating horse meat. Above all, I listened to their stories of remarkable resilience, courage and gratitude, stories that several men had not revealed before because they sounded too fantastic to be true.

I knew they were real because I knew what my ex-husband, a small child in Italy at the time, and his mother had witnessed. Also, by this time I had immersed myself in history books, literature and films on the Italian Resistance. But in order to form a more comprehensive picture,

I needed to return to Italy to discover how the Italians remembered the New Zealanders in their midst. I headed for the Veneto and Friuli regions where the majority of New Zealanders had been interned at Campo 57 at Gruppignano near the town of Udine in Friuli. From there, most of the men who would successfully escape had been sent to satellite working camps on farms dotted throughout the countryside.

Their stories began on 8 September 1943 when Italy, turning her back on her Axis partner, Germany, signed the Armistice and surrendered to the Allies. In the chaotic aftermath, the Italian Army collapsed and guards fled the prison camps. More than half the 80,000 prisoners-of-war managed to escape, despite being instructed to stay put and await their imminent release by the Allies. However, within days of the Armistice the Germans had poured more troops into central and northern Italy. The majority of prisoners were recaptured and sent to prison camps in Germany. The Allied advance up the peninsula was to take twenty months before Italy's liberation in May 1945.

Often prisoners-of-war were thought to have 'sat out' the war or to have had a lesser time of it than those fighting with the Eighth Army in the Italian Campaign. But most had known bitter fighting, the humiliation of capture, the unnerving ennui of prison life, and for those who escaped, the heady mix of fear and excitement. The demands made on them were diverse, complex, and required survival skills necessary to any battlefield.

My sources then are the voices of those men who were there 'behind the lines' and the Italian men and women who encountered them. Those voices heard through interviews, memoirs, diaries and letters are in turn sombre, humorous, outraged and emotional. They are always vivid and moving. They capture the authenticity of a time that stands out like a beacon at the end of their lives and connects the peoples of two countries, and the tragedy, the absurdity and the unquenchable humanity lurking in any war.

I arrived at my destination, a dark oblong slit that yawned back into a scarcely discernible dusty cavern. It was hard to believe that here, from the side of a cliff, steps had led down into a cosy domestic living space complete with bed, tables and chairs. I sat still for a while and looked out at the breathtaking sweep of valley below. Some flowering weeds were growing randomly at the mouth of the cave. Before embarking on my journey back up the cliff, I picked one to smuggle back to New Zealand.

For Jack.

CHAPTER ONE

Capture

1 May 1945. At 10 a.m. the trucks finally pass by on the road towards Trieste after a hold-up. Everybody admires the handsome New Zealand troops that Fascist propaganda had made out to be true and proper cannibals. The tanks proceed close by in an ordered way; they are full of handsome young men, healthy, robust and well-cared for; most of them are blond, and they smile, wave and joke with the cheering crowd.[1]

1942. The two truckloads of New Zealand prisoners from the 22nd Battalion captured on 15 July at Ruweisat Ridge south of El Alamein were still fairly frisky. The rigours of hunger and dysentery of the holding camp in Benghazi, wryly named 'The Palms', were yet to come. When they realised that their Italian captors had the honour of being visited by none other than Mussolini and that the man strutting in front of them, surrounded by half a dozen of his blackshirts, was indeed the revered *Duce*, all hell broke loose. Shouts of 'Go back to your mistress, you pot-bellied bastard!' rent the air. The Kiwis yelled and jeered and whistled to such an extent that Mussolini was visibly angry. His face went red and turning round, he reached for his gun from his guards and pointed it at the prisoners.[2]

This incident was recorded by Mussolini's son-in-law and Minister of Foreign Affairs, Count Galeazzo Ciano, in his famous wartime diary. In an entry of 21 July 1942, he reported that Mussolini's encounter with the New Zealanders made him feel the need for protection. 'He told me that he had found groups of fierce-looking New Zealand prisoners who were so far from reassuring that he kept his gun close at hand.' The original Italian version uses the term *facce patibolari* to describe the men, which literally means 'gallows faces', and can be translated as 'delinquents'.[3] Naturally, the Kiwis were chuffed that despite the indignity of being unarmed and under guard, they could still infuriate and unnerve the infamous dictator.

Perhaps it was this impression of wild, bayonet-wielding, colonial boys, added to a skewed view of Maori[4] that led to the propaganda posters appearing throughout Italy shortly afterwards. They depicted the New Zealanders as marauding primitives who ate babies and raped women. Sporting grossly exaggerated features and contorted facial expressions, the images were blatantly designed to terrorise the population and fuel the ugly racism underlying Fascist dogma. But Mussolini would have been even more apoplectic if he had known that, just over a year later, a handful of those belligerent New Zealand prisoners would be at large in Italy fighting against him and his Fascist system, liaising with and protected by thousands of ordinary Italians.

At this stage, Mussolini was in North Africa to spur his troops on and gloat over this latest crop of prisoners paraded before him, hoping that it was one step further towards bringing the war to a victorious close. Certainly it was not looking good for the Allies. Fought on a vast sweep of desert covering some 2400 kilometres from Tripoli in north-western Africa to Cairo in the east, the desert war was a bloody tussle that swung back and forth between the two forces. But the German juggernauts aided by their Italian sidekicks were winning major battles and capturing Allied prisoners in unprecedented numbers. Thousands of New Zealanders along with British, Australian, Canadian, South African and

Indian troops who made up the Eighth Army had already been taken in disastrous campaigns in Greece and Crete.

Many of the soldiers who were to end up prisoners in Italy were captured in the North African Desert in the battles of Sidi Rezegh in Libya in November 1941 and Ruweisat Ridge in July 1942. Those battles against the formidable armies of the legendary German Commander, Field Marshal Rommel, and his Afrika Korps were lost before they began. Most men expressed anger about the disorganisation of their commanders, poor equipment, the lack of reinforcements and being sent off virtually unarmed as cannon fodder, to be picked off like flies by the German Panzer Division tanks lying in wait for them. In the terrifying confusion as they charged wielding only bayonets or rifles against these tanks, they ran as much danger of being felled by shrapnel from their own mortar fire. Men taken prisoner were far more likely to be killed by their own side than by the enemy. Lucky to have survived the battlefield against appalling odds, they were then bombed by Allied planes as they were being taken as prisoners in trucks to Benghazi. Others did not survive the British submarine torpedoing of ships transporting them packed in stifling holds to Italy. Veterans have pored over military accounts of the battles where so many comrades died and have come to the conclusion that they were sent to fight on a virtual suicide mission.

New Zealand, the furthest colonial outpost of the British Empire, was renowned for its fine soldiers who distinguished themselves in the First World War. Although those who survived the trenches talked little of their experiences, these were not seen in terms of a military disaster. Even when an attack failed, as at Gallipoli, the New Zealand troops were always on the offensive and any evacuation of troops was successful. Their sons grew up through the Depression years resourceful, hardy and down-to-earth. New Zealand was an outdoors, sports-loving nation and many of its young men had worked on farms. When war was declared they hardly thought twice and large numbers eagerly volunteered. Patriotism and a desire to support England were also common motives. This was the generation of New Zealanders that called England 'Home', even if they had never set foot on her shores, who believed in the ties of Empire and the adage that 'where England goes, so go we'.

War, the ultimate 'boys' own' adventure, was the draw card but it masked a painful reality. Whether it was adventure, patriotism, boredom, an exploration of the meaning of pacifism or the lemming instinct of doing what everybody else did, the young Kiwis left in the expectation that they would be involved in action. They were confident that those in positions of high command orchestrating the battles would know what they were doing. That they should face years of imprisonment in droves due to incompetence was as unthinkable and absurd as the notion that New Zealanders were a bunch of cannibals.

The first battle in North Africa to yield a significant number of prisoners was at Sidi Rezegh in Libya.[5] Alarmingly, the New Zealanders found themselves being fired on by their own tanks.

'The afternoon was taken up dodging shellfire and attending to the wounded that were being brought in for medical attention. Three of our tanks came up shooting, and a number of our wounded were again injured. I ran across the ground and clambered up on to the last tank and banged on the turret and shouted that these were our own men. The officer popped out his head and then got in touch with the other tanks and they stopped firing. He said they had been given this map reference and told to attack it.'[6]

'The first action I was involved in made me aware that we were a big blundering mass of men, and that any idea I had that attacks were choreographed with skill was mistaken.'[7]

They developed acronyms to categorise the blunders: SABU, a self-adjusting balls-up and GAFU, a general army fuck-up. The capture of men of the 22nd Battalion at Ruweisat Ridge on 15 July 1942 belonged in the latter category.

'My battalion was meant to be providing rear support for the main attack. We had a company in reserve on our left and right. The password was Speights.[8] We went on through the night with gunfire ahead of us and a machine-gun on the right . . . We found ourselves in the middle of a contest between our own solitary anti-tank gun and the advancing tanks. They bowled the anti-tank gun out, the tanks came up and we were all taken prisoner.'[9]

A week later on 22 July it was the turn of the 24th Battalion at El Mreir.

'At daybreak the German Panzer Division unknown by our intelligence service, or to us, to be present, moved in towards us from the Escarpment above and without any opposition gave us a real plastering. Our tanks never turned up and I still believe to this day that there was no definite arrangement made for them to be there – just a request. That to me was a wanton waste of valuable men's lives.'[10]

'We were just run over. It was all the result of a misunderstanding (I suppose it's a polite way of putting it), a lot of the guys put it in a cruder way. The British were the attack regiment that was supposed to support us; according to the story they never got their orders and I think this is one of the things that prompted Freyberg into turning one of our brigades into an armoured brigade.'[11]

'For you the war is over' was the common refrain from their German captors. Being taken prisoner meant not only giving up one's freedom, but being relieved of personal belongings that expressed individuality and a tenuous connection with one's life before capture. It was a mark of pride as well as a small act of resistance to succeed in hiding and keeping such a treasured possession as a wristwatch.

Being captured was a traumatic experience for many of the men who later escaped. A sense of utter dismay and failure was one immediate reaction.

'Prisoner! Useless . . . and without having done any worthwhile thing . . . Not one bloody thing! We had followed orders, done what we were told and finished up in this ungodly shambles! Handed over on a plate!'[12]

The realities of war were compared inevitably with some of the previously held myths about honour and glory. Men were hungry, thirsty, dirty and sick at heart. They would offer their watches in return for a cup of water. Angry and humiliated, most were totally unprepared for even the notion of being taken prisoner. Relatively few soldiers in the First

World War had experienced capture.[13] Military training prepared men for combat rather than equipping them for the physical and psychological consequences of sudden, enforced inertia.

Gradually the lack of food and water and the exposure to extremes of heat and cold took its toll, and adjustment to their new circumstances became a necessary survival tool. The soldiers were herded into trucks with standing room only and transported for several days to a camp some kilometres south of Benghazi. Unfortunately, the convoy of Italian diesel trucks and trailers were mistaken for enemy vehicles and were targeted by Allied bomber planes. 'We lost a lot of blokes from the Air Force. They wiped out the rest of the 25th Battalion.'[14]

The Palms was a bleak compound at Benghazi about 50 metres wide and 350 metres long and earned its ironically elegant name through a number of tall date palms, which in the summer provided welcome shade, if you could get under them. It was far from a hotel though. The men had to sleep in the open on the hard rocky ground that was often damp because of the proximity of an oasis. The daily food ration was a piece of bread the size of a bun and a cup of black coffee made from burned wheat. Overcrowded conditions combined with inadequate food and sanitation brought on widespread dysentery. An open pit straddled by a long pole to perch on served as the latrine. One unfortunate prisoner who lost his balance and fell in had to be scrubbed to his bare skin and wait until his scanty clothing was cleaned and dried again. Two would-be escapers who attempted to slip out under the chassis of an Italian supply truck were punished by being tied to the gate-posts at the camp entrance with a pail of water placed tantalisingly close. Hunger began to erase self-respect and 'civilised' behaviour. A prisoner would keep his bread as long as he could in order to savour the pleasurable anticipation of eating it. If he managed an hour he could then slowly consume it, appreciating each tiny morsel. If he discovered his mate had been able to hang on longer than him and still hadn't eaten it, he would feel real hatred for him. Then would come the self-remonstrance, the struggle to regain some semblance of sane behaviour.[15] In December the cold breezes blowing off the sea chilled the windswept open spaces further, and the men huddled together for what little warmth they could muster. 'We slept on the concrete floor of a garage for many nights without anything over or under us, with the roller door right up to let a nice little gale blow over us in case it got too warm! It was winter of course.'[16]

After approximately two weeks holed up in The Palms the men were sent by ship to Italy. This proved to be another test of survival for those who had emerged intact from battle and relatively unscathed from the deprivations of The Palms. Several of the men who were to later escape in Italy ended up on two ill-fated boats, the *Jantzen* and the *Nino Bixio*, which were torpedoed by British submarines. When the *Jantzen*, an 8000-ton cargo ship with over 2000 prisoners-of-war crammed into three holds, was torpedoed three kilometres off the Greek coast on a grey December afternoon in 1941, the mayhem was indescribable. The first hold was completely destroyed in the explosion and all the men trapped in it died. Only five men in the second hold walked out of it alive. One had elected to perch on a platform jutting out about six metres below the opening, rather than descend the ladder to the murky bowels below. This saved his life, as he was able to scramble to the top before the ladders collapsed. The following chilling account reveals the depths of the horror that awaited the men who staggered, dazed and in shock, on to the deck.

'Struck in the starboard bow, the *Jantzen* lifted her stern as the forward hold filled. Many bodies, both dead and living, with the latter helpless and struggling, were sucked into the threshing propellers, where they were hacked to pieces and flung high into the air. A raft crammed with men was seen to go through that terrible mincer. The explosion had torn out the hatches of the first hold, blasting them and the men that lay on them with terrible force. Bodies and parts of bodies were strewn on the deck and in the shallow scuppers. One ghastly corpse hung entangled in the rigging over the bulwarks. A severed head lay between some piled hatches. Booms and rigging, planks and bent iron, and huge uprooted girders crushed and mingled with the remains of men. But to those who knew the carnage of battle, one thing was shocking – there were dismembered bodies, battered limbs and scalped heads, yet there was no blood. It was unearthly.'[17]

Over 600 men died. The Italian captain and senior officers had escaped in a lifeboat that a New Zealander had also managed to haul himself on to by diving overboard and fighting his way aboard.

On the *Jantzen* a German ship's engineer had taken charge and manoeuvred the crippled, heaving ship towards land. The ship had been hugging the Greek coast so closely that the rocky shore was about 40 metres away. But drowning was a distinct possibility as it was slowly sinking and heavy seas were crashing over the deck. Anxious to escape this fate, men slid down a rope shuttled to the ship from rocks on the shore, but the swaying and bucking of the ship caused the rope to tighten and slacken and many men were thrown into the angry black waters. Some dropped from sheer exhaustion and were dashed on the rocks. The lucky ones then had to face a night at the mercy of the elements. 'You couldn't believe the noise of the ship breaking up all night – bang bang. You never slept a wink of course, and the waves were coming over all night, all night, and we wandered around there seeing if we could find a feed. We found some apples and a bottle of grog and some sugar.'[18]

Aboard the *Nino Bixio* conditions were appalling. There were no toilet facilities in the holds, resulting in a putrid stench. Most of the men, who were suffering from dysentery, used their tin hats as receptacles and emptied the contents into oil drums, which were soon overflowing.[19] On 17 August 1942 at about 4.30 p.m. and just two days out from Benghazi, the torpedoes struck. One man, thrown into the air and thumped down again by the blast, could hear nothing except the sound of screaming from men trapped below in the hold. Moments before, another had refused his friend's offer to change places and thus be able to stretch out his legs. Thrown to his feet, he looked down at half a dozen men lying dead around him. Among them lay his friend, a steel hatch cover embedded in his forehead. There was chaos and horror on deck and in the sea with 'entrails on rigging and rails, pieces of bodies splattered and squashed against winches and other obstructions, the ship listing, heads bobbing in the sea all around, men throwing hatch covers into the water as rafts for themselves but hitting those already in the sea, men jumping overboard, Italian guards getting a lifeboat away which swamped . . .'[20]

The ship miraculously stayed afloat. An accompanying destroyer towed them to Navarino in southern Greece where they buried their dead and the wounded were taken to hospital. From there they journeyed to Patras and were handed over to the Germans. They balked at the short-back-and-sides haircuts they were given but it kept the lice at bay. Finally they embarked for Italy in a much smaller ship than the *Nino Bixio*, disconcertingly piled into a hold below deck at the stern of the boat.

These men finally arrived at the port of Bari on the south-east coast of Italy, where they were interned in a transit camp. It was here that they first reported sighting the posters representing the New Zealanders as cannibals. Italians jeered at the prisoners as they were marched through the streets in a show of propaganda before being herded to waiting trucks. One prisoner was humiliated when an Italian woman spat at him, a gob of spittle landing squarely in his face. But he was more infuriated he could not retaliate.[21]

Gaunt and suffering from amoebic dysentery, several men were hospitalised at Caserta. A team of nuns staffed the hospital and some charges dutifully became Roman Catholics during their stay, albeit temporarily. 'It was noticeable that when a rosary was hanging above one's bed, an extra large loaf or a double ladle of rice was given to the patient!' The most immediate problem for all patients was the lack of toilet paper but, already masters of improvisation, they used the wood wool packing from Red Cross parcels and old hospital patient charts.[22]

Many were in poor shape even when they had not been torpedoed. The worst of them were kept in a camp outside Bari for a few days while they were deloused and cleaned up. The fitter prisoners tried to help this pitiful new lot as much as they could.

'They were a mess. We were a mess but they were worse.'[23] A scheme was devised where the Kiwis in the camp would 'adopt' a Kiwi from this new bunch and take care of them.

Just about all the men had a poor opinion of Italians, both as soldiers and as prison guards. Their perceived lack of fighting skills and penchant for exaggerated elegance in military attire were derided by the down-to-earth New Zealanders. On board the torpedoed ships the instinctive attempts of the Italian crew to save their own skins did not endear them to their captives. At their worst, they were considered cowardly and cruel, at their best, excitable buffoons.

The Kiwis were not alone in their opinion. Prisoners recall the unconcealed contempt Germans showed for the Italians as fighters and as a race. Some Germans even apologised when they handed them over to the Italians. Both New Zealanders and Germans admired the other's soldiering skills. German captors often told their New Zealand prisoners that they should be fighting on their side against the common enemy – the Soviet Union. They were convinced that once this war was won, nations like New Zealand would unite under their German victors to defeat Bolshevism.

That Italy's entry into the war on the side of Germany in 1940 seemed unnatural was well known by the Fascist hierarchy. Two months before Mussolini signed the Pact of Steel with Hitler, cementing the Axis alliance in May 1939, Ciano had written, 'The *Duce* agrees it is now impossible to present to the Italian people the idea of an alliance with Germany. Even the stones would cry out against it.'[24] Anti-German sentiments were rife. The Austro-Hungarian Empire had a long history of authoritarian occupation of territory in north-eastern Italy; the battle of Caporetto in 1917 where the Italians had defeated the hated Germans was still fresh in collective memory and a source of national pride. Wrote a sombre Ciano, 'The peasants go into the Army cursing those damned Germans.'[25] Many Italian troops the New Zealanders encountered were indeed peasants. Little more than teenagers, they were impoverished, untrained, uneducated, ill-equipped and frightened. Most came from backwater villages and had been press-ganged into the army.

Predictably, the German-Italian alliance was an uneasy and often downright hostile one. Ciano noted how the army was 'anti-Rommel', adding that Mussolini, during his visit, bristled at being snubbed by German military personnel.[26] On the other hand, Italians had strong historical affiliations with the British who had supported their Risorgimento in 1861[27] and alongside whom they had fought in the First World War. It was odd to be against them.

The Italian reluctance for fighting was not only due to being on the wrong side. Italy had been constantly at war since December 1934. They had fought in Ethiopia during Mussolini's empire-building phase (Mussolini until then had been well regarded in England's eyes)[28] and in the Spanish Civil War where Italians fought on both sides. The Fascist government had sent army units to assist Franco's Falangist soldiers, while outlawed Italian anti-Fascists, specifically Communists and Socialists, fought against them in the International Brigade alongside the Spanish loyalists. After becoming an Axis partner with Germany in 1939, Italy had attacked Albania, invaded Greece, and had subsequently declared war on France and Great Britain in 1940, and on the Soviet Union and the United States in 1941. The military was ill-equipped, tired and unprepared.

Many New Zealanders, on the other hand, felt that they lived in God's own country. They had a strong sense of identity as rugged colonial boys and few places were considered better than New Zealand. Their geographical isolation often manifested itself in feelings of unsophisticated superiority to all those different peoples known as wogs, wops and dagoes who did not measure up to a narrow model of manliness epitomised by men of the British Commonwealth of nations and even their German foes. Seen as excitable, emotional and untrustworthy, the Italians belonged firmly in this inferior category. It was humiliating to be helpless in the hands of such an enemy, but they had no choice.

CHAPTER TWO

Prisoners-of-war in Italy

You have only recently become prisoners. We have been prisoners of Mussolini's Fascists for twenty years.[1]

The prisoners who arrived in the Italian ports of Bari, Brindisi, Naples and Taranto spent time in transit camps in the south before being sent on to more permanent camps in northern Italy. After the parched, dust-swept deserts of North Africa, the green hills, cultivated fields and lush vegetation were a welcome sight for the weary, often unwell men.

There were roughly seventy prison camps and ten military hospitals scattered throughout Italy.[2] Known in Italian as *campi di concentramento*, they were established in accordance with the Geneva Convention of 1929 regarding the treatment of prisoners-of-war, and should not be confused with the infamous Nazi concentration camps. Most camps were overcrowded due to the unprecedented number of prisoners flooding into Italy, 80,000 in all, but, although by no means comfortable, they were a huge improvement on the conditions experienced in North Africa.

By March 1943 the great majority of New Zealanders, some 1800, together with about 2000 Australians, were imprisoned in Camp 57 at Gruppignano situated on a vast stretch of plain near the town of Udine, in the north-eastern Friuli region close to the Yugoslav border. The snow-capped Dolomites, on some days barely visible, loomed in the distance. This immense camp contained rows of wooden barracks holding two-tiered wooden bunks, administration buildings, a recreation compound and a parade ground. An impenetrable, tangled barbed-wire fence five metres high surrounded it, while sentries in guard boxes manned each corner. Captain Calcaterra, the camp commander, liked to boast that no one had succeeded in escaping from his camp. Although several hardy prisoners tried to prove him wrong, escape attempts were foiled. One October night in 1942, nineteen Australians and New Zealanders had managed to escape through a 50-metre tunnel dug over some months through the floor of their hut, but they were recaptured within five days and harshly punished.[3]

Calcaterra was a stickler for discipline of the more irritating sort. There was talk that he had been hand-picked to deal with the unruly antipodean colonial boys flooding the prison camps. Breaches of iron rules such as saluting an Italian officer, standing to attention during the hoisting and raising of the Italian flag, or not talking during a check parade ensured that the solitary confinement cells were rarely empty.[4] Impeccably attired in his *carabiniere* uniform adorned with rows of gleaming medals, he was 'a perfect pompous clone of Mussolini';[5] for others he was straight out of a Gilbert and Sullivan opera.

But for most of the prisoners the real enemies were hunger and monotony. Food consisted of a small roll of bread, a bowl of skilly (a watery soup with a few greens), and an occasional piece of horse meat. They became scavengers, combing the cookhouse and picking up pieces of pumpkin and squash from the garden. Whereas in Egypt the conversation had revolved round the subject of women, by now it was food that occupied their talk, minds and fantasies. The desire for cigarettes could be stronger than that for food and drink. When Italians deliberately dropped their cigarette butts in puddles, prisoners raced to retrieve them.[6]

The food shortages and bleak prison fare were made bearable by the arrival of Red Cross food parcels with their cans of condensed milk, tea, jam, chocolate and cigarettes. Most prisoners believe they would not have survived without them. There was always some food that tasted better hot. At Campo 59 at Servigliano, 'The cooking was done on empty tins jammed together to make some form of stove. The only place these culinary arts could be practised was in the toilets which consisted of a 30 foot-long concrete floor, with about ten 8 inch-wide holes set at regular intervals along the floor.'[7] This practice was a punishable offence but before a guard came along there was usually time to kick the fire and the tin down one of the holes. As a result there were frequent blockages. The parcels also gave a boost to the already flourishing trading business. 'We were able to manipulate and even blackmail some of the guards there because of their fear of being sent to the Russian Front. When we did get Red Cross parcels, we traded cigarettes for bits of radio. Some of the men built radio sets.'[8]

The guards were just as badly off as the prisoners and often treated with disdain by their officers. Instead of socks the guards were issued with large squares of loose white material that they wrapped, then tied, round their feet. Scheduled for a hot shower, they were marched to the bathhouse under their own armed guard. The prisoners enjoyed creating a stir at the guards' expense. 'There were identical twin brothers in the guards at Servigliano. We named them the Rea brothers – Dia and Gonna. One day one of the POW cooks was having them on by tapping on the floor then making a great show of innocence. This immediately aroused the guards' suspicions and they straight away brought pick axes and broke up a section of the cookhouse floor which of course was concrete, much to the amusement of 2000 POWs.'[9]

At Gruppignano, the Catholic Church tried to alleviate the situation by sending envoys with gifts at Christmas and on other festive occasions. Their efforts were met with a mixed reception. 'They brought piano accordions and books and noticed we didn't seem to be very happy. That's very nice, we said, but we can't eat piano accordions and books. It's food we actually want!'[10] A prisoner recollected the surprise of an officer at the fact that all the men, including subaltern ranks, wanted writing paper. Many Italians could not read or write.

To keep minds occupied there was a small library. Art, music and drama groups flourished and crafts such as knitting, crocheting and woodcarving could be learned. A series of lectures was held on any subject a prisoner felt he could hold a discourse on for the best part of an hour. Courses in accountancy, agriculture and languages had the greatest following among the New Zealanders. With the welcome arrival of sports materials provided by the World Alliance of YMCAs, the vast sweep of ground could be used for cricket, baseball, soccer and rugby games and national teams were quickly set up.[11] With the idea of escape never far from their minds, some of the men decided to study Italian and began poring over books, listening carefully to the constant propaganda broadcasts over the loudspeakers, and haltingly practising on each other.

Initially reluctant to help the Italian war effort by joining a satellite work camp, although provision was made for this under the Geneva Convention, fifty Kiwis moved out of Camp 57 to go to a work camp at Torviscosa, Camp PG107. They caught the train from the nearby town of Cividale, and arrived at the station of San Stino di Livenza, a town in the plains north of Venice. It was a beautiful, golden spring afternoon and the men were in high spirits as they surveyed the green, intensely cultivated countryside blazing with colourful wild flowers. 'There were flat-top horse-drawn wagons to meet us. We piled on with our few belongings and headed downstream along the *argine* or the raised riverbank. It was a Sunday and we passed quite a few young people brightly dressed in their best who shouted what sounded like "Chow! Chow!"'[12] One of the young Italians watched the New Zealanders packed into two horse-drawn carts passing cheerfully in front of his house. 'We children were playing outside with a ball and they waved and greeted us.'[13] He was the son of the man who later was to hide two of those New Zealanders in that same home for over a year.

The majority of prisoners who escaped did so from these work camps on large farm holdings. The shortage of Italian manpower to work in the fields was offset by an influx of prisoners who, under the terms of the

Geneva Convention, could be used for such labour. Although some men had trouble with the notion of supporting the enemy war effort, most leaped at the chance to get out into the countryside. It meant double rations, fresh air and exercise which put them into good shape to take advantage of the events to come.

The men who worked on satellite farm camps were better fed, better housed and had more freedom of movement, despite being accompanied by a guard at all times. These guards were usually friendly and made it clear that they would rather not be at war. They professed surprise that the New Zealanders had volunteered for military service and not been coerced like they had. Sergeant Major Sergio Rigola, in charge of Camp 106 in the Vercelli district in Piedmont, was well aware of the good relationship between the prisoners and his soldiers, who were materially worse off than their charges. Among his guards were impoverished Southern Italians who had nothing above their miserable government stipend. They relished the cigarettes offered them. Even when prisoners threw away their cigarette butts, on countless occasions guards would swoop on them to extrapolate a few last puffs. 'At times I would intervene and remonstrate with them to show a bit of dignity. But these things happen. We all know that the Italian soldier is incapable of hating anyone. How can he be expected to hate those who give him cigarettes when he has none?'[14]

Activities on the large estate farm at Camp 107/4 included weeding rows of maize, pulling, topping and tailing sugarbeet, haymaking, digging potatoes, cleaning up the cowshed, scything grass, and stacking silage and hay.[15] At the hundred-strong working Camp 146 at Rosasco in the Vercelli area on the Lombardy Plains the farm was under the control of the Fascist leader of the district, about three kilometres from the camp.

'We started work at 8 a.m., went back to camp at midday for lunch and a snooze then back to the farm from 3 p.m. till 6 o'clock when we finished for the day and walked back to camp again. When the POWs first went to the farm, we were put alongside a group of women farm workers; presuming that by having our manhood challenged we would work twice as hard as the women. It did not work out that way, however, as our men had no interest in stimulating the Italian economy by putting in extra effort. So we worked only fast enough to maintain movement and by dragging our heels we gradually slowed up the Italian effort and brought the women's pace down to our level.'[16]

However, the presence of female co-workers, called *mondine*, challenged their manhood in other ways. In one of the 106 satellite camps the prisoners and the women slept in the same barracks, their separate headquarters divided by a simple, easy-to-scale wooden partition. Although any kind of contact was severely forbidden, 'you can imagine what happened. The sentry wasn't overly concerned and he couldn't stay awake all night with his rifle at the ready. I remember that when the first commander of the camp returned from his inspections of the dormitories he would often have some young devil in tow.'[17]

A gentle form of sabotage was rife whenever an opportunity presented itself. 'When the rice was cut and stacked into "stooks" in the fields, it was easy to screw one's boot into the head of rice before it was loaded on to the carts, thus wasting many pounds of rice.'[18] When hoeing potatoes the men cut the plants beneath the surface and threw rotten potatoes into the cargoes sent away, hoping they would cause the healthy ones to become putrid.[19] New Zealanders with farm experience were called upon to drive the small tractors, and at one camp professed mock dismay when a tractor ended up in the canal.[20]

At Camp 106/2 at Arro near Salussola the men convinced their guards that a ten-minute smoko every hour was normal work practice in New Zealand, but no one was keeping check on the time, especially their guards who would snooze alongside them. In barracks opposite to theirs were about eighty *mondine*, young women who stood up to their knees in water all day thinning the rice. The prisoners' job was to make little banks to contain the water that flooded the rice fields. When ordered to work in the irrigation drains the men went on strike, calling upon a non-existent clause in the Geneva Convention which allegedly stated that prisoners were not permitted to work in water.[21]

Another group made it their business to be constantly at war with the Fascist overseers. When they were expected to work weekends at harvesting time, in good New Zealand tradition they went on strike and not a man out of fifty would work. Such insurgency from subalterns was unknown in Italian army ranks. Although it resulted in imprisonment in a tiny jail for the ringleaders, a metal tube sticking through a hole in the wall served as a vehicle through which cigarettes, news bulletins, wine and hot drinks were passed, making it all rather a lark.[22] At other camps strikes came to an immediate end when the guards threatened to withhold the Red Cross parcels.

At Camp 107/7 at Torviscoso the dispensing of the services of one of their number as a translator resulted in the prisoners playing up. 'When Lilo spoke to them they just leaned on their hoes and looked at him or tried to repeat what he was saying, the way he said it. Soon every one except me had stopped working. Lilo came to me for help but I just looked blankly at him and shook my head.' The guard became frantic as carrots as well as the weeds between them were being hoed. One by one the 'chaps' went to the ditch at the side of the field and lay down. Finally, the desperate guard snatched the erstwhile translator's hoe out of his hands, threw it in the ditch and beseeched him to return to his interpreting.[23]

As the men of Camp 107/7 became fitter, they took up old pursuits. In the warmer weather they would strip off after work and plunge into the water of a small beach lining the raised banks of the Livenza river. Two things stood out for the Italians. Firstly, the fact that the New Zealanders could all swim, and secondly, the pallor of their skin. The propaganda posters of the *neozelandesi* had led them to expect 'black people with their faces all marked and contorted'.[24]

The prisoners began a rugby tournament between the upper storey barracks and the lower, 'keen to enlighten the natives with an exhibition of our national sport'. The cornfields provided an adequate if uneven field, and goal posts were staked out at each end with piles of clothes with two lines projected upwards from them. The referee had to decide if the ball was kicked high enough to constitute a goal. While the first game had been a bit of a frolic, the second game, watched by astonished guards and locals, became more 'fair dinkum' with both teams out to win. Although they were having great fun, there had been a couple of collisions resulting in blood noses, and one player had to leave the field while another played on limping after having been flattened. It was for the New Zealanders 'nothing out of the ordinary in a friendly game' but the sergeant-major ran over shouting to the interpreter, 'Arturo, Arturo,' and they thought, 'Gee. Beaut! This bloke's got the idea already and wants to join in.' But the white-faced Italian ordered them to stop the game immediately. He thought they were trying to kill each other.[25]

Life on the farm camps was generally lax. The corporal in charge of one group of prisoners had been issued with a bicycle to enable him to move around the gangs to encourage those who were not working to speed. Instead, he managed to access the workshop, ostensibly to do repairs on the bike. It was here that he swiped a couple of hacksaw blades, which were to come in handy later. [26]

At Camp 107/6 on the plains between the Piave and Livenza rivers near Venice, 'we operated an imaginary radio station, called Station G-I-N, the breath of the Lombardy Plains.'[27] But it was not all fun and high-jinks. The successful future escapers had a sense that learning the language would come in handy and borrowed an Italian grammar book from a visiting priest. 'Having learnt Latin at school and at university, I managed to leapfrog into Italian fairly easily. When I discovered that the local people spoke Veneto dialect I converted to that.'

They loaded sugar beet on to barges on the small canals traversing the area. Travelling to their area in bullock carts gave them the opportunity to get to know the local people. They got on well with their guards and set up a small business selling Neville Lodge's cartoons. 'He was already drawing cartoons for the *NZEF Times* but the first commercial sale of his drawings came about when the guards wanted to be caricatured.'[28] A deal would be negotiated for the drawing, such as two eggs – one for the artist and one for his business manager.

On their first morning at Prati Nuovi in April 1943, the New Zealand prisoners were ordered out on parade to receive a 'pep talk' from the landowner, Cugnasca. He was a handsome, nattily dressed man but was automatically suspect, because he was 'upper-class'. Cugnasca assured them they would be well fed and treated as long as they brought in the harvest for the Italian war effort. 'Don't even think of escaping,' he warned, 'because we have armed people keeping the roads under surveillance.' 'Okay,' muttered a prisoner, 'so we won't go by road.'[29]

A large farming estate stretching for 1000 hectares near the Adriatic Coast between Venice and Trieste, Prati Nuovi was an example of Mussolini's agricultural and social experiment of land reclamation. Malaria-infested swamps were cleared and subdivided into the 'new fields' from which Prati Nuovi derived its name. It provided work and accommodation for about forty farm workers and their families, about 400 people in total. Organised along strictly traditional lines, the estate was a microcosm of hierarchical relationships headed by the absent landowner, the administrator who directed all operations, and a sub-stratum of rapidly descending roles comprising the mechanic, the gamekeeper, the stablehands and the field-workers.

From April until October 1943, Prati Nuovi housed a satellite working camp, 107/2, for about fifty New Zealand prisoners-of-war. The New Zealanders and their five guards lived on the ground floor of a large three-storeyed building, part of which had been a schoolhouse. On the floor above them lived several families of the field-workers.

Although their living quarters were surrounded by barbed wire, life was generally relaxed. The men were responsible for their own cooking and washing, and relations with the guards were easy-going. Each night the men had to line up to be counted. They tested escape possibilities by getting someone to hide in the toilets to see if by doubling up they could confuse the old sergeant. But it never got beyond a light-hearted joke. Malaria was a constant health hazard, the land was as flat as a pancake and there was little vegetation to hide in.

Every day the men would go to work in the fields after receiving instructions on the day's tasks. One of their jobs was to turn over the grain crop on the wide, flat, concrete platform using large wooden shovels. An old steam engine with a big wheel ground the wheat up and poured it into sacks. The prisoners would then carry the heavy bags up a flight of stairs to the storehouse. They came to know the community well. A prisoner remembers the expertise of locals catching frogs in the canal. 'The frogs would bite and the men would flick the rod up; the frog would let go and was caught and bagged in one motion.'[30]

For the children of the farm workers, Prati Nuovi was a paradise where there was always an abundance of food provided by the produce from the fields and the prized cow. Having plenty to eat was a source of pride and gratitude when there were widespread food shortages in the towns.[31] Those Italians who lived with their families above the New Zealanders remember it as a happy time with everybody helping each other, regardless of status. The prisoners would sometimes march off to their work in the fields singing loudly and every Saturday night, after the day's work, a *festa* was held, a splendid feast with music and dancing on the terrace. The Italians felt sorry for the prisoners below behind the wire, wondering if the music made them feel nostalgic for their homeland.[32]

A highlight was the weekly Saturday trip to the station in the horse and cart to pick up the Red Cross parcels for the prisoners. The mothers of the boys would give freshly baked bread to the Kiwis who would in turn share out the contents of the prized parcels. As most Italian youths over the age of ten smoked, the prisoners used to give them Camel cigarettes or the Chesterfield ones with the picture of the little sailor on the packet. They tasted and smelt wonderful, unlike the foul, home-made Italian variety. The pungent aroma got one young Italian into trouble with the customs guard in the cinema at the nearby town of Latisana. 'Where did you get this from?' he was asked. 'The New Zealand prisoners,' he replied. He was ordered to stub it out immediately.[33]

But the motive for handing out the contents of Red Cross parcels was not necessarily altruistic. 'It was not from any desire to please the Italians, but because we all realised what excellent propaganda it was that prisoners-of-war should be in a position to give away such things as chocolate which the Italians had probably not seen since Italy entered the war.'[34] Some men still smarted from the jeers they received from Italians in southern Italy when dirty, half-starved and dejected they were being transported to their camp.

Being well turned out was a source of pride to the prisoners. On Sundays, as a chorus of church bells rang out over the countryside, the camp leader at Prati Nuovi would galvanise his men. 'Let's show these Eyeties.' The New Zealanders would don their uniforms, shine their boots and march briskly to the church on the estate. After sitting through the twenty-minute service in Latin, they would march out. They wanted to impress the Italians and show up their slovenly guards as well as counteract the Saturday Fascist martial parades dear to the administrator.[35]

But the chance to get out into the beautiful countryside on a horse-drawn wagon was a sufficient draw card for the high-spirited young men at Camp 107/4. When the sergeant said he had been given permission to take any Roman Catholics to the local church, 'we were all Catholics for the occasion.'[36] Another incentive may have been the chance to ogle the girls who used to bicycle near the prison camp to a chorus of admiring wolf whistles. Once the stomach was satisfied, sexual hunger returned.

In this relaxed, often carefree atmosphere, the war took a back pew as New Zealanders and Italians working together on the farms got to know and like each other. The men observed their new surroundings with curiosity and even affection. It was clear many Italians were pro-British. Whatever the motives, the Kiwis' friendliness and generosity with the contents of their Red Cross parcels were to pay off a thousandfold in a few short months when they would depend upon these same Italians for their very survival.

CHAPTER THREE

Escape

I left as soon as the gate was open. There was no way I was staying there as a sitting duck to be caught again.[1]

When Italy capitulated to the Allies on 8 September 1943, assuming a month later the ambiguous status of co-belligerent, the country fell into chaos. As the news spread throughout the country, delighted Italians began celebrating the end of a war that no one had wanted. Mussolini was increasingly unpopular. Disastrous defeats in Greece, the Balkans, East and North Africa and on the Russian front had destroyed any residual confidence in his leadership. Shortages of fuel, food, and rising inflation led to deep public unrest and in March 1943 strikes had erupted in Fiat plants in Turin, spreading to factories in other cities. On 9 July when the Allies invaded Sicily, the Germans largely defended it as the Italian army was in disarray. On 25 July Mussolini was forced to resign by the King, Victor Emanuel III, after a majority vote of no confidence by his own Fascist Grand Council, who had been secretly plotting against him for some months. To his great surprise, and to widespread rejoicing, he was arrested and imprisoned in quarters high up on the Gran Sasso mountain in the Abruzzi region.

During the forty-five days between the fall of Mussolini and the Armistice, negotiations between Marshal Badoglio, the newly appointed head of government, and the Allies were tricky. At first Badoglio played a double game, electing to continue fighting on the side of the Germans before changing his tune. This vacillation meant there were some lost opportunities for anti-Fascist Italians who wanted to prove their worth to the Allies and fight against the Germans. The British, deeply mistrustful of Italy, insisted on obtaining an unconditional surrender. Although the Armistice agreement had been signed on 3 September, it was not made public until 8 September, the day the Allies landed in Salerno in southern Italy.

Aware of the impending defection of their Axis partner, the Germans responded by immediately pouring more troops into northern and central Italy. Within a day of the announcement, the shaky, Allied-backed government of Badoglio, together with the King, fled ignominiously south from Rome to Brindisi, in fear of their lives. This resulted in the total collapse of the Italian army and with it all civil, social and administrative systems. The joy of the Italian people was short-lived. Betrayed yet again by an inept and opportunistic ruling class, they were about to witness their country become a bloody battleground between two foreign armies, played out against a brutal struggle that pitted Italian against Italian.

For meanwhile Mussolini had been rescued from his cliffside prison at Gran Sasso in a daring raid by crack German troops on 12 September. After a brief meeting with Hitler, he was ensconced in a puppet government at Salò on the shores of Lake Garda, in the northern district of Verona. There he tried to set up Italian armed forces under the banner of the Italian Republican Army known as the *Repubblichini* and continue his Fascist rule. It was clear that no move he made was without German approval.

At the same time, the organised resistance movement was born. Even before the Armistice, political groups, many of their members released from jail in a conciliatory move by Badoglio, had begun a plan of action.

On 9 September the six anti-Fascist parties formed the Committee of National Liberation (CLN) with their headquarters at Milan. The first partisan groups were established by the Action Party and the Communists. Within months it had swollen from a ragtag of political dissidents and disaffected patriots to a people's movement with the active participation and support of thousands determined to expel the Germans and eliminate Fascism. It was into this complex, explosive situation that 80,000 Allied prisoners-of-war were unwittingly propelled on the evening of 8 September.

There were varying responses in the camps, where prisoners were, in the main, largely unaware of these political developments. Because the Allies at this point were thought to be making great progress, nearly all Italian camp commandants had received instructions to keep the prisoners in their camps until the Allied forces arrived; there was a secondary instruction that they were not to be handed over to the Germans. These orders did not specify how this was to be carried out, given the fact that the Italian army had collapsed, the Allies were nowhere near, and German troops, fortified by ten more divisions, had swooped into Italy and taken over all strategic points of communication.[2] The natural outcome of this confusion was that the majority of prisoners were gathered up within days and taken on to camps in Germany, where they remained until the end of the war.

Most camps heard the news of the Armistice on the evening of 8 September through the reaction of their guards, who threw down their rifles, donned civilian clothes and left for their homes. Many of these guards, aware of their lowered status in the eyes of the Germans, fled to avoid the roundups of Italian men shipped off as forced labour to Germany. The accounts of New Zealand escapers reflect these responses. In most cases, the camp gates were opened by friendly guards bent on escaping themselves. This was the case for Arch Scott at Camp 107/7, who reports that the prisoners dispensed with the barbed wire and began to fraternise with the locals. Drunk on their newfound liberty, they tended to head for the wine shop for reinforcements and went on a drinking binge until they realised they would have more than enough with families only too willing to host them.[3]

At Cliff Manson's camp south-east of Rome there was no warning. The commandant told them Italy was capitulating. The interpreter was a pro-German Fascist, much disliked, who 'disappeared pretty smartly'. The commandant opened the gates before taking off himself. He advised the prisoners to make their way to the Sulmona working camp. 'We didn't take much notice of that at all. We had other arrangements.'4

Ian St George and his comrades at Camp 107/4 had used a purloined hacksaw to cut through the steel bars at the back of the ablution block. They had left them seemingly intact so as not to arouse suspicion. It was a simple matter one dark night to bend them up and slip out on to a small lean-to roof below.5

John Senior's escape, also from Camp 107/4, reflects the friendly relations that existed between the prisoners and the guards. The camp superintendent said he was under orders to keep them there until whoever arrived first – the Allies or the Germans. Anyone trying to escape would be shot. 'We weren't over-happy about that. Our acting corporal-interpreter went to see the *padrone* but no, those were his orders from above and we must stay under guard. As soon as they came back, that night Roy and I said, "Right, we're out." And we left.'

It was an easy escape. Senior had gone out with one of the guards on a social excursion the previous Sunday. 'He and I met two young Italian ladies – one was studying to be an opera singer – so I knew him quite well. So I went up to him. He was on guard at the gate. I said that very soon the troops would be here. We've made a lot of friends with the civilian labour people here, and we'd like to say goodbye. "Oh well," he said, "off you go. Be back by 5." I said yes, but he didn't say what day!'6

Laurie Read and his group were working when an Italian soldier arrived to talk to the boss. They were ordered to stop work, hand in their tools and were escorted back to the camp, 'seething with curiosity'. The officer informed them that the soldiers who had been guarding them were now there to protect them 'but did not say who from!' They were to stay in the camp to await instructions from the British authorities. For two days Read and his companions waited 'just sitting around enjoying the sun and talking to the Italian women who were husking the maize adjacent to the compound'. When, on 12 September, they heard that the

Germans were only five miles away and marching towards the camp, they wasted no time. They were not alone. Even before the prisoners could gather up their belongings, the guards had flung away their rifles, changed into civvy clothing and departed. Despite the desire of the Italian commanding officer to hand the prisoners over to the Germans to 'keep his nose clean with them', the men left for an outlying farm where some had earlier been employed.[7]

Doug Dymock walked out of his Camp 106/20 straight into a job in a carrying business in nearby Salussola, organised for him by one of the farmhands. Friendly relations with Italian labourers and the lack of manpower made it easy. Furthermore, the owner of the business was being well treated in a prison camp in Canada and his wife wanted to reciprocate. As he drove the big draught-horse and cart round town, Dymock tried to appear Italian by wearing a cloth cap. It hid his blond hair.[8]

Two things prevented John Abel and some of his comrades from fleeing right away. The first was finishing the New Zealand versus South Africa baseball test and the second was waiting until Saturday the 11th to collect their Red Cross parcels 'so you had something to cart off with for food'. When the gates were opened at 11 p.m. it was 'every man for himself'. But Abel could not believe the reluctant reaction of some comrades. 'The amazing part is that for all that quite a big contingent stayed. And some went out and came back again because they couldn't adjust.'[9]

In the first days after the Armistice the guards at Prati Nuovi had 'scarpered'. But for the New Zealanders a decision to do likewise was not so clear-cut. The Fascist administrator, Ghirardelli, had threatened to call the Germans in if they tried to escape. According to Paul Day, 'We were in a bit of a quandary. There were twenty-three cases of malaria and chaps were completely disabled. It was a very remote place.' They did not want to leave sick friends behind.[10]

It seemed wiser to stay labouring on the farm in return for food while they worked out what to do. Over the next week Day heard of a local, Elio Re, who had a couple of trucks that at night were used to ferry food to the partisans. It was not the first time Day and his companions had heard of the partisans. They were talked about all the time by the locals and even the guards, and alluded to in the phrase 'going up to the mountain'. When Day asked if he would take some prisoners up, the man agreed to get back to him in ten days' time when he'd fixed it up with the partisans.

Back at camp it was put to the vote. They could remain where they were, break up and make their way into the countryside, or go *en masse* to the partisans. All voted to go to the partisans but just before this was due to happen, German troops swooped on Prati Nuovi and rounded up all the prisoners. The Germans arrived towards evening one Saturday, in three trucks that crawled completely hidden from view behind a cart piled with hay, as it returned after the day's work. Benito Ciprian, the mechanic's son, remembers: 'If there hadn't been those carts we would have seen them arrive and they could have escaped. The Germans were cunning. They came behind the hay carts and no one saw them. They got down from their trucks with their tommy-guns – *alt, alt, alt*! We were all so upset.'[11]

Franco Ghirardelli, the son of the administrator, recalls the event as if it were yesterday. 'It was 6 p.m. and it was hot. I was a kid of twelve or thirteen with a ball. I was sitting on a fence outside. The moment I heard the noise of trucks I got down and I looked out to see who'd arrived. I ran back to the window and I gave a great yell inside. "Escape the Germans are here, escape the Germans are here," I shouted!'[12]

The Germans burst in while the men were having dinner and surrounded and cordoned off the building, holding people at bay with their tommy-guns. The stunned New Zealanders were ordered to pack up and be ready to leave in half an hour.

Paul Day attributes the notion of escaping to the secretary of the estate, Ilde Toniutto, who was Austrian and married to the postmaster of Cesarolo, Luigi Toniutto. Day, as interpreter, was in touch with her daily as she communicated to him the orders from the boss, which he then relayed to his companions. 'She was a big, tall, blonde girl, very handsome, self-contained. The whole Austrian platoon was clustered around her. There was nobody on guard any more.'

By this time, the prisoners had tossed their belongings on to the trucks and were standing outside, resigned to leaving. Ilde came up to Day to say goodbye, and as she did so whispered, '*È tempo di scappare*, it's time to escape. I saw she had twigged the guards weren't doing anything.'[13] While Ilde charmed her compatriots, Day asked the 'frazzled' captain if he could go back to get some belongings. Once inside he looked out the window. No guards were in sight. 'I stood there thinking for about twenty seconds – do I want a bullet in the back? Then I threw a window open, jumped out, and ran across to the hayloft, a huge structure with hay piled on top. I scrambled into the hay and put it over my head.' Day soon learned he was not alone. 'After I had been there about ten minutes, a little voice came out of the hay somewhere beside me, and said, "Is that you Paul?"' Sharing the haystack with him and clad only in a towel was Martin Hodge. He had been having a shower when the Germans arrived.

Bruno Blasigh and Benito Ciprian saw Paul Day's dramatic escape to the haystack from their window above the prisoners' quarters. They started squealing with excitement, 'Day *è scappato*, Day *è scappato*,' and were silenced with a belt over the head from the mechanic, Benito's father. The two fugitives stayed in the haystack until nightfall while the farm estate was searched. 'They went into every house, pointed guns at people and said, "Where are the New Zealanders?"' But no one had seen or heard anything.[14]

It was Ciprian, the mechanic, who at nightfall went to the haystack and called to Day and Hodge that it was safe to come out. He took them back to his house, fed them, hid their uniforms in the fowl house, and found them clothes. His stepson, Visentin, remembers, 'We were scared because we didn't know if all the Germans had left. Day had a fever of 40 degrees. I put him in my bed.'[15] Strategies to prevent discovery were inventive. Prominently placed on the wall was a picture. 'When the Germans arrived to take away the prisoners my father turned the picture round and Mussolini appeared. On one side there was the King and the Pope, and on the other side there was Hitler with Mussolini. When they saw it ... Heil Hitler ... and away they went!'[16]

How the Germans knew when to come still incites controversy. Most concur with Gino Fraulin. 'Ehh, there were Fascists around.'[17] Day believed that Ghirardelli, the boss of the estate, having heard that the

New Zealanders were preparing to flee to the partisans, tipped off the Germans. But his sons firmly deny this and are keen to set the record straight. Insists Franco Ghirardelli, 'After my father learned the reason . . . he found out and he was very angry.' He explained that an Italian colonel who was in charge of the prison camps informed the German command that there were prisoners out of his control at various working camps, among them Prati Nuovi. 'He told them to go and get them. This is what happened. My father only knew about this after they arrived.'[18]

Paul Day still maintains that it was highly likely that Ghirardelli called the Germans in.[19] Most other witnesses concur because of Ghirardelli's Fascist convictions and the superb timing of the Germans' arrival, hidden behind the cart. Such synchronisation required careful planning and prior knowledge of schedules as the flat plains of Prati Nuovi allow clear visibility for miles around. Yet by all accounts it was Ghirardelli who pacified the Germans when, after discovering that two prisoners were missing, they threatened to burn down the farm. And he would have known later of the presence of the escapers in houses round Prati Nuovi.

Maurice Cosgrave found himself in the unique situation of being shot at by fellow prisoners when he escaped from a British camp in the central Marches region. 'They shot the commandant who was a Fascist. Didn't like him very much.' But what happened next was an unpleasant surprise. 'Lo and behold, the Scots guards took over all the sentries' boxes and armed themselves with the Italians' rifles. They were originally prisoners with us! Well, this was a bit intolerable, so this friend of mine, Frank, who had been in the raid to capture Rommel – one of these commando fellows – well, we decided this was bad news.' They resolved to break out at the bottom end of the camp.

The camp was made out of concrete blocks with brick walls beneath them where the concrete finished. According to Cosgrave, it was a typical Italian construction that had not been cemented properly. At the very edge of the camp was barbed wire. A sentry box stood at each corner. Armed with home-made tools, Cosgrave and his companion crept out one night, made a hole in the brick wall and smashed their way through. 'So we escaped and the bloody Poms were shooting at the pair of us.' They dodged the bullets of their former comrades, who, obeying to the letter the order to remain, were soon on a train to Germany. The escapers laid low for some time.[20]

Jack Lang's escape was no less dramatic and shared by a number of men. The mass of New Zealand and Australian prisoners at Camp 57 at Gruppignano in the Friuli region of northern Italy had no opportunity to escape. Carefully guarded until the Germans arrived three days after the Armistice, they were herded off in groups to the railway station. Up until then they had been subjected to orders, counter-orders and wild rumours.[21] As most believed that the Allied arrival was imminent, they were furious when the ever-efficient Germans turned up to begin the process of evacuation of prisoners to camps in Austria and Germany. A belligerent Lang was given a beating for not moving quickly enough into the train. His parting shot to the guards was typical. 'There's no way you're going to get me through to Germany.'

With the sliding doors on each side of the train firmly bolted and the men packed in like sardines in the stifling heat, it must have appeared wishful thinking. Yet from the minute they were locked inside, men in every truck searched for ways to get themselves out. As the train pulled out of Udine, Lang and his close friend, Frank Gardner, huddled together to plot their escape. A small vent on the roof of the crowded cattle-truck provided an opportunity. Lang's shoulders supported Gardner as he levered himself through the narrow opening and leaped into the cold night. Then it was Lang's turn. The train was travelling at about 60 kilometres per hour. He stood for a moment on the steel foothold on the side of the truck, took a deep breath and jumped, landing unharmed on the gravel alongside the railway track, within a few steps of a bridge support. Gardner was not so lucky. In the fall he hurt his leg, but managed to crawl to a nearby farmhouse. Lang searched fruitlessly through the night for his friend before setting out on his own. They were not to meet again until after the war.[22]

Significant numbers of men escaped by carving holes through wooden carriages and releasing the bolt that held the sliding door. They were then able to simply walk off the trains when they halted for long periods of time or take advantage of the slow speeds uphill at night to throw themselves out. Apart from sustaining a few bruises and scratches, surprisingly few were killed or injured, but the Germans soon got wise. They wired the bolts and put sentries armed with machine-guns at the rear of the train ready to fire at would-be escapers.[23]

Bill Black's first escape was out of a second-storey window of the San Donà di Piave hospital. He had been sent there from his work camp prior to the Armistice, suffering from malaria. For the salt-of-the-earth Black, life in the hospital had its drawbacks.

'Of course all the nurses there were nuns and there was this long, long ward – it went for 100 yards, or it seemed like it. They used to give you a nightshirt that came up to your navel and nothing else, nothing on the bottom. And if you wanted a piss or a shit or anything, you'd have to walk the whole distance up the thing – practically naked in front of all those nurses. Most embarrassing.' But worst of all were the injections administered with a huge needle. 'When it went into your backside it would come up like an egg. A whole egg. You couldn't put your arse on one side of the bed. That's how much stuff they stuck in. And the pain was shocking!'[24]

The prisoners were soon removed to a room of their own with a guard outside. Their chance to escape was hatched by a friendly Italian visitor who spoke a little English and offered to meet them when they got away. In addition he possibly bribed the guard. Like any boarding school miscreants, Black and his comrade made up their beds one night to look as if they were sleeping soundly inside them. Then they squeezed out through the toilet window, manoeuvred themselves across the hospital floor to another window, and climbed out of that before sliding down two floors to the grounds below. While the patrolling sentry was out of sight, they scrambled over the hospital walls. Incredibly, Black was immediately reminded of home. 'It was a big long street like Hastings, like Heretaunga Street disappearing into Havelock.' But their problems were far from over. It was full of German soldiers.

One of the clauses in the Armistice Agreement stated that all prisoners were to stay put and await orders. An administrative requirement, it was designed to make their roundup and evacuation by the Allies as efficient as possible. Unfortunately, it was made months before the Armistice actually occurred and, presuming an immediate Allied take-over, the clause bore no relation to the current state of affairs. Even while they were defending Salerno, the Germans prepared the Gustav Line that cut the Italian peninsula diagonally from the Garigliano River in the west to east of the Maiella mountain. All prisoner-of-war camps were easily encompassed on the German side of the Line, which was not to be penetrated until the Allies won Cassino in May 1944. German might and tenacity combined with the difficult Italian terrain, a defender's paradise in the icy, muddy winter months, meant that progress for the advancing Allies was to be tortuously slow.

Although there were some attempts in the days before 3 September to rethink this policy of containment, if a decision was made it was not conveyed to the prisoners in the camp. The inclination of most Allied officers and leaders in the camps was to obey orders, understandable in the mayhem. It left them sitting ducks for the enemy. When, almost a week after the Armistice, the BBC announced that it was the prisoners' duty to escape and make their way south to the Allied lines, many thousands of able-bodied men were already on their way to Germany.[25] Of the 50,000 who did escape, their freedom was short-lived. Over half were recaptured within weeks. Of 3700 New Zealand prisoners, approximately only 450 successfully escaped, mostly from Camps 107 and 106 and their satellites.[26] At 12 per cent of their numbers, it was the lowest percentage of all the British Commonwealth forces.[27] This was because the bulk of New Zealanders were concentrated in the north-eastern area. Unfortunately, most were gathered up en masse from PG57, and except for a few dozen who leaped from trains, transferred to German camps.

After years of prison routine many men had become institutionalised, sapped of the independent thinking required to make decisions. The prisoners who successfully escaped were those who challenged military authority and had no compunction about disobeying orders. They possessed qualities of resourcefulness and bold initiative in judging the situation for themselves, and an unquenched antipathy to being imprisoned. But none would have escaped without the assistance of Italians, whether sympathetic or disinterested guards, or non-Fascist camp commanders who, correctly summing up the situation, took matters into their own hands and encouraged the prisoners to leave.

Abandoned once more to the luck of the gods in the wake of confusion, inept decision-making and conflicting orders, the New Zealanders who walked or clambered out of the prison gates and jumped from trains had no idea what was in store for them. What they would have all agreed upon was that getting out was the easy part.

CHAPTER FOUR

The Italian Resistance

The shame of our betrayal will not be expunged unless we fight the invader who contaminates our soil. Beyond the Garigliano you will find not only the bivouacs of the hard-faced British, but Americans, French, Poles, South Africans, Canadians, Australians, New Zealanders, Moroccans, Senegalese, Negroes and Bolsheviks. You are to have the privilege of fighting this witch's cauldron of bastard nations who respect nothing and nobody as they invade Italy.[1]

The thousands of prisoners spilling out of their camps became part of what has been described as the strangest tourist season Italy had ever known.[2] Combined with the troops landing in southern Italy, they represented over thirty-five different nations. But in far greater numbers the countryside was soon alive with Italian soldiers from their disintegrated army, eager to get home or join the newly formed bands of partisans. The Germans had wasted no time in demobilising the Italian army, disarming, interning and then sending its demoralised troops on to

Germany. Over 600,000 Italians were deported to work as slave labourers in Germany. Many never returned.

In the days following the Armistice, branches of the Committee for National Liberation (CLN) sprang up in every major city and town. Of the coalition of the six main anti-Fascist parties, by far the strongest and most organised was the Communist Party with Palmiro Togliatti at its head. Along with the Action and Socialist Parties, it refused to recognise Badoglio, an elderly moderate Fascist in Mussolini's former government, and elected the anti-Fascist General Ivanoe Bonomi, a former premier in pre-Fascist days and head of the Labour Party, as their representative. This was the first indication that Italy wanted to have a voice of its own in deciding its political future.

It is estimated that the real opposition to Fascism rose after 8 September. This was fuelled by the anti-Italian British Foreign Affairs Minister, Anthony Eden, who expressed the view that Italy changed sides only when they knew they were losing. This assumption that all Italians were Fascists is of course untrue. It ignores the fact that the Fascists achieved power with a minority of votes and, benefiting from a weak, divided opposition, from then on suppressed dissenters with violence.

Mussolini made it illegal for opposition parties to exist in 1925, after the murder of the Socialist Deputy, Giacomo Matteotti, by Fascist henchmen. Thereafter, anti-Fascism went underground. Many who opposed the regime fled to France while others were forced into internal exile under police guard.[3] Despite this, resistance to Fascism had never died, and it flourished in small acts and behaviours within the limits permitted by an omnipotent, watchful state. But as a political force, anti-Fascists were fragmented and ineffective and few Italians, let alone foreigners, knew of their existence.

There has been ongoing debate about how ordinary people felt about Fascism and the extent of consensus there was under the regime. Fascism had invaded and controlled all aspects of economic and social life so that overt resistance was virtually impossible. In order to gain employment, Italians had to possess the *tessera* or Fascist party card. This assumed a passive endorsement of Fascism, but for most people its primary advantage was guaranteed economic survival for their families. Subsidies were awarded to families who named offspring after Roman emperors or with names that reflected Mussolini's aspirations in North Africa. Although many Italians did not care for Fascist policies one way or the other, it cannot be denied that Mussolini was popular until 1937.

The regime was supported primarily by influential groups of the middle and upper classes, conservative army officials loyal to the King, the high-ranking Catholic clergy, titled landowners and business people. Yet wealth did not spare Italians from the clutches of Fascism. The previous landowner of Prati Nuovi, Max Oreffice, fell victim to the anti-Semite laws passed in 1938, according to which no Jews could own property. As a consequence he was dispossessed, his property at Prati Nuovi confiscated and his share taken over by his colleague.[4]

Like most Italian Jews, Oreffice was fully integrated into Italian society and belonged to the prosperous middle classes, considering himself primarily Italian rather than Jewish.[5] In 1939 he was arrested and while in custody suffered repeated beatings and was forced to drink castor oil. Among his documented crimes was that of having declared in front of dependants at Prati Nuovi that his horse Pasquina was 'more intelligent than Mussolini', and of having told jokes mocking the regime. He was put on trial, imprisoned and sentenced to five years in exile at Lipari. However, a month before Italy declared war in June 1940, he and his family emigrated to Ecuador where he set up a successful business selling, ironically, castor oil.[6] After the war he settled again in Italy. One day, according to several eyewitnesses, his son arrived at Prati Nuovi and threw punches at the person he believed responsible for his father's betrayal.

There were two types of activists who came to the fore after 8 September: those who had always been anti-Fascist and those who became anti-Fascist during the war. Without the war it is doubtful if the movement would have gained the momentum it did.[7] Its impact jolted Italians out of their passivity and young men were confronted with a choice. Most Italian soldiers who managed to avoid the early roundups just wanted to return to their homes and lie low. But awaiting them was the prospect of forced conscription to the Republican Army or to the

German labour force. The first nuclei of partisan bands were organised by the parties of the left and formed in the hills and mountains, assisted by groups of activists in the cities and towns. They were made up of disbanded soldiers, students and teenagers barely out of boyhood fleeing deportation. Escaped prisoners-of-war also joined the ranks. It has been roughly estimated that one month after the Armistice members of bands operating north of the Gustav Line numbered in the tens of thousands. Although there were many motives for joining the partisans, some less noble than others, it was apparent that Italians were undergoing a profound awakening. Even if it was just an awareness of what they did not want, this new consciousness became the seed of a popular insurgency that over the next twenty months spread to all sectors of society. For many, their participation in the Resistance was the most meaningful experience of their lives.

Aldo Camponogara's anti-Fascist ideas were very slow in maturing. An earnest, emphatic man who, since his partisan days, has been strongly involved in local body politics on the Communist ticket, Camponogara was brought up in a middle-class family, which professed no interest in politics and never criticised the regime. At school he took their universe for granted – the 'Fascist Saturdays' where young boys with wooden muskets were required to make militaristic marches and manoeuvres, and participate in collective gymnastic displays. Any knowledge of Italy's anti-Fascist history was suppressed. He sensed, however, the first whiff of covert dissent from some of the priests who ran the Marconi High School he attended. A certain Monsignor Lotzer, who had organised workers in factories during the uprisings of the 1920s, was known to be anti-Fascist. He had been placed 'in exile' by the Vatican; that is, shifted to an isolated rural community under the watchful eyes of his superiors where he would be unlikely to cause too much trouble. The curriculum was controlled by Fascist dogma, but this was often in conflict with the priests' agenda because of the time these weekend displays took away from established church-based social activities. Fascists had in fact shut down Catholic youth clubs in 1931, alienating a significant number of

Catholics. But generally, according to Camponogara, 'we were completely empty, completely in the dark', with no idea about Italy's recent history of worker struggles nor the existence of a militant, if fractured, anti-Fascist movement.

He was twenty when the Armistice occurred, a university student and therefore exempt from military service. He worked for a time at the German manpower organisation or Todt before joining the partisans in June 1944. He explains his choice in terms of a rejection of the moral bankruptcy of Fascism and his words are imbued with the idealism and sense of purpose felt by many educated young men attracted to the partisan cause.

'At the end we understood that there was an alternative to that life [under Fascism] and the choice to save your own skin, that is, to get out of this alive, a choice compromised by opportunism. When we understood that there were young people who were fighting for a cause to restore dignity to the country, freedom for us was a moral issue. The country had been humiliated and we felt that from a moral viewpoint, it was our duty to redeem this humiliation. It wasn't a political choice. We knew nothing yet of democracy, of justice. These things we understood only afterwards.'[8]

He gradually acquired his political ideas not only from seasoned anti-Fascists but also from people outside his middle-class origins, encountered for the first time in the ranks of the Resistance. Through contact with the sons of peasant farmers and factory workers, Camponogara learned of another world beyond 'our narrow intellectually snobbish horizons'. Thus began his education in the struggles of people on the social margins, followed by awareness that for them there was a stronger reason to fight than that of regaining their dignity. Their aim was to fight for a more just and equitable society. Camponogara describes his 'schooling' in terms of lengthy discussions on the direction the country would take in the aftermath of the war.

But the first contact he had with the war was with a group of New Zealand prisoners who had escaped from the Villanova camp at Torviscoso in the Veneto. Like the New Zealanders, he was hiding from the Fascists who were rounding up young men to recruit to the

Republican Army. They were all gathered in an underground bunker and 'although we were enemies and should have hated each other, in reality we found ourselves in a climate of great fraternity united by defending ourselves from a common enemy'. Camponogara had never seen a New Zealander or an Australian before. He found them 'different from us but interesting'. Language was a barrier but they managed to understand each other, so much so that all the Fascist propaganda hurled against the Allies could not dampen a strong sense of common humanity. Slowly the ties with 'their traditional allies' began to reassert themselves.

Italo Ziggiotti received a 'Fascist education' and recalls the month-long military-style 'Dux camp' he went on in the summer in order to be trained to transmit Fascist culture to his contemporaries. Much of this involved his being 'commander' of the marches, where young boys wielded wooden sticks in place of guns, and the gymnastic displays of 'Fascist Saturdays'. He jokes that had Fascism survived he would have had a good career. But the young Ziggiotti had a rebellious streak. He resisted the curtailment of independent thinking and the sense of having every aspect of life controlled. 'This is not the way you teach culture to a people, a people fenced inside a pen, like sheep, and the shepherds say, "Go and eat outside! Come back inside! Go outside again!"'[9]

Luigi Borgarelli was in the Italian army near Trieste. A medical student at Padova, he was allowed to continue his studies while serving in the military. Come the Armistice, he managed to get home to Rivarotto in the Friuli region and elected to wait for things to settle down before making any further decisions. When he realised that Hitler had plans to extend his dominion into Italy and that chunks of land that his parents had fought for in the First World War were being ceded, he did not hesitate. 'We had thousands of dead from that war and now this madman comes along and we have to follow him – not in your dreams!'[10]

For Bruno Londera, there were two main factors influencing his decision to join the partisans. A native of Gemona, a town nestled in the mountains in Friuli, he grew up in France to which his parents had emigrated when he was a baby. When the Germans occupied France he was sent, still a boy of seventeen and under threats of reprisals to his family if he did not comply, to guard a prison camp in Czechoslovakia.

In mid-1943 he was sent to Italy to join the militia at Tarcento. On 8 September, following the collapse of the Italian army, he set off with about a hundred others towards Gemona. Londera was one of only two soldiers with arms and his companions, fearful of being captured by Germans, told him to throw them away. 'Are we soldiers or are we not soldiers?' asked Londera. 'If we are disarmed, a German with a stick will be able to round us up.'

The Germans had already begun to occupy Gemona so with about fifteen others he went to a small cottage owned by family members in the countryside. There, as ex-military men joined them, they began to organise themselves, gathering arms and preparing to form a unit. Londera's choice to join the partisan cause was a deliberate, reasoned one. He attributes his decision partly to the fact that he spent most of his life in France 'in another culture, another education, another mentality, with a different sense of civic and political life'. In short, he had lived in a democracy. The second factor was that he was alone. By this time, both his parents were dead, so he had no family who could suffer cruel reprisals for his activities. This 'moral freedom' meant that he could act independently.[11]

Bruno Steffè, born in 1917, fought with an Italian unit in the Yugoslav Ninth Corpus partisan division. Having survived disastrous defeat in North Africa, Steffè was back in Italy in 1943 stationed at Trieste. The events of 8 September brought only a sense of relief. 'I came to 8 September with a precise sensation that the sooner we got out of the war the better it would be for the country because we were in no condition to defend ourselves, let alone be on the offensive. I was stationed at the Udine aerodrome at the time and I said, finally they are beginning to reason. Finally.'

He and four other officers formally offered their letters of resignation to the Italian Command. Escorted to the commander of the SS troops who were already stationed in Trieste, they were brought face to face with Colonel Globocnik, architect of the extermination camps in Poland and later responsible for the only crematorium in Trieste. It was spelt out very clearly to the young officers what their alternatives were. 'We are the most powerful army in the world. We don't use half measures. Who is not with us is against us and who is against us must be eliminated.' The colonel then asked for proof that his discourse had been understood. Those who were 'with them' should step forward. 'Of the four of us who had brought the letter, three of us did not move. One man stepped forward.' The mayor swiftly intervened, asking that the men be given until the next day to make their decision. There was much soul-searching that evening. 'I decided to go with the partisans. Besides, I had already compromised myself with the Germans who would be keeping an eye on me.'[12]

Querino Bullian sports a Stalinesque moustache and lives in a villa with views of Mount Ciaurlec rising above the town of Sequals in the Friuli region. He is disillusioned with the right-wing swing of Italian politics today and gazes sadly at the mountain where he fought with the partisans. 'I think of all my friends who fell there, and I wonder what was it all for.' Bullian served in the Italian army in Yugoslavia before 8 September. 'I spent three years in Yugoslavia fighting against the Slav partisans and then I came and joined the partisans in my own country,' he chuckles. He became an anti-Fascist during the war in Yugoslavia. His choice to become a partisan was based on his experience of surrendering to Tito's partisans after 8 September. He was impressed with their political ideals and their behaviour.

The Italians had raised the white flag, convinced they would be executed. 'We had been fed all this propaganda about the partisans and none of it was true. When we were withdrawing from Yugoslavia, the partisans had given the order that the people had to help the Isonzo Division and whenever we passed through a village we would be given a piece of black bread and a potato, anything they had. That was my experience and from then on I began to think with my own head. Not the *Duce*'s.'

After walking 150 kilometres through Yugoslav territory, Bullian returned home and immediately joined the Pisacane unit of the Garibaldi Brigade in November 1943.[13]

Gino Panont was one of the thousands of Italian soldiers who found themselves without an army after the Armistice. Disarmed and ordered to surrender, he escaped from a train taking him to Germany and returned to his hometown of San Stino di Livenza in the Venetian plains. He participated in the Resistance struggle from the beginning. His motive reflects the majority of those who joined the partisans.

'I never cared about politics. I didn't belong to any party. I was a patriot. I was defending my country. It was occupied by the Germans and I wanted them out. I did everything for this reason.'[14]

In 1943 Italian-born New Zealander Giovanni Nicolli was seventeen years old and working in the railways in Genoa when he was approached by a foreman inviting him to become a member of the Fascist Party. He refused and this refusal, combined with his association with other recalcitrants, blacklisted him.

'I hated it. I hate the *fascisti* because when I was young my mother was a widow with two kids, nobody to support her. The parcels would come for the parish poor people. The Fascists would give them out – one for you, one for their mates. But for the widow of Nicolli no food, nothing.' One day he decided to find out what was going on. His mother was too poor to pay for the Fascist *tessera*.

The locomotive driver told him he should pack his bags and go home. 'The Fascists have got your name. I'm sorry,' he said, 'we could do with you here.' But while he was home in Lusiana, in the Bassano del Grappo area, a boy from a Fascist family told him to escape. Nicolli quickly farewelled his mother and left. After hiding with his aunt, he joined the local partisans hiding in the mountains. There was nowhere else for him to go.[15]

The ensuing struggle that tore Italians apart was bitter and vicious. Both the young Italians who joined Mussolini's newly constituted Fascist forces and the partisans fighting in the Resistance considered themselves patriots. They wanted to redeem the spectre of a weak, incompetent Italy, despised by other nations and betrayed by the opportunism and indifference of its own people. Both sides drew upon the glorious ideals of the *Risorgimento* and a fervent national pride to fuel their struggle. Egged on by broadcasts from Radio London, the Resistance claimed the mantle of the 'second *Risorgimento*' and the Communists were swift to incorporate their divisions under the name of Garibaldi, its red-shirted soldier hero.[16]

Whatever political rhetoric was used, the reality was that by the autumn of 1943 Italy had three self-appointed governments with a complex network of competing allegiances, two budding Italian armies in conflict with each other, plus two massive foreign armies fighting a decisive battle on its territory. Not only Italy's political future but that of post-war Europe was at stake.

In the middle of this grandiose 'theatre of war' were ordinary Italians trying to get on with the business of daily living. For the thousands of fugitives who were thronging the countryside, whether Italians or escaped prisoners-of-war, it was crucial to discover which side these people were on.

CHAPTER FIVE

At large: the Hare Battalion

We were free and yet still among enemies. We were about as free as any defenceless animal liberated into a large area where predators abounded. We soon became known to the local folk as the Battaglione Lepre, the Hare Battalion. With a price on our heads, a bounty for each one collected and handed in, we soon learned what it was like to be 'The Hunted'.[1]

The New Zealanders who escaped had hazy ideas about where to go and what they would do. The thrill of being free was soon tempered by the practical necessities of finding food and shelter and working out whom they could trust in a country which, until a few days ago, had been an enemy. Those men who had spent time in the camp learning Italian were at a distinct advantage. Although they found that the standard Italian they had mastered was not much like the dialect spoken by the peasants, they could make themselves understood and soon acquired the correct patter.

For those fortunate enough to be in camps in central and southern Italy, getting back behind the lines to the Allies was a feasible goal. Cliff Manson's time as an escaper, in company with five other New Zealanders, was mercifully brief. Imprisoned in the Acquafredda camp, PG78 at Sulmona, he was close to the Gustav Line. It was still summer and sleeping out under the stars was not only possible but pleasant as well. On the way they picked up an old man with a donkey, two Italian youths and later, a young northern Italian couple. The Italian youths, keen to avoid the roundup of Italian males being taken off to German labour camps, proved, as Manson put it, 'handy', as they could find out from the local people where the Germans were. This meant the New Zealanders did not need to have contact with anyone outside the group. The party could not go near villages or cross bridges and they had to keep clear of the main roads, all of which were guarded. They sheltered in a monastery on a mountain, in haylofts, crossed gullies thick with undergrowth, and waded across low-level rivers. By the time they reached their final hurdle, the Sangro River which separated the German and Allied lines, they had spent only a fortnight on the run. Half way across the river, there was a rattle of machine-gun fire, scaring them out of their wits, but there were no splashes disturbing the smooth surface of the water. The action had taken place further down the river where another group was attempting to cross. One of the lucky ones, Manson successfully reached his own lines before the month had ended.[2]

For the men in northern Italy where the Germans were concentrated, there were three escape route options: head south to join the Allies, climb the mountains into neutral Switzerland, or try to go east into Yugoslavia. The route south to the Allies was under Fascist and German control and the Yugoslav option, although at first encouraged, was extremely difficult. They were soon to learn that their chances of escaping intact through Yugoslavia were slim. Tito's partisan bands were engaged in a bitter battle against the rival bands of the royalist Mihailovich as well as the German occupying forces. Moreover, the Germans controlled the coastline. Although the men did not know it at the time, it was safer to tackle the soaring snow-peaked mountains into Switzerland.

Those who had been labourers in the work camps were already aware that support for Mussolini was far from unanimous. All found welcoming shelter from local families in villages close to the camp; so much so that some were to spend the rest of the war in the locality. Initially they moved between safe houses and worked in the fields in exchange for food and shelter. However, once they realised that the Allied troops were a long way from arriving and the extent of the danger they placed their hosts in, they considered this a temporary arrangement. They planned to get out of occupied territory as soon as they could. The problem was, how.

After breaking out of his camp Laurie Read's experience was fairly typical. From September to December he remained in the district, fed by the people he had come to know and work with. Who to trust was always a problem, but those who managed to avoid recapture quickly learned strategies to protect themselves. Read and his companions were walking along the canal bank one day when they spied a man cycling towards them with a gun on his back. They turned and ran for their lives. When the man caught up with them he told them never to run away as a Fascist would shoot them. He was a game warden who thought they were poachers and the umbrella on Read's back a gun.

Like all the men, Read was taught to be wary of well-dressed strangers, as they were invariably Fascist. He and his friends lay low during the day. They dug a six by six feet hole in the ground by a stream and thatched it with leaves, branches and twigs. Here they slept until the snows came and alternative accommodation had to be found.[3]

Ian Millar describes his first few weeks after escaping as a paradise where he and his two New Zealand friends lived like lotus-eaters.[4] Made welcome by the Zanini family, they were given 'picturesque' civilian clothes and, to complete the fairy-tale, were waited on hand and foot by three beautiful daughters. The escapers refused to compromise the family's safety any more than they were already doing by camping outside under the grapevines about 100 metres from the house. Dressed only in khaki shorts, they spent sun-filled days, swimming in a nearby canal flanked by thick clusters of trees and eating ripe blackberries from bushes lining the riverbank. With all the food and attention, they quickly put on weight, much to Signora Zanini's delight at this obvious reflection of her hospitality.

When the rainy autumn weather came the family insisted on building a *casetta* or hut for them. Parties were held round the campfire every evening until it was realised that this could draw attention to their presence. Already patrols had visited the village demanding that ex-prisoners be handed over and offering a considerable reward for people to do so. This made the men keen to move on. However, the Zanini family vehemently opposed their plans and persuaded them to accept a new hiding place in a small forest near the canal.

At one point Jack Leydon made a trip cross-country back to Camp 107 to see if there was any useful information that could assist them. He was amazed to discover 400 of the original 1000 prisoners still living in the barracks guarded by only a single *carabiniere*. Each day German troops would take working parties out to labour in the fields and bring them back in the evening. The men, lulled into a false sense of security, were openly sceptical of his account of the warm hospitality of the Italians and were quite cool towards him. Convinced that the shortage of German transport and imminent arrival of the British would stall any attempt to move them, they were determined to stay put. Three days after Leydon's visit, they were loaded up and taken to Germany.[5]

In the end Millar and Stan Jones decided to move on. Despite the protests and pleas of the Zaninis who were sure they would not survive, the two men left on the next phase of what they felt was a grand adventure.

Keeping a diary was a risk that could cause trouble not only for the diarist if captured, but for his helpers if he named them. Major Hilary Evans of Auckland was one of a few escapers who managed to keep a written record of his experiences throughout the nine months he was on the run. He escaped from Camp 29 at Veano in the central Emilia Romagna region and headed south with his companions until he reached the small town of Vallepietra, about 100 kilometres from Rome. The diary, with an entry nearly every day, is a strong testimony to the ongoing assistance that he received from ordinary Italians from the moment that he escaped.

> 14th [September]. Were lucky to travel in the afternoon with a couple of civilians with mules. They put our hand luggage on the mules and helped us to get another barn at their village that night. The people put on a good meal for us that night in the local pub and gave us eggs in the morning with bread. The pub keeper helped us up the mountain in the morning.

The Germans weren't the only aggressors.

> 17th Fri. Just returned from a good wash. A cow ate my underpants which I had just put out to dry.[6]

In one town he and his companions were apprehended by a *carabiniere* and taken to the guardhouse. They thought that their freedom was over, but had not reckoned with the maternal sentiments of the *carabiniere*'s wife who was horrified at their ill-kempt state.

'*Poveri prigionieri!*' she cried. She persuaded her husband to let them go, even providing them with some of his clothes.

Initially Evans and his companions joined forces with two Italian soldiers returning home. They hatched a plan with one of the Italians who lived near the sea to obtain a small boat to sail to Naples or Corsica. This was foiled when, nearing the seaside town, they heard that Germans were living in his home. Evans starkly documents the confusion of those early days when the country was swarming with escaped prisoners of all nationalities and disbanded Italian soldiers. Men roamed in groups but often ended up separated for good after scattering when German troops or trucks were suddenly sighted.

> 2nd October Sat. Fine. Lost my companions twice. Never found them the second time. Perhaps just as well. Happier on my own.

Some men were unhappy and disoriented. They missed the camaraderie of the prison camps and found the loneliness and the lack of the language too hard. They handed themselves over to the Germans. Not Bill Black. Having scaled the hospital wall, Black and his companion were greeted with a bright moonlit night and the streets of San Donà di Piave thronging with Germans. Their only hope was to walk slowly among them and not attract attention. 'We must have passed hundreds of Huns and not one of them stopped us.' Still weak and sore after their ordeal, they hobbled along the road that led out of the centre until a young man came up behind them and said, 'You're British, aren't you? Don't go round the next corner. There's a bridge with a guard on it and you'll walk straight into him. He knows me because I live on the other side.' He offered to drive them across one by one, hidden in his wagon.

Like so many other evaders, Black was taken home by the Italian, fed, sheltered, then passed on to other safe houses. He spent the next few weeks crossing the Lombardy plains, learning quickly whom to trust. 'We had to watch where we went and who we saw. The well-to-do families were more than likely to be Fascists so we looked at the smaller more decrepit sort of homes and they took us in.'[7] All escapers echoed his mistrust of the bourgeoisie, the class that had fared better under Fascism.

Roy Johnston's opening line to the family he was to spend the next eighteen months with was a calculated risk.[8] A member of the Left Book Club at Victoria University, Wellington, he was familiar with recent Italian political events and had a shrewd idea where the sympathies of rural folk might lie.[9] He and Jim Locke had spent a couple of nights in a maize crop near his camp outside San Donà di Piave, observing a family engrossed in the process of wine making. Grapes arrived by bullock wagon and were forked into a large vat before being pressed by foot. Feeling confident that there was no subterfuge or strange activities going on, Johnston decided to test the waters. At dusk he approached the house and in his best Venetian dialect introduced himself as an English soldier from New Zealand. The old man welcomed him smilingly as the rest of the family gathered silently and watched. Johnston then took a gamble and asked, '*Conoscere Matteotti*?' 'Do you know Matteotti?'

Giacomo Matteotti was a socialist opponent of Fascism who was murdered by Mussolini's henchmen in 1924. Subsequently Matteotti had become the symbolic figure of anti-Fascism and regarded as a martyr.

The reaction was swift. After a moment's stunned silence the old man called out instructions and a woman disappeared into the house. She returned with a large framed photo of Matteotti from its hiding place and handed it to a male member of the family who then showed it to Johnston.

From that moment on, Roy Johnston became Raimondo and Jim Locke Giacomo, members of the family and a replacement for the son imprisoned overseas.[10]

For the three months following their escape, Paul Day and Martin Hodge lived clandestinely, fed by families at Prati Nuovi and the neighbouring localities of San Filippo and San Michele al Tagliamento. After some weeks Mick Hogan turned up, much to everyone's delight. He had jumped off the train to Germany and navigated his way back. The men worked in the fields at the Azienda Braida, blending in with a 120-strong work force of *contadini* who came from far and wide. Deep ditches lining the side of the road gave protection when enemy trucks rolled by.

Hodge (by now known as 'Martino') met up with another New Zealander and decided to set off for the Allied lines down south. Paul Day and Mick Hogan remained, living in several safe houses, particularly that of Gigi Paron. Often ill with malaria, Day was cared for by families and given quinine by the local doctor. When he needed some time to recuperate he was put up in the servants' quarters of a huge house and fed the classic Italian remedy for most ailments, 'white' mushy food.

They spent time at Cesarolo in the house of Luigi and Ilde Toniutto. Gianni, their son, remembers the escapers as shadows in the night. There was an unspoken pact among children to stay silent, although they all knew which families sheltered the New Zealanders. 'We instinctively knew it was dangerous to talk. So we ignored the whole thing.' Luigi Toniutto recalls Day as very blond, intelligent and cultured. But he sensed that Day did not trust him because he had friends on both sides of the political spectrum and fraternised with Germans. Yet he insists it was through him that Day met Gigi Mecchia, who organised for Day and Hogan to go to the partisans.[11]

Having dodged the bullets of the Scots Guards, Maurice Cosgrave and his British companion headed for a railway station about a kilometre away. They boarded a train headed for Amandola. The guard came along, looked at their boots and said, '*Inglesi?*' They thought they were for it now. But the guard went away and brought back another man who spoke English. He told them that Amandola was full of Germans and they did not stand a chance. However, before the train got there, they would stop by a mountain track. This was the signal for the two men to get off and head up the mountain and good luck to them. It was thus that the two escapers spent some days wandering through the hilly countryside. On the way they met an Italian who invited them home to dinner. It seemed to Cosgrave that all the Italians were keen to host an ex-prisoner, perhaps wanting to get on the right side of the Allies when they arrived. He and Frank were so starved they polished off an entire family's meal and the second lot that was cooked up too. Instead of meeting with disapproval, it only heightened their hosts' concern for the *poveri figli* ('poor sons') whose skeletal frames they felt it their duty to fill out.

Cosgrave and his friend stayed there for a while before heading to Meschia, a mountain village south of Comunanza, overlooking the town of Ascoli. On one side of the mountain soared a precipice which towered over a small mountain called Mount Fiore. From this vantage point Cosgrave describes watching students from Ascoli who were gathered on the hill. 'They were carrying on and I could see them from the top of this cliff. And the Germans ringed this little mountain and went up and shot the lot. A massacre. How many of them I don't know. I couldn't tell you. We saw it happening.'[12]

Arch Scott had a stint in the presbytery with the priest, Don Antonio Andreazza, and even hid out in a local school before joining the Antonel family on a permanent basis. They were country people who had land of their own, while working as share-croppers on adjoining land. Angelo Antonel was fourteen when Don Antonio brought the two New Zealanders to his family. His father Pietro used to go into the village every evening to find out what was happening. One evening he heard that the Germans were conducting a roundup that same night. Returning home, he took his scythe and went into the wheat fields and cut an opening of two metres, wide enough to hide Noel Sims and Scott. Later he brought them some blankets.[13]

As their home was dangerously close to the busy Venice-Trieste highway, Scott and Sims spent some time with relatives of the Antonels, the Cusins, who lived in more isolated surroundings on reclaimed swamp land. Maria Cusin never forgot the first time she set eyes on Arch Scott, who was brought to her home by the priest and Pietro Antonel. 'Up until that moment I had never seen such tall men. After my initial surprise I invited them in and we began to chat. That first night I didn't let them sleep in the barn because it did not seem very polite so I made them sleep in a bed.'[14] The ancient laws of rural hospitality operated even under such precarious conditions.

Scott and Sims spent many nights sleeping in the hayloft. During the summer, however, they often preferred to sleep in the open in a leafy-bedded hollow surrounded by weeping willows. Cusin made a straw mattress to keep them dry. Five neighbouring families took turns at feeding the men. It was the Antonels' turn on Saturday and Sunday. All the families soon became very fond of their charges and they used to compete in giving them the best meals of pasta, meat and potatoes. 'Every time the prisoners went to lunch at one of the families, they would not prepare the usual meal of polenta and beans. I remember the day Arturo told me to give him a plate of broad beans because he felt we were spoiling him too much.'[15]

The home of the neighbouring Boato family was ideally secluded for members of the Hare Battalion. From the high windows of the cookhouse they could observe coming and goings without being seen and, if necessary, make a hasty departure through the back door along a path of thick undergrowth to the fields behind the house. Seventeen-year-old Rosetta Gobbo became Scott's eyes and ears. She would act as a courier or *staffetta* taking messages concealed on her bicycle. She was always aware of the dangers and often felt afraid.[16]

Although Scott lived between the Antonel and Cusin families, he was frequently away. He travelled regularly around the region on his blue bicycle, becoming a familiar sight for the locals. Tall and rangy, he was an unlikely looking Italian, but he spoke the language well, having studied it in the prison camp. Some of his tasks were to organise food, clothing and money for his 'cobbers' in hiding and to arrange transfers for them if present living arrangements did not work out. His helpers admired his courage, calm, and his air of total self-assurance. However, Maria Cusin warned Scott not to tell her about any of his planned movements.

'I didn't want to know anything that I could carelessly let slip when I met the other women at the fountain where we washed our clothes.'

Meanwhile, from September to December Laurie Read and his companions were hiding in their dug-out, moving to a haystack when it became colder. The whole population conspired in looking after them. Even nuns from a convent in the district would ride over on their bikes carrying food for the men. Clothing was always needed, especially footwear. Rossana Rossetti of Latisana recalls a group of poorly clad New Zealand prisoners hiding in nearby maize fields. She and her grandmother took down the thick hemp curtains from their porch and made trousers for them.[17] The New Zealanders were very appreciative.

During this time proclamations were put out forbidding people to assist or co-operate with escaped prisoners. The penalty was death or confiscation of property. Germans who suspected people of harbouring escaped prisoners and sympathising with the partisans in the area began carrying out their threats of burning their houses down. In October 1943 Badoglio's government in the Allied-occupied Bari had declared war on Germany and Italians were treated as traitors.

At first Read kept low during the day but moved about freely in the town in the evening. One night the men went to the tavern, bought a bottle of wine and sat down in front of the open fire to toast their toes. When a 'cara' or carabiniere sat down with them they offered a polite 'buona sera' and beat a hasty retreat.

Every Sunday night films were shown in the local picture theatre. One evening Read joined the audience there. 'Most films were of German origin with "Eyetie" translations "dubbed" on the screen. The locals clapped and cheered when the locals won, and booed the villain in his dirty work – just like an old time music hall programme.'[18] But he never went back. Fascists had a habit of arriving suddenly. They would close off the exits and begin checking identities.

The escapers could never forget that they were caught in the middle of a war and that a battle was being fought around them. On their daytime excursions they were puzzled to come across strips of tin-foil about 15 cm long by 2.5 cm wide. Later they learned these were dropped by British bombers on night raids to fool the Axis radar. Aircraft were constantly droning overhead. Once they dived for cover under a tree when a German aircraft came across country, 'hedge-hopping' only a few feet above them. On another occasion British aircraft flew over the countryside dropping propaganda leaflets. Read was delighted to come across a bundle still intact. 'This was to be our main source of toilet paper for a long time to come!'[19]

They shared their haystack with rats 'the size of possums' and a big white owl, which would come swooping under the rafters to seize its prey. Well hidden in the depths of the hay, the men survived three searches of the farm but on the last occasion their hosts were shaken and visibly frightened. The men knew it was time to leave. 'They gave us some food, a St Christopher medallion, a picture card of St John of the Wood and some Gorgonzola cheese that they had been saving for their Christmas feast.'[20] Thus endowed, Laurie Read and his mates headed off on their journey towards Switzerland.

Ian Millar and Stan Jones's guardian angel was a well-off Italian who before the war was a contractor employing thousands of Italian workers on engineering construction projects all over Europe. He was instrumental in organising a series of safe houses and supplies for the men. He concealed his activities for the prisoners under a cloak of deep pro-Fascist sympathy, making friends with Germans and inviting them home for social occasions. He virtually ran the local black market so food was never scarce. He was one of many wealthy Italians who assisted the escapers out of personal conviction or with an eye to furthering business prospects after the war. Millar was under no illusions about his benefactor's motives. After handing over ex-prisoners fat and contented to the Allied armies he would be in a good position to gain some new British contracts.[21]

However, 'Giomaria's' assistance went far beyond the limits of self-interest of many well-off Italians, who provided anonymous donations of money but distanced themselves from overt activity. He never slept in one place for more than a night and there was a large price on his head under an assumed name. Soon he became a district commander of the partisan bands springing up in the area.

The support some men received was part of the network of organised assistance that materialised immediately after the Armistice. The *Ufficio di Assistenza Prigionieri di Guerra Alleati* or Allied Prisoners-of-war Assistance Service was an offshoot of the Milan-based Committee of Northern Liberation, governing the Resistance. It was established to honour one of the terms in the Armistice that prisoners-of-war were to receive every assistance from the Italian Government. Of the three self-appointed governments of Italy at the time, the Allied-backed monarchist 'government' led by Badoglio in liberated Southern Italy was ineffective and shunned by the Resistance; Mussolini's resurrected Fascist Republican 'government' was controlled by the Germans; and the six-party Committee for National Liberation directing the Resistance was regarded with suspicion by the Allies. However, the CLN-organised network was, according to Roger Absalom 'the single most effective rescue and relief agency to operate in Italy in terms of several thousand prisoners-of-war found and assisted'.[22] Agents were entrusted to find money, safe houses and guides to assist prisoners. No prisoner at large survived without help from their often invisible hand.

Ian Millar and Stan Jones found that their new friend's home resembled an army transit camp with its floating population of ex-prisoners who arrived, stayed for a while, then went off again for some weeks. 'It amused us very much that these men roamed about North Italy as if they owned the country. They would go off saying they would return in about two weeks. Their only luggage was usually a spare pair of socks.'[23] That they could roam so freely with so little was due to the generosity of Italians in taking care of their basic needs. It was unfortunate that some men showed arrogance in their confidence and took the assistance for granted.

CHAPTER SIX

Recapture

To tell you the truth, it annoyed me that they freely roamed round the town putting at risk the lives of the people who protected them.[1]

Although recapture was unavoidable for some, many escapers were careless. Going to the pictures, drinking in the taverns and wandering around the countryside in groups were commonplace and within three months over half their number had been recaptured. There were tales of drunken ex-prisoners singing the English version of 'Lili Marlene' at the top of their lungs as they staggered into the arms of a waiting German patrol.[2]

Some Italians reported that the New Zealanders they assisted did not seem aware of the danger they were placing their Italian helpers in and felt resentful of reckless, inconsiderate behaviour, too often caused by drunkenness. Drinking the plentiful wine helped relax the men, but it could unleash frayed nerves. Luigi Borgarelli remembers a scuffle breaking out among three New Zealanders he was sheltering after they had each consumed four or five glasses of wine. 'They drank wine like they drank beer but at 12 per cent [alcohol] you can't joke around!'[3]

Bill Black did not see eye to eye with an early companion. When they just about came to blows after getting drunk on the potent *grappa*, their Italian helpers insisted on splitting them up. In one case a New Zealander knocked his companion out when he drunkenly began arguing with their Italian hosts. They could not afford to offend those upon whom their survival depended.

The price paid by civilian helpers was much higher than that paid by the prisoners if caught. An incident in Marano Lagunare, a small fishing town on the Venetian coast, left a wound that is still raw to this day.[4] The people of Marano were sheltering groups of Allied prisoners, among them New Zealanders, who had spilled out into the countryside from the nearby Torviscosa camp. Italico Formentin, retired director of the Post Office, believes that the prisoners should have been more careful. As a result of the town's suspected assistance of prisoners, the Germans conducted a roundup and two well-known locals were executed.

A New Zealand officer thoughtlessly if unwittingly caused the death of one of them, the sharecropper farmer Giovanni Zulian, known as *il Cucchi*. The New Zealander, who was parachuted into the area, knew several languages and was often in the house of a man named Siro, the village sacristan and tailor, who possessed a radio. An unusually big man, the New Zealander was nicknamed 'Sandòn', a sobriquet given to tall people in Italian masquerade theatre.

One cold morning on 17 December 1943 a German platoon, among them feared Mongolian and Cossack troops, armed with rifles and tommy-guns, descended on Marano Lagunare. All the men over sixteen years were ordered to assemble in the fish market at the wharf and held at gunpoint. Soldiers burst into houses, rounding up even Formentin's 90-year-old uncle who was ill in bed. A fisherman called Antonio Corso had just returned from the lake with his fishing gear and a hunting rifle. Panicking at the thought of being found with a weapon, he tried to hide it and was intercepted by soldiers who arrested him for subversion. Formentin heard the sound of the man's sobs as they marched him past his window to the wharf.

The second person to be arrested was brought in shortly afterwards.

Sandòn, closely pursued by the Germans of the roundup, had fled into the surrounding countryside, following the river that flanked the valley. He came across Zulian who was chopping wood outside his cabin and asked if he could hide there but a terrified Zulian pleaded with him to leave. Sandòn appeared to head for the wooded area in the distance, but must have reckoned he did not have enough time to get there. Unbeknown to Zulian, he ducked back and climbed through an open window at the back of the cabin. Here he was found by the Germans and arrested together with Zulian, who was accused of harbouring the prisoner.

While the seventy or eighty men gathered together in the fish market were finally released, Antonio Corso and Giovanni Zulian were loaded into a truck and taken to a wooded area where they were forced to dig their own graves before being shot.

The murder of these two innocent men left a mark on the town. But the case involving Sandòn is particularly tragic as the sharecropper had no involvement with prisoners whatsoever.[5] Italico Formentin feels the New Zealander epitomises the thoughtlessness of the prisoners who, protected by their prisoner-of-war status, risked losing only their liberty. Ordinary Italians like Giovanni Zulian lost their lives.

Another man paid the ultimate penalty for protecting the escapers. Luigi Franzin was the gamekeeper and security guard of the Piva estate where New Zealanders were hiding with a large extended sharecropper family named Battiston. When Arch Scott initially ran into him in an isolated field, he confessed to feeling afraid of this armed man dressed in military attire. But it was part of Franzin's job to carry a hunting rifle and Scott quickly learned that he could be trusted.

Franzin had encountered the escaped prisoners by chance in the course of his daily patrol through the estate and his freedom of movement was ideal for providing them with food supplies and information. Sometimes he would return home and express annoyance at finding the prisoners roaming the countryside, putting others at risk. Luciano Franzin's memory of his father is filtered through the words of his mother, pregnant at the time with her fifth child. Forced for economic survival to join the Party, her husband had never 'survived twenty-four hours as a Fascist'.[6] As was often the case, his betrayal was motivated by personal rather than political reasons. Poachers, whom it was Luigi Franzin's job to chase from the grounds of the estate, gave vent to their grudge by denouncing his activities for the escaped prisoners to the Fascist authorities.

Luciano Franzin was three years old when his father was arrested in May 1944. Returning home from work on his bicycle Luigi was intercepted by a Fascist patrol lying in wait for him. He was not allowed to see his wife and children, who later collected his bicycle from where it was left on the canal bank. Three other men arrested with him were released on the same day. Franzin was initially taken to Portogruaro then transferred to prison in Trieste, where he remained for twelve days. He refused to co-operate despite brutal interrogation. An eyewitness reported that he was physically almost unrecognisable. Franzin did manage, however, to send a message to his family. Postmarked Milan, it may have been sneaked out while the train was en route to Germany, but no one is sure. This letter, addressed to his wife, asked her to observe two things. One recommendation was of a practical bent concerning the payment of taxes. The second has been a profound gift of grace and pride for his family and a measure of the calibre of the man. He wrote, 'I wish my children to grow up without carrying rancour for anyone.'

Deported to the Nazi concentration camp of Dachau, he never returned. His wife refused to give up hope until they received confirmation of his death. The family never knew how he died despite extensive inquiries. Scott is certain that if Franzin had collaborated he would have been released on the condition that he 'play along', resulting in the capture of all the prisoners.

It was this risk that made Major Hilary Evans refuse to remain in homes with families in the town of Vallepietra, north-east of Rome. During the freezing winter of early 1944 he went and lived in a cave. Initially in company with an Englishman, he spent most of the time on his own. Evans recorded his experiences in his diary, but was careful not to record names or places. An entry of 3 February 1944 is revealing of the tough, no-nonsense Kiwi, who invariably began with a brief report on the weather.

> Fine again. Tragedy! I learned the following when I went down at 6 pm to _____ casetta. This morning at daybreak Jerry surrounded the village and then went in searching for prisoners, rooms were turned upside down and a great deal of food was taken. The podesta (mayor) was arrested and later released, _____'s brother was shot while trying to leave the village to go to his farm and another man was wounded in the leg. _____ was much affected needless to say. Loftus and I returned to the cave instead of going into the village for our evening meal as usual. This is exactly what I have told the villagers would happen if they encouraged prisoners to live in the village. It is no comfort to see my words come true. I blame the whole affair on Fascist spies.
>
> I will go down after dark for our food.[7]

Tony Jacobs was philosophical about his betrayal to Germans by an Italian who put him and his weary companions up for the night. 'The Germans had promised the local farmers a big reward for handing over POWs.' It was well publicised that failure to do so would result in being shot. But he did believe that his Jewish surname caused him to be roughed up more than his friends.[8]

Despite the often quaint experiences of many men, their situation was always highly dangerous. The longer they remained at large the more people knew about them and, if caught, the less likely their status as prisoners-of-war was respected. It is amazing that, overall, so few Italians engaged in spying despite the incentives. The financial rewards for providing information leading to the capture of escaped prisoners-of-war could lift a struggling family out of poverty. The amount was usually 1800 lire but could be higher depending on whether the prisoner had already made a name for himself and was a 'good catch'. Other devices to invite the co-operation of the population in handing over prisoners were subtler. One of these was to offer the repatriation of Italian soldiers in concentration camps in Germany in return for every prisoner handed in to the German Command.

Some men had been at large, protected by families for weeks or months, before they were taken again. Most were put on a train for Germany where they were interned for the remainder of the war. Others looked for opportunities to escape again.

'For you the war is over' was a phrase that Ian St George heard several times between capture in North Africa and his escape into Switzerland in February 1944. After 8 September, like many escapers, he lived with a family and helped with the winemaking. He became a 'human juice extracting machine' as clad only in underwear he hopped on the wooden vats filled with grapes and 'walked them down'. He sampled frogs fried to a crisp in olive oil and found them delicious. But his freedom was short-lived. During the intensive early roundups for escapers he was bailed up near a shallow canal by a fierce dog, captured by its German owners and taken to Treviso. Here with other recaptured prisoners he embarked on a train for Germany.

Italian train carriages have doors on each side. As the train pulled in to the station of Verona, the seat of Mussolini's new Fascist government, both doors opened to allow the flow of human traffic. Guards were engaged in offloading their charges on to the platform on the right-hand side, while civilians were clambering in from the opposite side to claim the seats vacated by the prisoners. It was a split-second decision. 'I dropped to the floor, crawled under incoming legs and out on to the opposite platform.'[9] He looked up and saw that his companions, Rex Ryman and Gordon McLeod, were there too. Egged on by Italian civilians who closed ranks around them, furiously beckoning to them with the distinctive rapid hand gesture, while hissing *via, via* (go, go), the men managed to get down the ramp, through the foyer and out the main entrance of the railway station. They paused for a second to watch 'our boys' being loaded on to army trucks before heading back along the railway track in the direction the train had come from.

Deciding to stay together, the three New Zealanders set out for the mountains. People were usually helpful, and although fearful about the consequences, put them up in barns. They lived on the staple diet of polenta, a thick porridge-like paste made from maize stirred in boiling water and cut when cooled into wedges, chestnuts and hazelnuts. They kept themselves passably tidy with one razor and three blades between them and a pair of scissors for rough haircuts. The higher they climbed the colder it became and they had to break the ice on streams to wash. At Schio, close to the Swiss border, they encountered a family with a radio. It was a great treat to hear the Radio London news and the lilting voice of Vera Lynn. Their diet improved when a motherly woman with a son away fighting gave them a huge thick cheese which they cut into three slabs. This and the plentiful grapes on the vines kept their hunger at bay. But they were ill-equipped for the snow and high country of the Alto Adige, so like many escapers they retraced their steps eastwards in a vague hope of getting to Yugoslavia. On the way the men split up and spent several weeks cared for by three families near Crespadoro in an area that in July 1944 was burned by Germans and Fascists. After a brief spell with partisans who arranged for them to go to Switzerland, they were issued with train tickets for Milan. There was standing room only on the train and they found themselves crushed against German soldiers and Italian civilians. Fortunately no one spoke.

At Milan the men followed the instructions of the partisans, looking out for a girl in a red coat on a corner, whom they followed at a distance to a safe house. On another train leg of the journey a man wanted to make conversation with St George, probably because he stood out like a sore thumb. But when they arrived at a small place called Sondrio, border guards ordered the men off the train and arrested them for not having passports.

For the third time they were 'in the bag'. They spent about five days in the local jail with a frustratingly enticing view of the Swiss Mountains from their window, before being handed over to German SS soldiers. These 'nasty characters with three pips on their shoulders' escorted them, butting them with their rifles, to the railway wagon. Resembling New Zealand cattle trucks, such wagons were completely boxed in by a locked sliding door with two small ventilation openings high up at either end. 'But the lining on both inside and outside was wooden tongue-and-groove.'[10] At night after the guards had checked them and returned to their more comfortable carriage ahead, the men began kicking a hole through the inside lining. After surviving a further brief torch inspection by guards at the next station, they broke through the outer lining and clambered on to the bumper. The train was travelling about thirty kilometres per hour. They pulled their sleeves down to cover their hands and jumped to the side to miss the sleepers, aiming to fall as loosely as possible and roll. All three sustained mild bruising and scratches. Regaining their freedom was nothing compared to their elation at the thought they had put one over the brutal guards. 'All we could talk about were those guards losing their pips the next morning and laughed accordingly with typical Kiwi sense of humour.'[11]

If they were in civilian clothes, recaptured men lost their prisoner-of-war status and were treated as spies by the Germans. Walter Willis had his first introduction to the notorious political prison in Via Spalato in Udine when he was recaptured after his initial escape.[12] Together with a South African, Eddie O'Connell, he was put into an underground cell fit for one man. These cells measured about 2 by 2.5 metres but had a very high ceiling of approximately 3 metres. One wall of the cell was the exterior wall of the prison and was flanked by a small oblong window crossed by heavy bars. Although it was impossible to reach the bars even by standing on the wooden bed, every two hours day and night, two wardens would come into the cell with a ladder. 'They used a heavy steel rod to "sound" the bars. We could doze off in that cell but never sleep.' There was no water and no basin for washing. The latrine consisted of a small bucket, less than 25 cm high, which fitted into a recess in the wall beside the door. This recess, which was the exact shape of the bucket, went right into the interior walls to the passageway outside. 'We learnt through experience that the bucket was not emptied unless it was pushed into the recess as far as we could reach. The interior walls were at least two feet thick.'

On their first day in their new accommodation fastidiousness caused them to miss their initial meal. Standing on a small wooden shelf were two aluminium containers that resembled the receptacles used to make milkshakes in New Zealand. Both contained old vegetable soup with a grey scum floating on top. 'No doubt the previous occupants had left in a hurry. The first day when the warden arrived with the soup we had nothing to put it in. We could not imagine that we would be expected to use the containers already there. The warden pointed to the containers – we showed him the interiors – he shrugged his shoulders and went on his way. We got the message. We emptied the contents into the latrine bucket but we had no way to clean them. By the next day we were so hungry it didn't seem to matter.' The 'soup' consisted of cabbage leaves and turnip boiled in water. There was no spoon.

The cell had one doorway but there were two doors. The inner door served as a gate. It was made of steel rods about 15 cm apart with a narrow opening for the food containers to be passed through on a small metal shelf welded to the bars of the gate. The exterior door that opened to the passageway was made of solid steel except for a covered peephole. When the warden came with the rations he opened the steel door and filled the containers that were waiting there. Despite the steel-barred gate separating the warden from the prisoners, the men were required to retreat to the far wall. All these operations were conducted in complete silence. 'I never heard a warden speak. I never heard a warden walking down the passageway outside. They wore rubber-soled boots and could thus approach the peepholes in the door without being heard. To escape from those cells was completely impossible.'

There was no visual contact with the outside world. The window openings were all covered, although one opening below ground level received ventilation from the outside. One day the men heard the sounds of children at play. But for Walter Willis it was like a strange dream fracturing the horror that had become their normality.

'I will never forget the terrible cold. I will never forget the terrible screaming, at night ... In our cell Eddie and I never did find out the cause of the screaming. We did not even speculate. We were afraid we might find out first-hand.'

A handful of New Zealand escapers, like those of other nationalities, did not survive their time in the Italian countryside.

In March 1944 two New Zealanders, Private Percy Bartrum and Private Len Corless, were reported killed by *carabinieri* 'for robbery and violence' near Salussola in the province of Vercelli, north-western Italy.[13] The reason given is that they used violence to get alcohol so were shot after an exchange of fire. Curiously the two New Zealanders were reported to have pistols, which would have been most unusual. Corporal R. J. Hemsley noted that both men used to regularly pass the house where he was staying but he never saw them again after the news was given him. He reported that as long as New Zealand personnel behaved well, *carabinieri* who knew they were in hiding would leave them alone.[14]

His account, which appears in both the New Zealand and Italian archives, is likely to have been falsified. The report originated from the GNR or the National Republican Guard, the Fascist militia affiliated with the SS, and not the *carabinieri*. The two forces had different allegiances. As a rule, the *carabinieri* maintained loyalty to the King, did not fire at prisoners and often helped them to escape. Significant numbers joined or assisted the partisans or allowed their weapons to be confiscated by partisans.[15] Although escaped prisoners were wary of *carabinieri*, they often mentioned that they turned a blind eye to their presence. Ian Millar noted that when their whereabouts was reported to the local *carabinieri*, they refused to do anything about it.[16]

In the archives of the Carabinieri Piras headquarters at Salussola there is, tellingly, no mention of this incident regarding the New Zealanders and the Marshal agrees that the circumstances were likely to have been invented.[17] This and the subsequent slurring of the memories of both men in the historical archives of two countries should at least be open to question.

Private James McLeod was killed in March 1944. He was seen together with another New Zealander talking to an Italian by the name of Davide Onor on a road near Passarella di Sopra in the San Donà di Piave area. A few minutes later a car stopped nearby and Fascist troops of the San Marco Brigade alighted. McLeod attempted to escape and while running was shot in the back by the Fascists. He died shortly

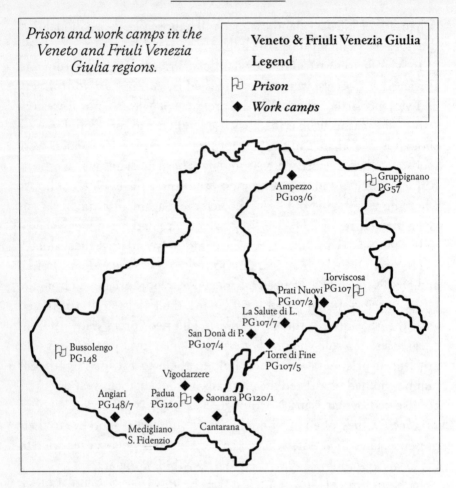

Prison and work camps in the Veneto and Friuli Venezia Giulia regions.

Veneto & Friuli Venezia Giulia

Legend

⚑ *Prison*

◆ *Work camps*

Ampezzo PG 103/6

Gruppignano PG 57

Torviscosa PG 107

Prati Nuovi PG 107/2

La Salute di L. PG 107/7

San Donà di P. PG 107/4

Torre di Fine PG 107/5

Bussolengo PG 148

Vigodarzere

Angiari PG 148/7

Padua PG 120

Saonara PG 120/1

Medigliano S. Fidenzio

Cantarana

afterwards. His companion, who put up no resistance, was captured. Onor allegedly betrayed the two ex-prisoners.[18]

These incidents occurred in early 1944 when the men's survival chances had deteriorated sharply. After October 1943 conditions steadily worsened for prisoners and Italians alike. By the end of the year with the onset of winter, men had made some sort of decision on whether they would stay or move on. Two New Zealanders being sheltered on the Piva Estate voluntarily gave themselves up to the Germans rather than continue to expose their families to further risk.[19] Those who did stay with their families were to be the most active members of the Hare Battalion.

CHAPTER SEVEN

The Kiwi peasants:
'They too are sons of mothers'

We didn't have much to eat ourselves. But what else could you do? We couldn't let them die of hunger.[1]

At the intriguingly named Busa del Morte (Mouth of Death), Roy Johnston and Jim Locke settled into their new life as Raimondo and Giacomo, sons of the Pizzocaro family. It was a typical *famiglia patriarcale*,[2] comprising nono and nona, their four sons and their wives and a fifth wife whose husband was a prisoner-of-war in South Africa. Numerous children, ranging from toddlers to teenagers, swarmed around, completing the family. Nona, tiny, shrill-voiced and black-garbed, was the undisputed head.

After a night's luxurious sleep in the soft warmth of the hayloft, Johnston and Locke offered their services for pressing grapes in the vat. Having worn their boots and the same socks for some days, they headed towards the canal indicating that they wanted to wash their feet before pressing the grapes. Nono was horrified. 'No water in our wine,' he remonstrated. So Johnston, deciding that the adage 'when in Rome' should here be judiciously applied, obligingly took off his boots and socks and set to. That night at dinner he tried to tactfully bring up the subject of hygiene. But his lack of knowledge was made painfully obvious when the males of the family, aghast at his ignorance, explained that fermentation acted as a natural cleansing mechanism, causing skins and dirt to rise to the top. Later that evening, as they went up to the hayloft, Johnston hoped that it was true. A horde of hens was roosting around the edge of the vat with their rear ends perched above the pressings.[3]

They were given civilian clothing and wooden clogs and the women turned their wool uniforms into garments for the children. Gino Pizzocaro, a boy at the time, remembers Johnston as tall, cheerful, with a lot of respect for the family and a great fear of the Germans. Like all the New Zealanders, he was keen to pull his weight and pitch in with the farm work. He helped milk the cows, gather maize and make wine. Young Gino used to run along the deep drains to warn the men when a German patrol was in the area.

Some aspects of family life took time to adjust to. A lack of modesty about bodily functions was one. 'When we first got there and were working in the field I would say, "*Scusami.*" "*Perchè*? Why?" they would ask. "I have to *pisciare.*" And I'd go way down to the other end of the field and *pisciare* and then I would come back and they would all be laughing. And they'd say, "Raimondo, you have some bloody silly habits in New Zealand. We all *pisciare.*" Then one of the women would be called over. "Go on, show him." She'd squat down and she could pee further distance than a man. And she'd have a bet with us and we'd be straining to keep distance with the artillery.'[4]

The stable, heated up by the cows, was the main place of congregation after dinner. Often joined by neighbours, the family would gather to play cards, knit, darn, drink wine and discuss the day's events. 'In the stall it was like a lounge. If you had to widdle you went over to the corner of the stall and pushed a cow out of the way. I was particularly fond of little Maria. Once there was just Maria, her mother and I in the stall and I went over to have a pee. And Maria came over and started swinging between

my legs. And the mother said, "Maria, Maria *sta attenta*, you'll get wet."'
Johnston knew that he had become an Italian when he could continue
and not have to stop, embarrassed.

When a woman came round to administer quinine injections to
combat malaria, Johnston was concerned. 'This is awkward,' he said to
nona. 'What if they question us?' 'No,' she said. 'You go in, take your
pants down, bend over and they will give you a *spunga*. We don't think
the arses of you Kiwis are any different from the arses of Italians.'[5]

Women in the Veneto region are reputed to be very strong, while the men
are *dolci*, sweet and gentle-natured. All the New Zealanders who lived
with peasant families confirmed that women controlled their
households. Tiny, black-garbed nona made all the crucial decisions in
Johnston's family, while nono was 'huge and used to hover', awaiting
orders. One frightening incident stands out. 'It happened out of the blue.
The alarm went out. *Tedeschi*! So we only had one option – to go up
through the trapdoor to the inside of the haystack.' To avoid being
pierced by the long-pronged forks plunged into haystacks to force out
escapers, they crouched in the corner. From his hideout Johnston saw the
whole incident unfold.

'On this particular evening all hell breaks loose and there's a German
patrol complete with helmets and machine-guns and hand pistols. The
whole family's brought out and lined up against the wall. They were after
arms and it was the women who spoke out. They were the ones who held
the fort. The men would talk but the women would really do their bun.
They would say we are a peaceful family. We have no arms round here.
They would really frighten the hell out of them.' After that Johnston
called a meeting with the family and suggested that he and Locke
(Giacomo) should leave as it was too dangerous to have them there. Some
of the men in the family thought this made good sense. But nona would
not hear of it. 'Fortunato is in South Africa. He is a prisoner of the
English. He is our son. These two are sons of mothers too. We will look
after them.' The matter was closed.

Nona was a great character. Through her, the curious, open-minded

Johnston learned much about the intricacies of Italian peasant culture, its ambiguities and wry humour. Religion was a topic that would often come up. Nona had firm views. 'Raimondo, you talk religion. Cesira [Fortunato's wife] is the daughter of a priest!' 'You're joking!' replied Johnston. And she said, 'No, no, no, the church is not good. They have gold in their churches and we are hungry outside.' Next day Johnston, always conscious of the need to keep fit, was up early working and walking vigorously. 'And I'd see this little thing like a Van Gogh painting in a black hood heading off down the road, going to Mass. So later in the day I'd say to her, "It was a very good discussion we had last night, but you puzzle me. I see you going to Mass." "Oh, Raimondo," she said, "just in case, just in case."'[6]

The primitive conditions of the rural families the New Zealanders lived with were always obvious. Maurice Cosgrave reflected that 'peasant people have a different outlook. They've got an ox for ploughing the field. They've got a couple of rabbits for killing for meat. And they've got a pig they divide up with the *padrone*. Life is miserable. It's the only one they've ever known so to them it's all right. Yet it's stepping back in time.'[7]

Four families – Botosso, Martin, Furlanetto and Pasqual – protected John Senior and three fellow Kiwis for eighteen months in the neighbourhood of San Giorgio di Livenza. Ines Martin, who resembled Senior's older sister, cooked, sewed and did his washing. But at times she had to be firm. She told Senior there was too much drinking, too much laughing, too much talking and too much English. 'We fear for our safety.'[8] Senior tried to avoid being sent away by saying that the Allies would soon be arriving but it is doubtful he ever fooled the Italians.

'Even if we knew the risks how could we not take care of them when they didn't want to leave, as they were fond of our families as we were fond of them. John, in particular, was like a brother and I was his sister, one of his family. I was always afraid but I could never find the courage to send him away.'[9]

The world of the Italian peasant was governed by tireless work in the fields according to the rhythms of the seasons where the cycle of planting, tilling and harvesting had changed little in a thousand years. The 'invasion' into this archaic world of hungry, disoriented young men from the furthest outposts of the British Empire resulted in a mutual solidarity between peasant and prisoner that has been termed 'a strange alliance'.[10] At odds with the Italians' status as enemy and the profoundly negative image many prisoners harboured of them, the generous warmth of the welcome they received surprised and moved even the most cynical. Hunted and forced to beg for food and shelter they were received with a simple dignity and humanity that was humbling.

Most peasants were sharecroppers contracted to give half of all the produce to the *padrone* whose land they settled and worked on. Roy Johnston once watched this halving being done, amused to note that 'some halves were definitely bigger than the others!'[11] Some were small tenant farmers who paid the landowners a fixed rate in exchange for the fields and house they rented. Other groups were formed by small landowners and the most precarious of all, farm labourers, who went wherever they could find work. Dependent on the abundance of the harvest and the generosity of landowners, many needed to hire out their services as casual labourers to supplement their meagre income.

Everyone in the family was expected to work, including the children. For Novella Bigotto at Teor near Rivignano, whose family fed Pat Moncur and two other New Zealand escapers, 'there wasn't much time for playing.'[12] She would often spend three hours in the fields before going to school. Among her chores were picking broad beans or corn, taking the turkey, goose or the family's sole prized sheep to pasture, and in the winter, gathering wood in the forest. It was considered a waste of time educating children whose lives were destined for the fields. The children of peasants sat in the back benches and were often ignored unless they offered the teacher a chicken or some eggs. Novella Bigotto recalls those times as harsh, but with a spirit of solidarity and harmony lacking in today's world. Everybody gave a hand to each other. 'There was the occasional scuffle but how beautifully the young people used to sing together in the square!'

This vast underclass of poverty was a fertile ground for the leftist forces who were mobilising the country on the attractive premise of sweeping away the old unjust institutions and an economic system that generated poverty.[13] Yet many peasants were wary of the present ruling order being replaced by another equally repressive one. In the north-eastern corner where boundaries had been contested for centuries, and Communist partisans had aligned themselves with Tito's bands, resistance to Communism ran particularly high.

However, a family's economic dependency could be a key factor influencing their disassociation from politics. Fraulin and Perosa, the sons of the sharecroppers at Prati Nuovi, explain. 'The administrator at that time had all the power. You had to say yes even if it wasn't right.'

Confirms Bruno Blasigh, 'You had to work and keep quiet. If something went wrong the landowner could send you away. Our families didn't know anything about politics. You worked and you ate.'

While many peasants ignored politics they instinctively identified with those suffering oppression. Traditionally, Italian peasants were distrustful of authority and did not take regulations seriously. Centuries of exploitation and neglect had spawned a sub-culture that, while paying lip service to authority, liberally bent the rules and tended to side with the underdog. The prisoners, young men engaged in a daily struggle to survive while being hunted by a common enemy, must have struck a chord. The women in particular saw them as replacement sons for their boys away. Perosa recalls his mother telling his father they had to do something because she would hope another family would help their older son who was a prisoner of the English. Countless escapers from all countries testify their Italian 'mamma' referred to them as sons of mothers. In this maternal, moral exchange economy that connected mothers across geographical boundaries and the divisions of war, women believed that looking after one woman's son would result in another woman taking care of her own.[14]

Nonetheless, because of their self-sufficient economy and the ability of the women to make a little go a long way, food was more plentiful than in the towns. The escapers were generally polite and friendly; immensely grateful for all the assistance they received, they were eager not to be a burden. For their part the peasants found themselves being treated respectfully as equals, rather than as a despised subaltern class at the bottom of the heap. They were fascinated with a collection of photos Ian Millar carried in his pay-book. When they saw a photo of the Millar family beside their 1938 Chevrolet saloon they shouted, 'You're rich!' It took all his effort to dissuade them from calling him '*signore*'. For several days Signora Zanini insisted on bringing them meals on dainty traycloths with table napkins.[15] That these young men from distant 'developed' countries depended on them for assistance against the hated Fascists and Germans gave them not only a common purpose, but, for the first time, a sense of active participation in influencing events around them.[16] Down-to-earth New Zealanders who prided themselves on being from a classless society would have had less 'class' baggage than others and may have had more in common with the rugged, practical peasants than at first met the eye.

In Italy the landowners of the vast properties knew nothing about the care of livestock. As one New Zealand officer confronted with an Italian intelligence officer who tried to make much of their shared country background stated, 'His knowledge of livestock was confined to the family racehorses, mine to the earthy skills of dairy farming.'[17] Farmers in New Zealand, no matter what their background, worked the land and had the rough calloused hands of the peasant. Because many New Zealanders had grown up or worked on farms, animal husbandry was a hot topic of conversation. When Ian Millar told his helpers that in New Zealand farm animals lived outside all year round they were incredulous. 'They thought us very cruel, for their farm animals lived a very sheltered life inside barns almost all the time.' A single cow was much treasured and tenderly nurtured to produce a calf on a certain date, an eagerly awaited event. Stan Jones, in civilian life a farmer with a flock of over a thousand sheep, was regarded as an authority on all farming matters, so he and Millar were invited to assist at the birth. 'When the calf's front legs began to appear, they tied a rope to them and the four of us were ordered to pull the other end. Stan was horrified!'[18] But following the unspoken code of deference to Italian customs, the two men did as they were told and after the successful outcome were plied with double rations of wine. Eight days later the calf was killed to avoid the requirement of German authorities to register the birth. This was one of the many ways peasant families managed to beat the system, obtaining more food for themselves.

Even in these harsh conditions, ceremonial occasions were celebrated and Italian culinary skills produced remarkable tastes for the unsophisticated Kiwi palate. Maurice Cosgrave still remembers the beautiful meal prepared to celebrate the epiphany and its symbolic figure, *la befana*, the benevolent 'white witch', in January 1944. They ate a boned turkey stuffed with sausage meat and truffles. The killing of the pig in December was a memorable ritual. 'The pig was put on a sloping board with its head down. Somebody cuts the throat and an old lady catches the blood with a basin. The blood is coagulated and chopped up into bits and fried with onion. Delicious. I suppose it's something like black pudding.' Onions could be eaten like apples with big chunks of dark bread. The *provolone* or sheep's cheese was exquisite. 'They milk the sheep and put it in a big clay pot beside the fire and it curdles itself with the warmth.' Nothing was ever wasted. Once Cosgrave saw a woman squirt milk from her breasts into the pot. 'She had too much milk so she put it in with the cheese.'[19]

Bill Black participated in a wonderful feed on New Year's Eve in 1943. 'They get a great big sort of – it looked like whitebait nets – and they slam these against the haystacks outside and all these sparrows fly into them, thousands of them. And they wring their necks and stick them on a skewer and cook them over an open flame. And they're beautiful. Oh, they really are!'[20] His reminiscences are peppered with comparisons to life in New Zealand. In this way, as an outdoors man used to hunting in the bush, Black could maintain a sort of psychological control over an unfamiliar environment. And he commented many times on how the Italians loved their wine and enjoyed getting people 'shicker'. This easy identification of New Zealand landmarks with the Italian allowed him to move more confidently in a foreign environment.

The peasants' intimate knowledge of the land enabled them to devise ingenious hideaways to protect their charges. Initially Senior, Johnston and their companions were sheltered in the vineyards in a *casotta*, a small shelter made of maize stalks lined with hay and hidden inside the vines. However, it was effective only until winter when the leaves fell off the vines. In the plains escapers hid in haylofts, barns and huts on game reserves, while in the mountains and hills they found shelters inhabited seasonally by occasional labourers, shepherds and charcoal burners. But by 1944 when the danger escalated, more unusual places were sought. The Zanella family helped Black to hide in a sump, a hole 2.4 metres square by 1.8 metres deep. They burned bundles of straw inside it to dry it out. To disguise the entrance to his new abode, Black built a 'shit-house' out of cane on top of the sump. It sufficed for some time before the water started seeping back in.

In the summer the Kiwi Italians of the Hare Battalion went barefoot, but when winter came their feet were frozen. John Senior's army boots had long since worn out so he had the upper leather taken off the soles and tacked on to wooden clogs, worn habitually by the peasants. These kept his feet protected from freezing ice or snow although it was impossible to run if pursued.

Most of the men living on the swampy Venetian plains suffered from bouts of malaria. When they did their families would allow them to sleep inside. Once John Senior was so sick that the Furlanetto family worried he would die. They were also frightened that if Senior died on their premises they would all be shot. The priest arranged for a doctor to provide an injection and quinine pills to Senior at his vicarage. As German headquarters were next door, Senior completed the last phase of the journey crawling to the front door out of view of the sentries. Clelia Furlanetto, aged fifteen at the time, remembers Senior preparing for his visit. 'That evening John got out from his bed, washed himself and put on a suit. He said that dressed like that he already felt better. He took the medicine and was cured in a week. He would always say that if he died we should bury him under a grapevine as he would make the wine taste better.'[21] Ines Martin, a member of one of the families protecting John Senior, Roy Ryan, Toby Pierce and Bob Anderson, recalls the constant fear of Fascist patrols finding the prisoners. They usually arrived at night and banged and thumped on the door until she opened it. Ines would say, "Come in and look wherever you want but they're not here. Go on, lift up the covers and check they're not underneath!" They never found them of course because we had them hidden in the fields.' They were crouched in huts made of maize stalks under the vines.[22]

Carnival in Venice is a time of feasting, merry-making and licence often associated with the amorous exploits of one of Venice's most famous sons, Giacomo Casanova. It precedes the austerities of Lent with its forty days of abstinence from meat. Arch Scott and Noel Sims decided to relieve the tension and frustration of the past months and bring some cheer into the Carnival week of February 1944. One night they dressed up as women complete with make-up and wigs and, for the next few hours, romped across the fields from household to household, singing, dancing and drinking liberal quantities of *grappa*, the potent brew made from the pulp of grapes.

'The awful thought had crossed our minds of the possibility of our being taken thus dressed by the Germans, but this thought did not persist beyond the first house.' The news of their imminent arrival had spread through the community and families waited up for them. Scott has no memory of how he arrived home at his hayloft at dawn. He had apparently crossed a very wide canal while remaining perfectly dry. 'It seemed that (i) I was the unrecognised world champion broad jumper, or (ii) I was the second one to walk on water, or (iii) *grappa* was magic. Based on subsequent experimentation and observation I tend to favour the third option.'[23]

A few kilometres west at Santa Maria Cessalto near San Donà di Piave the Varaschin family was also celebrating Carnival. It too was to be unforgettable. Some months earlier 11-year-old Maria Varaschin had heard of the escaped prisoners living under a bridge. 'And people were saying how can they possibly live there? What are they eating? We were all against Fascism. But we were forced to put up with it.'[24] It was the much-loved local priest, Don Pietro Buogo, who organised the placing of the four New Zealanders in people's houses. Their Italian names were Arnaldo, Giorgio, Guglielmo and Arturo. Guglielmo, who was Bill Black, lived in a little outhouse separate from the main dwelling. Because he was ill with malaria, Arturo, the smallest of the tall New Zealanders, came to live at Maria's house. He slept inside on the second floor of the adjoining barn where the silkworms were hung. He was much favoured by her grandmother who used to bring him *caffe latte* every morning. A man used to bring him quinine hidden in a hole in the saddle of his bicycle.

Maria remembers the New Zealanders as being very kind and good-natured young men who enjoyed playing games with the children. They used to gather in the huge stable where the cows were kept because they provided warmth. After a few glasses of wine the New Zealanders would sing their special song. To illustrate this she broke into the *Yi, yi yippee, yippee yi* chorus from 'She'll be Coming Round the Mountain'.

One night in February during the week of Carnival the New Zealanders attended a big gathering of family and friends. They had eaten the traditional *fritelle* and drunk wine and everyone had been singing and enjoying themselves. At 3 a.m. they were all in bed when there was a loud banging at the door. A Fascist patrol burst in and accused them of hiding an English prisoner. 'My father said, "No, there is no English prisoner." He thought he was safe because Arturo was outside the house.' Maria was frightened as the Fascists began to search the house. Her father pleaded with them to deal with him if they had a problem but not to touch his children. They went to the stables but found nothing. 'Papà was so relieved until one of the squad saw the ladder leading up to the second floor. They went up the ladder and they found him asleep.' Both her father and Arturo were beaten up and taken away, tied to each other with a rope. But not before the squad took all the salami and any other food they could find.

All four New Zealanders were rounded up that night. Bill Black was among those taken off to the local jail after the platoon burst in 'bristling with bloody guns'. A spy had betrayed them to the Fascists, even though Black thought some of his companions mixed a bit too freely with the villagers, going to church and being generally indiscreet. According to Maria, there were about four spies in their area who wreaked havoc on the largely anti-Fascist local populace. Their identities were discovered at the end of the war. Two of them were women, one a seamstress, and they were meted out the usual treatment. Maria has no sympathy. 'Do you know what we did to them afterwards? They shaved their hair and it was a Sunday and they had to go to Mass. Think of the shame of it. But they brought such misery to people.'

Her father was taken to prison in Treviso. A few days before he was to be deported to Germany, the Allies bombed the prison and Riccardo

Varaschin was able to escape through the rubble. Dodging the main roads, he walked back home from Treviso. 'My mother was in bed. She heard the sound of someone clearing his throat from outside the window. She said, "Riccardo, is that you?" And he said, "Be quiet, be quiet," because he was frightened that the Fascists were waiting for him. Then he came up the ladder. We slept on the second floor. I was the littlest. He kissed me and he said, "Listen, it's a miracle I'm here."' He hugged them, took a blanket, and went to sleep in the fields. Her father was able to work in the fields during the day, but he kept away from the house until evenings, a routine he maintained until the end of the war.

Black recalls, 'We were a bit worried about the old man because we didn't know what was going to happen to him, whether they were going to shoot him or burn the house down.'[25] After his second escape from a train heading for Germany, Black eventually returned to the area and was cared for by the Zanella family. He was pleased to learn of Varaschin's breakout from the prison.

The Garibaldi partisans often came to the farmhouse at night requesting clothes and food. Once they killed a cow. They did not mind them taking the cow, but Maria's father was reluctant to put his family under further risk, given his own status as a fugitive. One night the partisans brought in three captured Fascist soldiers. Maria's grandmother was asked to prepare some food for them. One man kept repeating 'Long live the *Duce!*' while another asked for some paper and a pen. He said that there was only one thing he regretted and that was leaving the four-year-old son he had never seen.

When Maria and her friend discovered their bodies in a shallow grave three days later, the priest, Don Pietro Buogo, organised the burial. He fiercely swore everyone to secrecy. 'If the Germans find out they will kill you,' he said. 'What terrible secrets we children had to keep!'

Maria Varaschin still thinks of the man and wishes she could tell his now adult son that his father before dying had spoken those words of remembrance. But she does not know how to trace him. She also wonders if Arturo managed to return safely home. He was so frail that she doubted he could survive further imprisonment. Only Guglielmo returned to say he had escaped from a train. But of Arturo she never heard again.

Not far from Maria, Raimondo and Giacomo were ensconced happily with the Pizzocaro family. They embarked on regular nighttime raids to forage for food. In particular, the scarcity of fresh fruit deprived the children of an important source of nutrition. Fruit trees groaning with succulent produce were kept locked up in the *padrone's* orchards under a guard and dog patrol. To arrive at the furthest reaches of the vast property meant a considerable hike, including fording a couple of canals. However, a preliminary reconnaissance informed them that the guard had a girlfriend. When she arrived for a night of passion the guard and dog would enter his quarters. Acting upon this crucial bit of field intelligence, they regularly pulled in a successful haul of fruit for the delighted children.[26]

Losing one's modesty over bodily functions was only a partial step towards assuming a new identity. Johnston had really become an Italian peasant when he began devising and carrying out schemes to outwit the wealthy Fascist *padrone*. For a New Zealander the latter came far more naturally.

CHAPTER EIGHT

Survival strategies

*I told him I was a Kiwi but he didn't know what a
bloody Kiwi was.*[1]

Successful escapers learned very quickly to cast aside any preconcep-
tions or arrogance. Being physically fit and able to get by in the outdoors
was not enough to ensure survival. Adapting to their environment
required skills of imagination and sensitivity that initially may not have
come naturally to many Kiwis. There were hours of forced monotony
when it was too dangerous to move outside. During their months under
Giomaria's protection, Ian Millar spent three hours every day studying
the Italian language. Assisted by a medical student who brought him
grammar books, Millar could soon read a newspaper and certain novels.
However, when he tried his skills out on the locals they had difficulty
understanding him as they spoke a dialect that differed considerably,
especially in the verb endings. Millar enjoyed spending evenings at
Giomaria's house where everyone spoke good Italian and 'the general
standard of conversation was higher than we were accustomed to'.[2] His

efforts to practise and master some of the formal intricacies of the language caused a hero's reception. 'The first time I used a subjunctive mood in my conversation they seemed to be so pleased over my progress that I had to wait for the uproar to die down before carrying on!'[3]

But the New Zealanders could never get rid of their English accents. John Senior and Roy Ryan had by this time become shrewd and played on Italy's famous regionalism. When Venetians, trying to place their faulty Italian, asked where they came from, Senior would say south of Rome. For a people who had never ventured beyond their village, southern Italy was another country. 'That explains why your dialect is different!'[4] Maurice Cosgrave in the central Marches region was advised to say he was from Bergamo, north-east of Milan, if captured by the Germans. 'Nobody can understand those people anyway.'

While he was staying with the Bianchi family in Comunanza, Cosgrave, now known as Pietro,[5] attended the small school across the road to improve his language. Despite being over six feet tall, the New Zealander shared the benches with half a dozen seven-year-olds. He joined in the chanting of the alphabet. 'G is for Gesù, M is for Maria, that sort of thing.' But he made a lot of mistakes. If he encountered hunters setting out on a shoot, he would wish them *buona fortuna*, words guaranteed to cause a dismayed reaction – functioning in opposition to its meaning, it is like wishing someone bad luck. He quickly learned that *in bocca lupo* (in the wolf's mouth) is the suitable phrase in wishing good fortune for any intended endeavour. At a dinner party of a wealthy *padrone* who helped him out with money, 'We got talking about English whisky and I said Vat 69.' There was a deadly silence. 'And I was trying to explain that it wasn't that hot. And later on Francesco said, "Eh, Pietro, 69's something a man and a woman do!" Jesus Christ, oh dear, oh dear!'[6]

Arch Scott came to love the children of the Antonel extended family. An entourage of about twenty youngsters was constantly around them. 'They were our constant cobbers, even the tiny ones. They were never cheeky, never a nuisance. We used to talk and sing and play with them.'[7] The children ran messages, brought food and helped them more than anyone to learn the Venetian dialect. The language lessons were mutual. Nine-year-old Ida, whose job was to look after the geese, was a special favourite. One day Scott and three of his compatriots were sitting under the grapevines ruminating in a desultory fashion, as they often did, on their extraordinary circumstances. As usual, a silent, attentive Ida sat close by. She asked suddenly, 'Cosa vuol dir 'sto – what means this – "Far Key Nell?"' She enunciated the words carefully. 'Always is being said, "Far Key Nell."'[8]

All through the cold winter of 1943–44, Ian Millar and Stan Jones talked about what they would do once the spring arrived. They were determined to achieve something 'instead of this negative occupation of waiting and waiting for our armies to arrive'.[9] Whatever direction they decided to head in they wanted to avoid 'the horror' of being put behind barbed wire again. They even rejected escaping to Switzerland on the premise that being interned there would be comparable to prison camp. Such a fallow, inactive time could, however, be put to good use. Visits to the mountains to meet up with the Kiwi group comprising Paul Day and Pat Moncur were an ideal opportunity to practise disguising themselves. If it was difficult to look like an Italian, behaving like one was essential. Italians taught them that if they wanted to be taken for peasants they must not talk to each other or walk abreast. Walking slowly with their heads down was another tactic. Any suggestion of a military bearing in their walk must be replaced by the peasant slouch with one or even both hands in their pockets.

On one of their journeys back and forth to the mountains Millar and Jones decided to take a short-cut running behind the village in order to gain the main highway, rather than the long route. 'If we were to look like peasants who knew every inch of the country, we must certainly save ourselves any walking.' Men and women were busy working in the fields and the Kiwis felt very conspicuous 'tramping about the countryside'. In order to avoid suspicion the men adopted what might in their own culture have appeared a brazen demeanour. They found themselves in a fortified area manned by two Fascist soldiers sitting in a weapon pit. As it was customary for most Italian peasants to stare at people they did not know, the New Zealanders stared boldly at the Fascists 'in the Italian

Top left: Celebrating Easter 1944 in the mountains above Sequals, protected by partisans. L–R unknown ex-prisoner, Ernie Clark, Ossie Martin, Italian helper and Pat Moncur – with an egg over his shoulder and holding a bottle of special Easter wine.

Middle: The Botosso and Furlanetto homes in the plains of San Giorgio di Livenza in the Veneto. The two families looked after John Senior and his friends.

Below: Douglas Dymock's prison work camp near Salussola, Vercelli, in front of the barracks. The Italian sergeant is on the left, face turned away because of a swollen jaw due to toothache. Back row, Douglas Dymock fourth from left (pipe in mouth), second row, Bill Gyde fourth from left, front row, George London first from right.

Left: S. Giorgio di Nogara – three escaped prisoners in their hideout.
Bottom left: David Russell.
Bottom right: Owen Snedden (left) and John Flanagan with Alwyn Jagusch, an old school friend in Rome after the liberation. Flanagan's weight loss is evident here.

Left: Jim Locke (Giacomo) (left) and Roy Johnston (Raimondo), loose in Italy behind the lines, enjoying the vino they may have helped to make!
Below: Bill Black (Guglielmo).
Bottom left: Bill Black and Don Pietro Buogo, the priest of Cessalto.
Bottom right: Riccardo Varaschin, arrested and imprisoned for sheltering New Zealand escaped prisoners.

Left: Before and after – the summary execution of a young partisan by an equally young Fascist soldier.
Below: The 'Mondine' – women who worked up to their knees in water in the rice fields, alongside the prisoners in the Vercelli work camps.

Left: Defend her! She could be your mother, your wife, your sister, your daughter. Fascist propaganda to counter the Allied 'invasion'.
Bottom left: John Senior.
Bottom right: Ines Martin (left, seated) and her family.

Above: Arch Scott (centre) with members of the Antonel family. Angelo Antonel is third from left. His father Pietro is second from left.

Below: L–R Ernie Clark, Ossie Martin, Pat Moncur, Paul Day, Mick Hogan. Kiwi 'partisans' in Northern Italy.

Opposite: Arch Scott and partisan Gino Panont in St Mark's Square, Venice.
Left: Roy Ryan (left) and Dave Taylor (centre) with members of the Francescon family.
Below: Ian St. George.
Bottom left: L–R Ian Millar, Dick Partridge, Stan Jones.
Bottom right: Laurie Read.

fashion' and walked nonchalantly past. In this case they received barely a glance but further on, two well-dressed civilians stared hard and fast back at them, their gaze boring into their backs as they walked on.[10]

Arch Scott learned to scrutinise any environment he was in for a quick exit, a habit he was never to lose. There were so many false alarms that he adopted a calm, impassive manner as a technique for dealing with any eventuality. Another strategy was to act in a light-hearted way as an antithesis to fear, so much so it became natural.[11] One evening he was dining with an Italian family when two German soldiers knocked at the door. Invited to share the meal, the Germans later pulled out photos of loved ones and Scott, in his guise as head of the family, sympathised with their desire to return home as soon as possible.[12] As each adventure was confronted and successfully overcome, Scott began to notice being drawn to 'the fascination of danger, to the irresistible challenge of it'.

The men who stayed in the area established an informal liaison network with other escaped prisoners that ran from Udine to Venice. They regularly visited each other to swap information on roundups, the progress of the Allies, and to organise supplies for fellow escapers. At first these were social occasions to catch up on the gossip with mates. Often unbeknown to them fellow Kiwis would be hiding only a short distance away. Bill Black would walk miles just to have a chat with a friend, while for Ian Millar and Stan Jones, who met up by chance with Pat Moncur, it served the dual purpose of keeping fit. They enjoyed many 'happy hikes' climbing in the mountains and although wary of talking with people found that if they did, 'they invariably seemed to know more about us than we did ourselves!'[13] It also helped combat the loneliness that often assailed those men who chose to be on their own.

Sometimes a well-adjusted couple decided to split up for their own safety. Eventually it was the most sensible decision for Millar and Jones who had a close call with a 'trigger-happy' band of young Fascists who would now be searching for them. By travelling alone they reckoned they would have twice the chance of returning to their Allied forces as would the two of them travelling together. It would also increase the chances of at least one of them being able to send a message to their families in New Zealand after months of silence. But it was a wrench to split up after being close friends since their earliest days in the army. At 11.30 a.m. on 30 April 1944 they parted on the highest peak of the mountainous district after scrupulously dividing their meagre possessions. 'We cut our towel in half and also our cake of soap.'[14]

Maurice Cosgrave was wary of hanging around ex-prisoners for another reason. Germans had captured two English escapers outside the gate of the Comunanza cemetery. From his hiding place behind a tomb Cosgrave watched as they were made to dig a hole beside the road, then when it was deep enough, forced to stand in it. They were shot through the belly, then the hole was filled up. 'You get to the stage where fear just disappears. All you're thinking of is survival.' He heard later that a fellow ex-prisoner, who had been captured with a friend, was responsible. 'Where are all the other English?' he was asked. When the man said he didn't know, he was ordered to go and look for them. 'They told him if he didn't come back, they'd shoot his mate. That's how the two I saw got caught. They were betrayed by their own people.'[15]

Later on Johnston and Locke made contact with a Socialist partisan group belonging to the Matteotti Division run by an Italian lieutenant endowed with contacts and cash. By now prisoners, peasants and partisans were actively working together and liaising with the British Special Forces Missions or American OSS operating in the mountains. In the last few months of the war when planes were constantly flying overhead on bombing raids to Munich, several pilots whose planes had been hit managed to parachute safely to the ground. If it was in Johnston's corner he and Locke attempted to get to them before a German patrol did. Their job was to hide the pilot and his parachute before handing them over to the partisans. One British Spitfire pilot, alarmed by the sight of two dishevelled peasants racing towards him, pulled out his revolver. He received a tirade of abuse advising him what to do with his gun. When asked who they were, Johnston retorted, 'We are bloody New Zealanders of course'. 'You New Zealanders appear to be everywhere in this bloody war,' the pilot replied in his crisp, 'plummy' Oxford tones.[16]

Bill Black was first on the scene to greet an American major who was stunned that he had been shot down by small arms fire, an apparently impossible feat according to the rulebook. With his leap into enemy territory, however, the old rules no longer applied and the major had to take orders from a ragged New Zealander, a lowly private to boot. 'He couldn't speak a word of Italian. "Americano," he said pointing to his boots.' Black was unimpressed. 'I said, "Don't be such a bloody idiot. Come on, I'll get you out of those clothes." I told him I was a Kiwi but he didn't know what a bloody Kiwi was!'[17] These highly trained airmen had grandiose notions of what was feasible in their new situation and could be a liability. 'He wanted to go out there and flog a bloody plane from an airfield and fly straight out of the joint. It wasn't going to work.' The major needed re-education. Black got him into some civilian clothing and 'took him round and showed him exactly how we were living and how we'd been doing it for months'. He emphasised the need for patience, and told the major to stop broadcasting his rank, 'otherwise you'll have everybody in the world around you.'

John Senior and his companions also took responsibility for some American airmen who had baled out of a burning plane and were hiding in neighbouring fields. Senior organised more comfortable accommodation in an enlarged hole in a haystack and provided them with books and cards. Even in the haystack, formal military discipline was maintained. To Senior's amusement, the aircrew stood to attention when addressed by their officer. The fact the New Zealanders had been at large for so long astounded them. With their tanned, weather-beaten skins, command of dialect Italian and easygoing demeanour the New Zealanders blended into their environment in a way that the Americans seemed to find disorienting. Although appreciative of their assistance, the aircrew remained aloof. 'They appeared to be alarmed and frightened and kept to the confines of the haystack, gazing at the sky as hundreds of their planes went over to bomb Germany.'[18]

Towards the end of the war, John Senior had a close encounter with the enemy of an unusual kind. Word was received that two Germans were hiding in the haystack at the back of the farm. The New Zealanders'

Italian families were worried they were spies and asked them to sort them out. Senior was curious but also wanted to show off his soldierly prowess in front of the Italians. It was an opportunity to reverse the usual dependency experienced by the protected ex-prisoner. 'We said never mind, we'll take care of it.' At dusk Senior and his companions, armed with pitchforks, surrounded the haystack and yelled at the Germans to come out. 'If they reach for their guns, stab them!' Two men emerged with their arms in the air. While they were baled up at the point of pitchforks, Senior searched them for weapons. Having found them unarmed they marched the men into the fields and sat them down for questioning in a clearing encircled by cut maize. He hoped the Italians were watching. One man was a Pole who had been drafted into the German army when Germany invaded Poland. Neither man spoke English but the Pole spoke some Italian dialect and translated it into German for his companion, a navigator with the German airforce who had fought on the Russian front. In civilian life he was a conductor with the Berlin Symphony Orchestra. It was obvious the men were deserters and fed up with war, convinced Germany was defeated. They insisted that Germany had never wanted to fight England and that the two countries should have joined forces to fight the Russians.

Two of the New Zealanders then went off to collect flasks of wine from the nearest farmhouse. When they returned the pitchforks were put away and they all drank to each other's health. The six men, communicating in the only common language native to none of them, the Venetian dialect, proceeded to get roaring drunk. A high point of the revelry was when the New Zealanders provided a rousing chorus of 'Toreador' from the opera *Carmen* while the German, delighted at the opportunity to practise his former profession, vigorously conducted.

But the deserters knew that if caught they would be instantly executed. They told the escapers that their POW status might no longer hold up because they had been at large for so long. They too risked being shot if captured. At evening's end, 'with our arms round each other's waists, we escorted them back to their haystack.'[19] Next morning they had disappeared, perhaps not willing to trust in their continued safety beyond that night of fraternal revelry.

Paul Day's group was unsure what to do with a German deserter who had been picked up by Italian partisans and handed over to them. The man said he had jumped out of a truck laden with reinforcements heading towards Cassino. Answering to the name of Peter, saying he was of German-Swiss parentage, he tended to wander around shouting obscenities about Hitler. The South Africans were very wary of him but he teamed up with a man called Paul Schwartz when they split into pairs to try and reach Switzerland. Both were never heard of again and Day believes they were shot as German spies by the same partisans he encountered in a village en route to Switzerland.[20]

But so-called German deserters could also be decoys planted as spies, as many partisans found to their detriment. There is a curious case of a man called *il Neozelandese* (the New Zealander) who joined the partisan Tiger group commanded by Lieutenant Egidio Cardona operating in the mountainous area round the town of Fabriano in the central Marches region. After the Armistice three different groups had gathered in this area to form partisan bands: anti-Fascists who organised the movement, groups of ex-prisoners-of-war, and disbanded Italian army soldiers. Among an exclusively Italian partisan group was the so-called Luigi Neozelandese, who passed himself off as a New Zealand escaped prisoner-of-war. On 2 April 1944 he took part in an operation to capture ten Fascists at Sassoferrato where suddenly the partisans found themselves surrounded by twenty Germans. They had been ambushed and were outnumbered; an Italian partisan, Alessandro Orsi, was wounded and brutally killed, while Luigi Neozelandese, also wounded, was spared and taken away in a German truck. Some weeks later *il Neozelandese* reappeared. He claimed he had miraculously escaped from the German hospital after hearing that a German military tribunal had condemned him to death. He also told the group that their commander, Cardona, had been captured and shot. This piece of false information caused great uncertainty and confusion and it was only later that they learned it was not true.[21] An order had been received to retrieve some arms which had been buried at Murazzano and take them to the village of Piaggiasecca. The partisans arrived at Piaggiasecca on 9 June but found themselves surrounded at 2 p.m. by German forces. Leading them was 'the New Zealander', and an Italian Fascist. Three partisans were killed in this attack and 'the New Zealander', after this second betrayal, disappeared, now exposed as a German spy. Although a small group of German deserters fought valiantly with the partisans, many partisans were understandably not willing to take a risk with them or anyone they remotely suspected of being a spy.

It was not unusual for Fascists to turn a blind eye to ex-prisoners in their midst. In some cases this was because bonds of friendship with protectors rose above politics or self-interest. But a desire to keep on side with the eventual victor was common. When Gastardo Borin, head of the San Giorgio di Livenza Fascists, arrived at the Bottosso home decked out in black uniform and boots and armed with a revolver, he had come to arrest the four New Zealanders and march them to German headquarters. It was common knowledge they were hiding in the area; in fact he had encountered them at the Bottosso family's wine shop a few days earlier. Accompanied by two henchmen, he summoned the heads of the other families plus the prisoners to the Bottosso's kitchen. Borin, a father of six who happened to be a grandson of the *padrone* of all the farms in the area, knew the families well.[22]

It was September 1944. John Senior and his friends had been living with families in the area for nearly a year. Senior instructed his companions to ply the henchmen with wine. Then he and Borin settled down to a serious discussion. When he learned that Borin had a cousin who was a prisoner-of-war in England, Senior bluffed that although well treated for now, this cousin would be executed if they were handed over. Like many Italians who sat on the fence, Borin offered a deal. In return for not turning the men in to the Fascists, 'Will you promise to stay in the zone and say to the English and Americans when they get here that Gastardo Borin befriended you and is not a bad Fascist?' Under his protection the men would receive clothing, good food and prior warning when a *rastrellamento* was likely to occur. Often members of his family would send word of a roundup and arrange for a new location. Borin would then report back to his superiors that attempts to capture the prisoners were unsuccessful. As head of the roundups he was believed. This continued sporadically until the end of the war.

Borin, like many who played a double game, had a thirst for its edgy risk-taking. Once he invited Senior along to witness a Fascist meeting at his house. In the sidecar of his motorbike was a spare Fascist uniform wrapped in brown paper. Senior, although tempted, declined the offer.[23]

Partisans were scathing of men like Borin. They were often singled out for punishment at the end of the war in the conviction it was their moral weakness that caused Italy to buckle under Fascism in the first place.

In the spring of 1944, well after Paul Day had made his escape to the partisans and eventually over the Swiss mountains, a platoon of German soldiers occupied Prati Nuovi. At this point the civil war between the partisans and the Fascist militia and the Germans was at its most brutal. Yet regardless of their political affiliations, everyone testified that the Germans were 'good' and did not hurt anyone. The Germans occupying Prati Nuovi were older veterans of the Wehrmacht who probably hoped to sit out the war in relative tranquillity.[24] The commander, slyly nicknamed 'Stalino' because of his fulsome moustache, used to stride around snapping his whip against his boots. But he organised immediate medical attention for Bisioli's sister when she scalded herself with boiling water and other small kindnesses were acknowledged. The degree of turning a blind eye was evident one New Year's Eve where Germans and Italians at Prati Nuovi joined to welcome in 1945. 'Stalino', who had been drinking heavily, turned on Bisioli's father, who was also drunk. 'I know you're a partisan,' he shouted, 'and I know you gave food to the prisoners!' before a German officer intervened, admonishing both men to calm down and forget about politics.[25]

For many Italians accommodation to changing circumstances and uncertainty was necessary if the war was to be survived. Getting on with everybody was a crucial factor. The sons of Fascists made no distinction between the New Zealanders and the Germans and stressed their distance from politics. 'We were friends with everybody – English,

New Zealanders and Germans. We were on neither side.'[26] Even the Communist Bisioli had little quarrel with individual Germans. It was a German he had befriended who warned him there was an order out to kill his father because of his association with the partisans.[27]

The story of Prati Nuovi is the story of ordinary Italians dealing with extraordinary circumstances. Yet under the surface of necessary accommodations and humour, the tensions and violence of war were lurking. Alongside great acts of generosity flourished small acts of spite and betrayal. Political divisions snaked through the underbelly of relations at Prati Nuovi. After three months in the area Paul Day was getting nervous. He knew he had to leave the area and reach the partisans, fighting against the Germans and liaising with Allied Special Forces.[28]

Time and again the figure of a priest looms large in the network of both organised and spontaneous assistance for New Zealand escapers. Although a common attitude among the advancing troops was to compare the poverty of the people to the sumptuous wealth of the churches and their 'well-fed' priests,[29] men behind the lines, especially those brought up as Roman Catholics, found solace in the familiar rituals of the Church. It was a point of recognition in a culture that in other respects was quite alien. Even lapsed Catholics like Maurice Cosgrave took the opportunity to go to Mass. So strong was his friendship with the local priest that Jack Leyden, who had escaped with Ian Millar and Stan Jones from Camp 107, elected to remain in the village. The priest commented warmly on the New Zealander's devoutness in attending church every day. However, his visibility probably led to his recapture three months later.

Yet priests were not always trustworthy and the men learned to be wary. 'Some were Fascists and some weren't,' recalls John Senior. 'When we were hunted we couldn't get sanctuary in the church because you never knew whether they would give you away or not.'[30] However, in the rural areas priests who often came from peasant families themselves were key figures in organising safe houses. Their prestige and authority in some parishes was so high that people would do anything they asked.[31]

At San Giorgio di Livenza, Don Fausto Moschetta was a great ally of the prisoners. He had fought against the Germans in the First World War and was very pro-British, entertaining his listeners with stories of the Scots soldiers who looked like women in their skirts. A round, jovial man in his sixties, he resembled Friar Tuck and possessed some of the fearless feistiness of that great character. Recalls John Senior, 'He had two private motorcars and on one occasion the Fascist patrol came down the street wanting his cars. And he chased them out of his property and across the bridge with a walking stick.'[32] Don Fausto made no bones about where his political sympathies lay. After a massacre of civilians occurred in the mountain village his people came from, he banned Fascist militia soldiers from attending his church. Senior was not surprised to learn after the war that Don Fausto was a partisan. His code name on Radio London was *Pippo dai capelli bianchi* (Pippo with white hair).

The fate of Don Antonio Andreazza, the singular most important contact for Arch Scott in supplying shelter and supplies to escapers, has elevated him to hero status for both prisoners and Italians alike. Don Antonio was active with the liberation groups and had friends in high places. He created for Scott his two false identity cards and organised accommodation and money for the prisoners. He told Scott on more than one occasion that he knew the Germans were after him and sported a tiny Beretta pistol he was rather proud of.[33] In April 1944 he was arrested at the cemetery after he had finished conducting a child's funeral. Taken to Santa Maria Maggiore prison in Venice he was subjected to brutal torture. One method was to repeatedly douse him in buckets of ice-cold water. Even then his ingenuity did not abandon him and he pretended to be mad. Despite this, he was condemned to death. A campaign to have him declared mad by the prison doctors was subsequently waged by his friends. Even Scott was asked to use his considerable influence with an Italian count and the services of an astute lawyer were engaged. The ruse succeeded and, judged insane, Don Antonio spent the next year in a mental asylum at the island of San Giorgio in Venice. When he was released in April 1945, Scott learned that the Germans knew a surprising amount of details, including the activities of the so-called 'English captain' and were never far behind him. After the war, the priest continued his ministry and even became deputy mayor of Cessalto. Sadly his health, never robust due to an angina condition, was permanently broken by his ordeal. He died at the age of 48 in 1953. Despite being repeatedly told by his bishop to stay out of matters political, Don Antonio saw his involvement as an extension of his Christian duty. In response to those who cautioned him, he would say, '*Vedo la strada diritta. La seguirò*. I see the straight road. I'll follow it.'

Although priests were at the forefront of organised help for escaped prisoners, the nuns were just as active. Because they ran essential services such as hospitals and schools they had access to funds, useful contacts and could disguise many of their less orthodox protégés. Key organisers of assistance in the Rivignano area were Sister Giuseppina and her Mother Superior, Gabriella Cordani, of the Order of the Sisters of Charity, who lived in a convent close to the main road. Even as late as 9 September 1944 there were still over a dozen New Zealanders hiding in the zone.[34] When groups of prisoners began appearing in the district the nuns supplied them with food and clothing and shelter in the convent if the weather was bad and the men were ill. Concerned that the military trousers with the distinctive pockets would give away the identity of her charges, Sister Giuseppina and her cohorts replaced them with priests' trousers, 'ones without pockets'. When she learned that one of the prisoners, a New Zealander, Swainson, was ill with an infected leg, she called her Mother Superior who had grown up in England to come and speak to him. They took him back to the convent.

A German recruitment centre had taken over the kindergarten building in front of the convent, while at the back sick escaped prisoners were nursed. German personnel and New Zealand charges would exchange polite greetings when they encountered each other in the corridors, but the Germans, engineers of a mature age, 'real gentlemen' according to Sister Giuseppina, were not interested in knowing who they were.

Sister Giuseppina lives in a retirement home for nuns at Trecesimo. Still vigorous at 93, she remembers her special favourite, the bearded wild-looking New Zealander Private Swainson. He used to come and go wandering the countryside for months at a time, mysteriously saying that he went from the mountains to the sea, from home to home. His name appears in a testimony by a man who said that a certain Swainson had courted his sister but her disapproving family had nipped the budding romance in the bud.

After the Liberation in May 1945, Swainson presented himself to the Allied authorities but he was without documents and physically unrecognisable. They needed proof of his identity so he brought them to the convent to Sister Giuseppina. 'I was in the orchard killing a rabbit and my hands were soaked in blood. And my name was called and I saw these two officers and what looked like a poor old man, with a long white beard and a limp. I stared at him. Who is it? I wondered. And he comes towards me and embraces me. I recognised him from his voice. Swainson! Yes. Even the officer cried at such an emotional scene.'[35] Sister Gabriella Cordani then provided a written affidavit testifying he was indeed who he said he was.

Another New Zealander, a small red-head known as 'Ginger', became ill with appendicitis. A desperate Sister Giuseppina went to a renowned surgeon in Udine and begged him to operate. He was a Communist from Rome who instead of being banished into exile to an isolated community under police watch, the common punishment for dissidents, was sent to Udine and allowed to practise freely at the hospital. This was because he had once successfully operated on Mussolini who had decided his talents should not be wasted. The surgeon agreed and allayed Sister Giuseppina's doubts. 'Of course I can do it. I am the chief surgeon and I do what I want!' He warned her only not to let the prisoner open his mouth. In the end, however, before the arrangements could be made, Ginger was successfully operated on at a smaller hospital.

Sister Giuseppina's courage was boundless and she knew how to exploit her religious status. Her father, caught unwittingly in the middle of a skirmish between Germans and partisans, had been captured 'because he wasn't able to run fast' and imprisoned in Udine. Sister Giuseppina decided to intervene. 'I was a bit nervous to go there to the SS captain who was the terror of the whole province.' She persuaded a small child who was playing nearby to accompany her. 'I said to the little girl, "Listen, little one. I'll buy you some sweets if you come with me. I must go and speak with an officer. You don't need to say anything. I'll speak, but you need to stay close beside me."' She alighted from her wagon to find a pistol pointed at her. Brought before the captain, he wanted to know why a child was with her. 'Because my order requires me never to present myself before officers on my own,' was the demure reply. After her father's documents had been checked, the nun was told she could collect her father in three days. That same day, shortly after she had picked up her father, two partisans threw a bomb into the prison entrance. 'And then nobody could get out.'[36]

Sister Giuseppina believes that her Mother Superior, Gabriella Cordani who spoke English perfectly, was far more at risk than her. The authorities came once to investigate claims that Cordani 'had something to do with the English'. 'We said, you have mistaken *suora* with a *signora* who lives at Latisana. But she's not there any more now.' Sister Giuseppina remembers to this day the woman who denounced her beloved mentor and spits out her name with disdain.

Maurice Cosgrave, known as Pietro, stayed a couple of times at an ancient Franciscan monastery in the Appignano mountains. Only one father and two brothers remained out of the original seventy. Cosgrave arrived one snowy evening. In the main room the tables, seats and long benches built into the wall were all carved out of stone. A huge fireplace dominated the room, but the fire burning inside it was small and the wood supply was scarce. It was freezing. 'They were talking about going to some farmer's place to get some wood.' Cosgrave offered to go as he was wearing good boots. 'They only had these things made out of old tyres.' But the brothers refused. When Cosgrave insisted, one whispered, 'No, no, Pietro, you see we have to steal it.' Cosgrave finally understood. 'If I did it, it would be a sin, but they could get round it.'[37]

CHAPTER NINE

Fighting with the partisans

*You're likely to get a gun and told to fight. You can't understand
what the hell they're talking about so you're really in the shit and
the shiver so just be careful what you do.*[1]

There was no other option, Gigi Mecchia informed an increasingly
nervous Paul Day. 'Wait while I get you some bicycles.'[2] It was time for
him and Mick Hogan to go up the mountains to the partisans.

It had become too dangerous to continue living with families on the
plains round Prati Nuovi. Spies were everywhere as were, by this time,
Germans. The only bicycle he could find for them was a tandem. The
tall, long-limbed Day couldn't work the pedals from the front so Hogan,
'a little roly-poly chap', took the steering position. They were an
incongruous pair as they set off. 'Mick wore a cheese-cutter hat and I had
on a long raincoat and a felt hat.' Mecchia rode about 100 metres ahead
to warn of any potential trouble and they made a note of side roads that
they could nip down if necessary. As the New Zealanders rode their
tandem through the town of Spilimbergo, 'buzzing with Germans', a

109

soldier pointed at them and made a loud remark to his companion. Both roared with laughter. It was an electrifying moment, 'But we just had to carry on.' A few days later they were delivered to the partisan head-quarters above Castelnovo del Friuli where they met up with Pat Moncur and Ossie Martin.

Most New Zealanders commented on the disorganisation and chaos of the early partisan formations they encountered. They felt that they were an undisciplined bunch that would have benefited from some rigorous training. There were few arms or supplies and the motley assortment of people in their ranks, some teenagers, did not inspire confidence. Ian Millar reflects a common view. 'They had no ambition to fight the Germans, for if a German patrol appeared they panicked. Their main occupation seemed to be stealing the butter and tobacco from the *magazzini* round about.'[3] Although invited many times to join Giomaria's partisans they refused on the grounds that it didn't seem to have any real purpose. For trained soldiers certain aspects of partisan warfare were perplexing. Giorgio Bocca writes, 'The ex-prisoners of other nations often wouldn't understand. They would go down with the rebels into the plains at night expecting to fight Germans and Fascists then they would arrive at a stockpile in a salami factory to be told, "No, John, don't shoot. This is our friend." They feel frustrated. "So this is the Italian partisan war?"'[4]

In the early months following the Armistice it could hardly be otherwise. All wars of liberation against occupying forces involve civilians and establishing friendly relations and networks of supplies with the population is one of the key tactics to survival. Many bands began with three or four young men huddled in a stable at night plotting how best to resist the German occupiers. The origins of the Battaglione Boatto (later renamed Pellegrini after a member, Antonio Pellegrini, was hanged in December 1944), operating around San Stino di Livenza, are typical. Five men led by Gino Panont formed a clandestine group called the Gruppo Combattimento Livenza intent on sabotaging the enemy, but they only had one gun between them. The first few months were spent stealing weapons through disarming local Fascists or *carabinieri* and arranging for food from the peasants to be supplied for the partisans fighting in the mountains, as well as organising safe houses, clothing, supplies, and transport.[5] As Bocca put it, 'fifty people laboured so that ten could shoot'.[6] Conditions were often desperate. When Querino Bullian arrived at his partisan unit in the mountains above Spilimbergo, he was advised, 'So you don't have a gun. Go kill a German and take *his* gun!'[7]

There were thus two kinds of resisters in the Veneto and Friuli-Venezia Giulia zones, each of whom depended on the other – the partisans who operated in the plains carrying out acts of sabotage and organising supplies, and those who fought in combat units in the mountains. The flat, bare plains were totally unsuitable for combat with no forest, rocks or mountains for hiding, while the mountains although providing cover were cut off from the means of sustenance. While partisans in the mountains served as protection for prisoners passing through, partisans such as Panont on the plains worked alongside Arch Scott, looking after the needs of escaped prisoners lodged with families. The reaction among the partisans to the influx of Allied prisoners in their bands was mixed and depended on the geographical location and supply of arms. Gino Panont remembers various escaped Allied prisoners-of-war joining his brigade but later on it was too dangerous to have them there. 'They spoke little Italian, they stood out easily, and they didn't know the zone as well as those of us born here.' As a result they became a burden and Panont felt they were better off without them.[8]

Paul Day together with a group of twelve ex-prisoners spent over three months with partisans on the slopes of Mount Ciaurlec, north of Spilimbergo on the Tagliamento River north-west of Udine. Although relations with the partisans were cordial, the men were wary of getting involved in their operations. 'Don't go near them,' Day was told. The partisans were 'absolutely without discipline' and had few arms.

However, Pat Moncur had only admiration and affection for these same Garibaldi partisans he spent several months with on Mount Ciaurlec. Known as Patrizio, Moncur never knew their names, a tactic that ensured a measure of safety. If captured and tortured, the confession of names could lead to the deaths not only of the partisans, but also of their families. 'If there was an Italian, I'd call him Bill.' He was not expected to join the battles but stood guard and assisted where possible. 'It was great. I sat in the sun and watched the birds go by. We were fed. The food was all right. They were in charge.' He was free to roam, though a clandestine visit to the town of Sequals was unsuccessful. 'I came down with the idea of going to Mass. A German truck pulled up and about fifteen Germans trotted into the church. So I went back up the mountain.'[9]

On Easter Sunday 1944 partisans and escapers celebrated with a rich feast of poultry, butter, brandy and cake. Locals came up the mountain bringing painted eggs and wine for them. Moncur is still moved by the memory of their abundant generosity. Ian Millar and his friend Stan Jones, staying at the time in the Praforte mountains, hiked over to join them for the festivities. On the evening of Easter Saturday, enlivened by a large supply of wine, 'we had a great time with all of us sitting round an open fire drinking and singing to our heart's content.' They were nonetheless on a sober mission. A distraught woman had begged them to take a message to the partisan leader. The Germans had threatened they would burn down her house if she did not produce her son. Although the leader spoke to the woman, 'it was our guess she received little satisfaction.'[10]

Moncur participated in two raids. The first was on a cheese factory where the objective was to supply the hungry locals with cheese before the Germans could get their hands on it. 'They were absolutely astonished we were giving away all this cheese.' But Moncur says the operation 'wasn't very brave'. He now sees it as an arranged job with no shots fired and sympathetic guards who gave themselves up easily. The cheese was already stockpiled ready for transport on the packhorses.

The second was an attack on a German convoy. The group they were with had held up the convoy, looted the lorry, and shot a German who tried to make a breakthrough. The Yugoslavs failed to turn up to help them and they were outnumbered. 'They started blobbing us with mortars. We resisted until it got too hot.' It was only a matter of time before the Germans came up on a manhunt. Moncur and his companions

Paul Day, Ernie Clark, Ossie Martin and Mick Hogan scattered and regrouped at their pre-arranged hiding place in a cave in a rock outcrop where they secured the entrance with a large stone. To their surprise and terror ('I lost all my dandruff'), a party of German soldiers stopped outside their cave and ate lunch, laughing and joking. A trickle of water coming through a crack in the rock added to their consternation. It was a soldier relieving himself. When the men returned to their barn and found it ablaze they knew it was time to go.

After intense discussion, the New Zealanders decided to split into pairs and head for Switzerland. Before he did so, Moncur went up to see how the partisans had fared. They were all packing up. 'And I said, what are you going to do? *Dove andare*? And they said "shhshh". They wouldn't say. Fair enough. If I got captured and gave away what was happening to them, they'd be shot. So we all had a hug.' This took some getting used to for a Kiwi bloke. 'The first time I wondered what was going on, you know. But I came to like it.'[11] Of the twelve who left only four of them made it into Switzerland: Pat Moncur and Ossie Martin who set off on 1 May and Paul Day who paired up with Ernie Clarke. The rest were captured.

Maurice Cosgrave, like most of the Hare Battalion, never stayed in one place very long. It was a case of being where it was least dangerous. He spent two brief stints with friendly Communist partisans in the Marche, returning again when things got tough. When they heard he was a radio technician they asked him to build a radio so they could talk to Moscow. But he could not get the parts or the power. He found them a cheerful, optimistic bunch, if disorganised. 'Everything was about the new era that was coming and how they'll get rid of the Germans and they'll all be Communist. They would drink the local wine singing *"Bandiera rossa, per la libertà. Viva communismo e la bandiera"*.' Cosgrave would sing lustily along with them. The leader of one of the groups, in reprisal for an attack on a German convoy, was hanged by his heels in the square in front of his family and slowly stabbed to death. He was buried outside the cemetery, 'even better, on the road where people walked over the body every day. The Germans were *pigs*.'[12]

A group of New Zealanders who had escaped from Camp 106 near Vercelli headed for the rugged mountains in the Valsesia district, bordering north-western Italy. Here they came into the orbit of Vincenzo or Cino Moscatelli, the most fêted of the legendary heroes of the Italian Resistance, and one of the first to form a partisan band after the Armistice. Laurie Read was keen to get to his group because he had heard of his exploits and wanted to find a 'band of practising *partisani* [sic]'. After leaving Grignasco, he passed through small villages such as Mulino Jannetti, Ara and la Colma, situated north of Grignasco. At one village their group gathered up three young men who were on their way to join the partisans. Emotions ran high as families embraced their teenage sons, perhaps for the last time. 'At the end of the village street they stopped and waved to their folk, calling farewells to papà, mamma, aunts and God knows who else, half a dozen times before we got out of sight and proceeded upwards, ever upwards.'[13]

Soaring above them was Mount Fenera, presided over by a haunting figure of Christ on the Cross. Visible for miles around, it jutted out on the spur of a rocky outcrop. But for the pragmatic Read it represented another milestone in their climb. 'We thought, "Fancy climbing there!"' Progress was swift. At the end of the day they were above the statue, looking down on it.

The partisans encountered at these first headquarters were very young. When Read's group arrived they had just been given a pep talk by their captain and had decided on 'Death or Glory' as the band's motto. The next day Read joined a party that went down the mountain to a village below for supplies. He clambered back up carrying a wicker-covered flagon of wine over half a metre high on his back. If he had been able to get to it, he would have consumed most of it on his journey up the mountain. 'So near and yet so far. It took the rest of the night to get my breath back.'

That night while they were all asleep in a mountain house, a sentry had seen a procession of lights bobbing up and down on the lower slopes and unable to discern what they were, panicked. 'We did not know either, but it rather disconcerted us to see how the Death or Glory boys went to pieces.'[14] Read's group then decided to move on to join a more 'established' band, much to the annoyance of the commander Mario Vinzio, battle name *Pesgu*. He was trying to build up his disparate band into a more organised fighting force and was later to become commander of the 82nd Garibaldi Brigade, the Osella Brigade.

Cino Moscatelli's brigade was already very effective and had a fearsome reputation. It had raided an aerodrome, obtaining two cases of .303 munitions, and had made a number of sorties round the zone, 'confiscating' the revolvers of *carabinieri*, who then had to go on patrol unarmed. One of Moscatelli's right-hand men was an Australian escaped prisoner, Frank Jocumsen, who remained with him until the end of the war. While walking along the tracks towards their headquarters, Read encountered Jocumsen and another Australian driving a jeep. They briefed them and told them where to report.[15]

Moscatelli was the fourth son of seven children of a railway worker. His education was limited. At the age of twelve he was working ten hours a day, but spurred on by the misery and social injustices he saw around him, he became politically active. At seventeen he marched at the head of a strike he had organised and shortly after, he enrolled in the Communist Youth Movement. He had by this time met Pietro Secchia, a long-time Communist and future political leader of the Garibaldi partisan formations. Moscatelli became a key figure in the underground anti-Fascist groups and was imprisoned for five years. He escaped and spent time in Moscow at the Communist International School. Clearly Read admired Moscatelli, but like most New Zealanders he had some reservations. 'The Captain was educated and trained in Russia and indoctrinated with communistic ideals which he practised, and whenever a Russian victory was announced on the radio we flew the "hammer and sickle".' Significant victories such as the Leningrad battles were celebrated with the issuing of wine and tobacco for the men. Although accounts from those close to Moscatelli have stressed that he believed in a consensual proletariat revolution, Laurie Read was not so sure. Many jobs and positions were already allocated to different supporters of the partisan unit, and the property of noted opposition leaders earmarked for sympathisers. Comments Read wryly, 'It was obvious that the ordinary Italian was only going to have a change in bosses after the war.'[16]

Read and his fellow escapers were assigned to outpost duty. From their mountain outcrop they looked over a railway line that circled the undulating countryside in a wide arc, making trains visible for well over a kilometre whether they were headed north or south. When the ex-prisoners were on outpost duty they practised their marksmanship using the train engine as a target. This was done with the full co-operation of the engine driver who, as the train pulled out of range, would stand up and wave. The engine would whistle a 'raspberry' as it chugged on its way. One day two ex-prisoners were stopped in the village and questioned by a couple of *carabinieri*, who arrested them and then loaded them on to the next train. Men working up a telegraph pole observed this incident and immediately notified the partisans. At the next stop four heavily armed men including the 'Aussie', Frank Jocumsen, boarded the train, held a gun to the driver's head and went through the carriages until they found their boys. The train was then allowed to go on its way. The *carabinieri* were taken prisoner, stripped and tied spread-eagled to the roof of the truck that then sped off up the mountains to headquarters. They arrived scared and frozen stiff. 'The *cara* were given the choice of being shot or doing the camp chores.'[17] Not surprisingly they chose the latter, and from then on they took over the irksome tasks of drawing water and cutting wood. Read and his companions became good friends with them. 'Whenever there was an issue of vino or cigarettes to celebrate something special they let us "Britishers" know so we could ask for our share of the "goodies".'

The partisans lived on a staple diet of boiled apples and mushrooms. Their meal on Christmas Day 1943 was unforgettable. To celebrate the festive season a packhorse mule was slaughtered. When Read went to headquarters to collect their rations he found it consisted of the lungs and head which were to be boiled up with rice. Read was on cooking duty that day and kept stirring the 'mess of pottage' to prevent it from burning. 'Every now and again a mule's eye would come to the surface with a baleful glare, before subsiding into the "stew" again! However much the lungs were cooked they remained uneatable, and it was like chewing a rubber tyre.'[18] Finally they were thrown down the mountainside, where even the goats were unable to digest them.

Dances provided a welcome break from the tensions and boredom of war. Because they had no footwear other than their old army boots, Read and his comrades were initially reluctant to attend a dance in the village hall. They need not have worried. The women wore mountain boots heavier than theirs. 'We were the ones who came home with the bruises!' A startling incident occurred during an 'excuse me' dance when a prospective 'excuser' who attempted to break in on a couple was refused by the young woman. The ginger-haired Italian pulled out his revolver and shot the girl's ear off. Pandemonium ensued and the perpetrator ran off into the night with everyone in hot pursuit. Taken before Captain Moscatelli the next day, his punishment was surprisingly light given the iron discipline generally operating in the better-organised Garibaldi units. His revolver was confiscated and he was not permitted to carry a gun.[19]

Moscatelli was twice kidnapped by Fascists but rescued by his men before he could be taken for trial and execution. On a third occasion his abductors and their spies were caught and executed in the forest and reportedly buried by Moscatelli's Australian bodyguards. Three men and a woman had paid the price for these kidnappings, but the father of the executed woman had sworn to 'get' Moscatelli so Read's group was always 'on the lookout for trouble'.

The first real battle occurred in Valsesia on 12 December 1943 when a Fascist patrol arrived to collect its manufacturing output. They ran into a partisan ambush at Varallo and it was in this furious shoot-out that 'Frank the Australian' cemented his legendary status. He ran into the middle of the piazza, his face uncovered, and targeted a bar packed with Fascists. Wielding a heavy Breda tommy-gun, he sprayed them with bullets. 'This was like a red rag to a bull,' writes Read. Ten days later the Fascists of the 'Tagliamento' division arrived, armed to the teeth with recruits also drawn from the criminal underworld. Their commander was Merico Zuccari, infamous as a sadistic torturer. In the meantime *Pesgu* had attacked a Fascist patrol on the road towards Borgosesia, killing one man. In reprisal Zuccari imprisoned ten citizens of the town of Varallo Sesia who had nothing to do with the partisan action. Among them was the mayor, Giuseppe Osella, a trade unionist, an 18-year-old student, and a boy of fifteen. Read grimly describes what these innocent victims had to endure before being executed. 'These were tortured by having their fingernails pulled out, their arms were broken, they were hit in the mouth by rifle butts, then shot in the stomach. Their throats were then cut before the Fascists left. This was in front of the villagers and their families, who had been forced to watch the proceedings. They were then told that the bodies had to remain in the square for a week as a warning to the district.'[20]

Such atrocities could not go unpunished. Moscatelli refused to be intimidated. As soon as he learned of this proclamation, he went straight down the mountain to the village. The Fascist perpetrators had by now fled, although Read heard they were intercepted and killed by another group of partisans further away. Despite the opposition of terrified locals, Moscatelli ordered the bodies to be decently buried immediately.

The fighting that followed was fierce, what Read called 'dog eat dog with a vengeance'. Two battles occurred in quick succession. The first was at Camasco, a few kilometres east from Varallo in the mountains, and the second was at Roccapietra, a town on the outskirts of Varallo.

Moscatelli's forces proved such a strong match for the Fascists that German reinforcements were regularly being trucked in. Read gleefully reports that 'on 12 January 1944, four trucks of Germans arrived at Borgosesia to pick up four wounded Fascists – and wasted no time in getting out again!'[21]

Moscatelli's divisions contained about 180 men including sixty from the Gramsci Brigade. Added to this were between twenty and thirty Allied ex-prisoners, among them Read. The combined Italian Fascist and German forces totalled up to 500 men who were further bolstered by armoured vehicles, mortars and heavy machine-guns. One night while on guard duty overlooking the village of Cellio, Read and his companions were pounded by mortar fire but there were no casualties or direct damage. Nonetheless the rebels were being driven back, so Moscatelli sent out an urgent appeal for reinforcements from other units. The partisan forces at Omegna led by Captain Filippo Beltrami were called in, increasing the combined force by about another hundred men. This led to 'a bloody scrap of three days'. The partisans were driven from the villages of Castagnea and Cavaglia but the rugged mountainous terrain as always favoured the defenders who, in this case, were familiar with the area, and the Germans and Fascists incurred many losses.[22]

On 13 January after the battle at Roccapietra, further brutal reprisals were carried out by Nazi-Fascists on the people of the surrounding towns. 'Three or four local villages were burned out and we saw these occupants streaming up into the nearby hills. On the second day I was half a mile up the mountain on a spur overlooking the village below, watching for any troop movements, when I noticed that these villagers had gathered on the outskirts of their village to watch the battle. Suddenly the Germans fired some mortars amongst them and the Italians, realising the battle was for real, ran helter-skelter back to their houses!' When Fascists suddenly made an advance behind them, Read and his companions were nearly trapped. 'We had to scram for our lives. I was unable to return to our mountain house to retrieve my possessions, such as they were. I only had what I stood up in.'[23] They slept that night in a room in the overcrowded partisan headquarters. On the third day of the battle the group of escaped prisoners had had enough. There are differing versions of what occurred. According to Read, 'Captain Moscatelli told his Aussie bodyguards to scram as things looked bad for the partisans. This seemed good advice, and we reasoned we owed nothing to the Italians or to Italy, and we were not prepared to suffer winter chills, ice, snow and hunger, or to shiver for the Italian cause.'[24]

However, Moscatelli's comments on this final day of battle express annoyance at this decision. He wrote, 'The only black mark of the hard day was caused by a group of Allied ex-prisoners who were part of our formation. At the first blows of the enemy they scattered as fast as they could towards the Swiss Frontier, with the exception of a few, among whom the popular Frank (Jocumsen) who remained with us until the end of the war.' Moscatelli scorned their 'poor discipline, lack of a spirit of sacrifice, and their unwillingness to fight'.[25]

Clearly Moscatelli felt betrayed by this desertion which meant the depletion of sorely needed numbers to shore up their defences. From his point of view, they were men that the partisans had fed and sheltered and who thus in return owed them loyalty against a common enemy. The ex-prisoners, caught up in a civil war they barely understood, were battle-weary and wary of the Communist fervour with which Moscatelli inspired his troops. The atrocities being committed on Italian citizens in reprisal for partisan actions did not help. Read found a reluctant but more supportive ally in Captain Beltrami, leader of the Giellisti, the Justice and Liberty group, a republican-leaning non-Communist party.

'On 18 January I had a yarn to Captain Beltrami, leader of the Omegna rebels, who did not want us to go, leaving his troops, but nonetheless gave us some hand grenades – we had to leave our guns behind. He gave us rations for five days, then fifteen assorted personnel with two Italian guides.' Thus generously equipped, they left the partisans at 4.30 p.m. and headed towards the Swiss border.[26] A month later on 13 February, Beltrami was killed at the battle of Megolo. He received posthumously a gold medal for valour.

A New Zealand officer noted the uneasy relationship between the partisans and escaped prisoners in north-eastern Italy. The latter were reluctant to serve in a foreign army with different aims, different tactics and different equipment from the one they had signed up to. 'Thus to the officers of the partisan battalion we were an embarrassment. We were a hindrance to their mobility, a threat to their security, a drag upon their food supplies. And what officer of a guerilla force needs soldiers of a more sophisticated army watching patronisingly as he trains his force?'[27] He observed that private soldiers who had been in the work camps related easily to individual partisans as they spoke fluent if ungrammatical Italian, whereas commissioned officers who had not had this experience were ill at ease and disadvantaged by their stilted Italian. However, few escaped soldiers of any nationality or rank chose to remain and fight with the partisans. Most New Zealanders stayed on sufferance, grateful for the protection but keen to move on when there was a chance.

Just a few kilometres south from Laurie Read, in the labyrinth of valleys, hills and thick woodland of the Biellese countryside, another New Zealander was fighting with the partisans in the bitter winter spanning

1943–1944. He was to stay until the end. Like most New Zealand soldiers, Frank Bowes regarded the Italians he encountered in the North African desert with contempt. 'The Italian is the poorest example of a man that [it] has been my misfortune to contact,' he wrote. Just over two years later, lined up before a Fascist firing squad alongside fellow partisans, he was to give his life for them and their country.[28]

Corporal Frank Bowes had fought with the 26th Battalion in the disastrous Greek campaign before being evacuated to Egypt. In November 1941 he was wounded at Sidi Rezegh and hospitalised with severe head injuries from an exploding shell. Overcrowded with wounded men from both sides, the hospital camp was soon surrounded by the enemy. Initially in the hands of the Germans, they were then handed over to the Italians, whom Bowes judged 'a disorganised rabble, a different proposition to the Hun who at least showed something of manhood about them'.[29] Apart from enduring the Italians' looting of medical equipment and personal possessions, conditions were grim in the makeshift field hospital. Bombs were falling round them and the sick men were in as much danger as they had been in the front line. In fact, as Bowes discovered, no front line existed and battle raged wherever there was contact between the highly mobile forces. They did what they could to protect themselves. 'Shrapnel was falling in our encampment and we who were in any way capable, dug in for ourselves and all our comrades who could be put into holes. Then we felt a trifle more comfortable.' Yet despite the tension, 'when our fellows shelled the Eyeties and they would stampede in terror into our tentments, we would always raise a cheer.' The lack of food and water, though, was agonising. 'I can't walk about the hospital now to see chaps I know who are badly wounded. They ask for a smoke or beg for water. I can see how much they suffer but I can't help them.' He made friends with a man who was wounded in the arm. 'Between us we were able to do most things a little at a time.' This even extended to raiding a supply truck when night fell and they could hobble past the guard, unseen. They feasted on precious water, tins of tomato soup, milk, beans and tobacco. It was a case of every man for himself.

Released shortly after by the British and returned to Egypt, Bowes was back training in the desert after a spell of convalescence. In July 1942 he fought at Ruweisat Ridge. Wounded again, this time in the thigh, he recuperated in Palestine before rejoining his battalion in September. Given his battle history and injuries, it seems incredible that he should have been considered fit to join the fray again. In October 1942 he fought in the Battle of El Alamein which marked the first decisive victory and the turning point of the war for the Allies. From then on the enemy was in retreat, and from October until May 1943 when fighting in North Africa ended, only about 90 New Zealanders were taken prisoner.[30] Captured at Alamein, Frank Bowes was among them.

However, letters from Camp 57 in Italy show him in good spirits, taking pleasure from reading books and looking forward to returning to his family. 'I picture your garden as I think it will be now you have summer,' he wrote to his wife in January 1943. 'I think often of my arm-chair beside yours and an open fire.'[31] Men sensed that the war would soon be over and nostalgic thoughts turned to the life they had known and hoped to return to in New Zealand.

By the spring Bowes was working in Camp 106 in Vercelli. His health and spirits improved even more in the picturesque countryside and he relished the work in the open air. 'I find I have not forgotten how to milk a cow, haymaking is much the same the world over and altogether this life is quite familiar to me.'[32] He was taking keen note of his surroundings. 'It is interesting to discover so many beautiful flowers I have never previously seen, growing in profusion. Reds and pinks predominate in this country.'[33] No mention is made of Italians. The letters had to pass through censorship but like the other men in 106, he would have learned the language and become friendly with the locals. 'I am quite reconciled to this life now,' he wrote, 'and will not, in my state of optimism, be worried about the time I'll be here.' The divisions of 'us and them' disappeared in his gradual acculturation, replaced by a curiosity and empathy for the world he was now living in. One of his last letters home is telling. 'Life at present is not uninteresting and I find it rather an education to learn the methods of this country which are a rare combination of the very old and most modern.'

From 8 September his last months can be sketched only through Italian sources, as there were no more letters. He escaped from Camp

106/2, eventually reaching the Crestani household in the tiny village of Giardino near Mosso Santa Maria. Like so many others, he was welcomed and treated as one of the family. Although his letters always spoke in positive terms of his health, he was not robust. Weakened through malaria and battle wounds, he was nursed by the mother, Signora Paola, for some weeks. Bowes would have fitted in to the household of these olive-skinned, down-to-earth people in more ways than one. Years later, his son John was to notice a striking physical resemblance between Girolamo Crestani and his uncle Alan, Bowes' brother.

The Crestani were staunch anti-Fascists. Family members had been employed in the textile factories at Biella and were active in the worker campaigns for social reform in the early part of the century. Involved in the trade union movement smashed after Mussolini took power, they responded immediately to the call for insurgency after 8 September. When the partisan band was formed at the end of November, 20-year-old Francesco Crestani joined up immediately. It would have been more than gratitude that compelled Bowes to join him, although a sense of loyalty to the family he was now part of would have prevailed. He probably felt at ease in the rugged countryside round Biella, with its similarity to the Canterbury landscape in New Zealand's South Island where he grew up. This sensitivity to the environment could have persuaded him not to attempt escaping into Switzerland. Given his experience of mountain conditions and his fragile health, he may have reckoned that his chances of success were low.

At thirty-seven Bowes was nearly twice the age of the Crestani sons and a hardened veteran of campaigns in Greece and North Africa. Perhaps he welcomed the chance to do some fighting again. In the desert he had considered going into action 'an opportunity to justify us being here'. Bowes may have felt these amateurs needed sorting out and he could put his skills, honed in extensive training in the desert, to use.[34] But whatever his young companions lacked in experience was made up for in zeal and courage, qualities Bowes admired.

He was part of a band connected to the Piave unit, a division of the Garibaldi, and fought under the battle name *Folgore* or Thunderbolt. Together with ten companions, one of whom was another escaper, an

Australian from Perth named Kenneth Osborne, he was stationed in headquarters in the mountains north of Mosso Santa Maria, near the Margosio woods. The Garibaldi partisans operating alongside Moscatelli's division were very active in the zone. They had confiscated the arms of local *carabinieri* and descended on the woollen mills, organising strikes and threatening factory owners who supplied the Germans.[35] Whether Bowes shared their leftist political views is debatable, but he would have supported the Crestani family's fight for social justice and despised the Nazi-Fascist squads who were terrorising the zone. Whereas Read and his fellow escapers lived in separate quarters from the partisans, Bowes was fully integrated into the band. Unlike Laurie Read, he was personally involved. Every so often, when the coast was clear, Bowes, Osborne and young Francesco would return from their mountain hideaway for some rest and nourishment to the Crestani home.

Snow lay thickly on the mountains the morning of 20 February 1944. Heavy mist shrouded the countryside like patchwork, occasionally lifting and shifting. The poor visibility was perfect for the full-scale military operation to rout the bands of partisans stationed in the mountain strongholds. The attack was organised by Moscatelli's nemesis, Merico Zuccari, infamous commander of the Republican National Guard division. It was co-ordinated with the combined forces of the 63rd Tagliamento Battalion led by Centurione Ravaglia and a German platoon. While the Germans ascended from the west, the Fascist patrols arrived from the east then separated to stealthily cover all areas of the mountains in a circular net. Guided by a local, they alighted from armoured trucks to proceed on foot up winding stony mule tracks.[36] In the early afternoon Ravaglia's battalion surrounded the stronghold on Monte Prapian defended by Frank Bowes and his group.

Eros Martinetti, battle name *Falco* (Eagle), was making his way back to join his band on Monte Prapian when the sound of gunfire shattered the stillness. Alerted to the trap he managed to slide through the snow to safety, despite sustaining a wound to his arm. Up in the headquarters a fierce exchange of fire took place and the partisans, outnumbered and outgunned, fought furiously until they had exhausted their supply of munitions. When Astro Tortelli or *Lupo* (Wolf), the 18-year-old captain, was wounded, he shot himself through the throat. Although suicide was a common tactic to avoid brutal torture before inevitable execution, as captain and leader of a fighting band there was an unspoken expectation that he should have remained with his comrades to the end.[37]

The remaining eight partisans, among them Bowes and Osborne, were captured. Taken to Fascist headquarters at Vallemosso, they were subjected to the customary beatings and torture before undergoing a summary trial. As expected, they were sentenced to death. One man was spared because he had only been with the partisans for three days and had not taken part in any actions. Immediately after the verdict the seven men were taken by truck to the Santa Liberata cemetery, located a kilometre north-west of Mosso Santa Maria. It was no coincidence that here, a few days earlier, partisans had executed twelve suspected spies.

Meanwhile, the mother and sister of Francesco Crestani made a desperate attempt to save their men through a relative, Tranquillo Crestani, a Fascist sympathiser. But when Crestani reached the village of Pray to plead for the lives of the partisans, mistakenly thinking they were still there, he encountered an infirmary full of wounded Fascist soldiers. The officer remonstrated with him, 'But who are you trying to fool? Look at what your lot has done to us!' By this time, the seven condemned men were being transferred to the cemetery. Young Luciano Crestani was standing by the road among clusters of sombre locals as the truck passed by. He was the last in the family to see them alive.

At 12.30 p.m. on 21 February the men were lined up against the left wall of the church flanking the entrance to the cemetery. In front of them were the Fascist soldiers of the 63rd (Tagliamento) Battalion. The condemned men were ordered to face the wall as the Fascist punishment for 'traitors' was to be shot in the back. Before the volley of shots rang out, one man, Corrado Lanza, turned his head. In a last act of defiance he shouted 'Bastard!' to the commander and spat in his direction. Some members of the firing squad may have deliberately fired to miss as bullet holes perforated the wall above head height. In a conflict that pitted Italian against Italian, many of whom had grown up together in close-knit communities, there was sometimes a reluctance to aim straight. But it could have devastating consequences. Two hours after the executions, a woman saw a sign of movement from one of the bodies which, under orders, were left exposed as a warning to locals. She informed the Fascists in the futile hope that someone could be saved. But they delivered a mercy bullet in the nape of the neck of each body.[38]

They were buried unceremoniously in a common grave in the cemetery, denied religious rites. But the partisans had secretly arranged for the bodies to be placed in such a way that each man could be later identified. Subsequently they were disinterred and claimed by their families. A memorial service was held, followed by a solemn funeral procession through the village carrying the seven coffins. After the Liberation the Allied occupying forces disinterred the bodies of the two 'foreigners' and transferred them to a war cemetery in Milan where they lie today. For the Crestani family it was a heartbreaking double loss. Girolamo Crestani, who three nights before had slept in the large double bed alongside his 'fraternal friend' Bowes, took over his battle name of *Folgore*.[39]

Today a memorial plaque in the cemetery commemorates the fallen fighters. The name of Frank Bowes, *Neozelandese*, is at sixth place. The majority of those executed were aged eighteen.

The events that led to Frank Bowes' death bring into stark focus the ferocity of the civil war raging through the country. The climate of reciprocal denunciation and revenge set in motion a chain of reprisals between Fascists and partisans that culminated in the 21 February execution. Just a week earlier Vincenzo Variara, battle name *Turin*, one of the founders of the Piave division, was shot after being captured by Republican guards at Biella where he had gone to organise a supply of boots. This prompted three partisan commanders of the Piave to take action against the civilian spies they felt were decimating their ranks. Twelve alleged spies were captured but during their transfer the three leaders turned back to the town of Cossato to check on a patrol that had not yet arrived.[40] Their movements were betrayed by an anonymous phone call. After being ambushed, all three were killed in a furious shoot-out with a German patrol. As a result, on 19 February partisans executed all the suspected spies, including five women, at the Santa Liberata cemetery. In another tragic twist, the commander of the *carabinieri* at Mosso Santa Maria, Marshal Alfonso Tavenar, committed suicide on 20 February. Tavenar had tried desperately to prevent the execution at the cemetery and it is believed that his anguish at his failure, coupled perhaps with his sense that he could be next, led to his taking his life.

In the days that followed, a funeral was held 'with forced pomp' in the piazza of Mosso Santa Maria for the twelve civilians executed by the partisans. All the villagers were made to attend, including schoolchildren. A woman who, during the funeral service, loudly inquired, 'And what about the others?' in reference to the partisans, was arrested.[41]

The death certificate reveals that religious rites were denied the men before their execution. Yet the priest of Mosso Santa Maria, in a letter to Frank Bowes' wife in Christchurch, stated he had received the comfort of religious sacraments.[42] This must have been out of a gesture of pity for a widow in a distant country, who need never know otherwise.

The consequences of these events were devastating. If it was difficult to destroy partisan units, which, even when decimated, sprang up again like mushrooms, it was easier to carry out acts of terror on the local people in order to rob the partisans of their support. The Resistance bands were inundated with recruits who were fleeing Mussolini's decree of 14 February that they join his newly established Republican Army.[43] But reprisals on the villagers were so brutal that spurred on by their frightened families, many young men in the Biella zone joined Mussolini's troops. In addition, the Germans were making increasing demands for Italian manpower to add to the beleaguered German forces.

After the war Rhona Bowes tried to find out more about the circumstances of her husband's death. She met a wall of reserve. There was diffidence and no little ignorance about the Italian partisans, especially the Communist groups, and Bowes' participation in their struggle fell outside of the accepted framework of military action. We can only speculate what his last thoughts were but his letters give a clue. He would have stoically reconciled himself to his fate. During his first convalescence in the desert, he expressed pride in the way a small force could boldly stand up to a much larger enemy. 'I think that one of the reasons of our successes was that no matter what strength of enemy came in sight we would be in boots and all!' he wrote. Fighting with the partisans against the vastly superior Nazi-Fascists would have embodied this David-and-Goliath ideal. Furthermore, Bowes had been wounded enough times to know that luck played a significant part in survival. This time his luck had run out, as this enemy took no prisoners. But standing alongside his young comrades on that tragic afternoon he had made another kind of journey, one that took him beyond the prejudices that slated a whole population upon the reprehensible actions of a few. But the man who wrote, 'Tell John I will soon be taking him down to the beach, swimming and walking on the hills. Keep the garden and cupboard well stocked and leave the rest to me,' would have saved his last thoughts for his beloved wife and the son he would never see again.

CHAPTER TEN

The partisan struggle

There are three Allied Armies fighting in Italy. The Fifth and Eighth in front of the enemy need no introduction but the Partisans fighting a less conventional struggle in the enemy rear have been the subject of so much tainted enemy propaganda and so much ill-informed scribbling from this side of the line that it is not surprising to discover how little of the truth is known about them by most people.[1]

It was the summer of 1944. Don Pietro Buogo, the priest of Cessalto, directed Bill Black towards the partisans. Although his means of transport wasn't a tandem, it was almost as bad. 'We rode these bloody old bikes and they were old bikes. Right along the main roads and they didn't stop us. Eventually we got passed to another guy then we were changed over to two or three other guys. And then we started up this bloody mountain and that bloody near killed us.'[2]

Black found himself with a brigade of the Nino Nanetti Division and the Allied Special Forces presided over by the English Special Major

.....Siamo costretti rinchiudere i partigiani

PARTIGIANI DIETRO ..... IL RETICOLATO

'Partisans Behind the Wire.' German propaganda leaflet to discredit the partisans.

Harold 'Bill' Tilman. The Nino Nanetti Division was one of the most redoubtable partisan forces, consisting of some nine brigades and five thousand men. Named after a Communist hero killed in the Spanish Civil War, it had relocated *en masse* from the Apennines above Bologna to a more defensible zone in the Venetian Pre-Alps.[3]

By this time, the British Special Operations Executive (SOE) and American Office of Strategic Services (OSS) secret missions were sending in agents to assist the partisan struggle. Their numbers had increased to 50,000; initially dismissed as 'rebels' or 'brigands' before being elevated to the more respected status of 'patriots', it became increasingly clear that they were a force to be reckoned with from the German perspective, besides providing invaluable assistance to the Allies. But views on the partisans continued to be divided among military authorities, mainly because it was feared that the movement could become a separatist one, 'incite' the people towards Communism and warrant the same brutal suppression by the British that had crushed the Greek Resistance Movement in 1944. Once an area was liberated the partisans were disarmed and encouraged to join the new Italian army, commonly called Free Italians, formed under the auspices of the Allies in the south. The Fifth Army even put many partisan bands in the Apennines into internment camps,[4] much to the glee of the German propaganda machine. John Senior was working in the fields of San Giorgio di Livenza when a leaflet distributed by the Luftwaffe floated down.[5] It trumpeted this fact as evidence of how the Allies regarded them and advised them to join their 'brothers' against the true enemy. But reports from Special Mission agents who had been parachuted in to the mountains to ostensibly 'control' the partisan formations were unanimous in requesting more support for them and in trying to soften the views of the military hierarchy.

It was an international mix stationed in the freezing snow-covered mountains near the town of Belluno. American airmen, Russians, English, Rhodesian, Mexican and even German deserters were among the partisans. New recruits were being dropped in all the time, including a zealous American officer, 'a brave man but as silly as a chook', who hatched a 'mad' but fortunately foiled scheme to go after Kesselring. Although it was a makeshift organisation, hierarchies of rank were observed as closely in these mountains as in more conventional military sectors. There were about twenty officers and Black was put with the aircrew. Like most Kiwis, he found all this nonsense over rank amusing. 'Didn't worry me. I called a spade a spade and they – the Yanks couldn't understand that. I hadn't seen [one of the airmen] for a couple of days and he wandered out one morning and I said, "G'day Jack, how are you?" and these four aircrew said, "Jesus, did you hear that?" And they said,

"Oh well, they don't seem to stand on ceremony up here apparently," and let it ride at that.'[6]

Black's group was constantly on the move, passing from one partisan band to another. They lived in abandoned barns and huts and cowsheds in the warmer weather and when the winter of 1944 set in, one of the coldest on record, they camped in log cabins and caves they blew out of the mountains with dynamite. They were under continuous attack. 'We fought and we ran most of the time. We were chased by the bloody Germans all over the place at different stages.' While on guard overlooking a village, Black saw a truck with the Red Cross insignia arrive in the village. Men in white got out. He was suspicious. 'I think they're bloody Huns in camouflage whites,' he told the second-in-command who came to relieve him, but 'he didn't seem to be too worried about it.' Black's hunch was to prove correct. The next morning he decided to get some sausages from outside and while he was there, use the makeshift toilet. 'The snow was about six feet deep outside this bloody place. Freeze your bloody balls off. I dug these sausages out of the snow – we'd a cache there. I'd just dropped me tweeds to have a shit and all of a sudden the bloody roof lifted off. I nearly got smothered in bloody snow. They'd seen me and fired bloody mortars at me!'[7]

It was time to leave. They walked for days to find another partisan unit but it was cat-and-mouse all the way. 'We got away but it was a mighty hard trip. They were right behind us from one hill to another. You could see each other for some considerable time.' On another occasion Germans surrounded them on top of a basin covered in snow, 'just like Christmas'. He and his two companions dived into a 'slitty' where across the gully they saw a German creeping through the small scrub. The men had a Bren gun between them and gave him 'a bit of a shot to see what happens', but they were in white-out conditions, unable to work out distances, so they were shooting into a void. The man was scared off but they had given their position away. Black and his companions were crouched in the two metre-wide trench when a couple of mortar rounds came screaming over. Both sides of the trench were blown in, blackening the men with mortar dust. 'If they'd put one in the middle they'd have got the lot of us. But they didn't. They only fired the two shots. How lucky can you get?'

He was angry to find that the partisans had disappeared when they heard the shooting. 'They'd left us holding the bag, the bastards. They'd asked us to take a Bren and they'd put us right out the front.'

Allied personnel, who lived in separate quarters, were not expected to fight with the partisans, especially when arms were scarce, but they took on peripheral tasks such as guard duty and sabotage actions, mining roads and bridges. This kept them separate from the partisans and their 'cause', which most ex-prisoners were unwilling to risk their lives for. Yet there were pamphlets circulating in the villages with substantial rewards offered. 'They knew our names and where we were. They knew I was a Kiwi.'[8] In the areas where fierce fighting was going on, arms were a necessity and not just for combat. Bruno Steffè: 'I always carried a pistol and a knife on me. I was an officer. If they captured me they'd butcher me to make me tell them things I didn't even know, then they'd kill me. I had made up my mind. If Germans surrounded me, I would shoot myself.'[9] Laurie Read agreed. 'The main thing while living here was to have a revolver, so that if cornered by the Fascists – and torture was inevitable – one could use the revolver on oneself. How much pain one can stand is questionable.'[10] Arch Scott often debated what he should do if caught. Although the idea of suicide was anathema to his Catholic faith, he hoped he would never be put to the test.

To prepare for an aerial drop, Black used to listen to the BBC radio twice: firstly at six o'clock at night, when a list of names in code would be transmitted, then again at eight o'clock for the confirmation. 'My code was *The Major is without a Beard*. If I heard that come over it meant I was going to get a drop and I would tell the blokes to get themselves organised and we'd go out and light the fires and wait for these planes to come over ... I used to have a little poem. And the first letter of the poem – I used to put the fire out in an "h" or an "l" or a "t". And the "n" letter of the poem I used to Morse code this with an old lamp and they would reply and they would know it was us.'[11]

The partisans had little control over the contents of the drop and when it arrived sometimes wondered if their benefactors were living on the same planet. Maurice Cosgrave's poor opinion of the British did not improve during his three weeks with the partisans in the Marches area. One clear, crisp evening they were called together by their Italian lieutenant and told a plane would be arriving with a drop. 'This aeroplane came droning over – it was exciting – and it dropped over a whole lot of stuff and we rushed for it because they'd said we were going to get arms. . . they were chests of tea. That was the first occasion and we got chests of bloody tea! And the second time we got boots.'[12] For the Italians it was a quickfire immersion into the curious tastes of a different culture. 'When you wanted arms you got boots,' confirms Aldo Camponogara, battle name *Lemene*. 'And then they give you tea. We didn't know what it was. We had to learn to drink tea. And to eat tinned fruit. We'd never seen it before.'[13]

It was not uncommon, either, to prepare for a drop and then to be bombed by their own planes, unconnected to the organised drop. Bill Black wryly recalls one such stuff-up. 'Twice they came over but they weren't the same outfit. They were our blokes all right but they bombed us. They dropped a load of bombs on us, heavy stuff. Another time they dropped anti-personnel bombs. They were worse than the big ones because they were going off for days later. They were sort of butterfly bombs. You only touched them and away they went. So with our subs knocking us off and our airplanes knocking us off I had a bad time from our own army!'[14]

To be fair, the Allied agencies were operating under difficult conditions, which meant that particular supplies were not always available. Underground organisations in Warsaw, France and Yugoslavia had prior claims on reinforcements. Weather conditions in the north, especially during the winter, were overcast and delays were unavoidable. In the mountains supply drops were hazardous with one peak or valley looking like another. To make matters worse, decoy fires were lit by the enemy or even rival groups which confused pilots and infuriated the rightful recipients. Charges of favouritism based on political preferences were rife. The Garibaldi groups believed with some justification that they received fewer supplies than the Monarchist or Osoppo groups because of their Communist sympathies. This rankled when their armed bands were by far the most numerous and widely considered the most effective fighting force. However, by the end of the war these supplies were far more evenly distributed with the Communists receiving more than 40 per cent of all aid.[15]

For Luigi Borgarelli, battle name *Sandro Sandri*, commander of a band of Osoppo or non-Communist partisans back down in the plains in the Latisana district close to the Veneto-Friuli border, the code name was *Maria Filomena dell'aceto*. When he heard the familiar *ta ta boom, ta ta boom* signal from Radio London, he knew that three evenings later there would be a drop. Strong flares were laid in five cone-shaped holes two metres deep. In this way they could be clearly seen from the air without being visible at ground level. The drop consisted of about twenty metal boxes, each one attached to a parachute. The boxes contained materials for sabotage – explosives, detonators, nails, steel pliers as well as boots, socks, chocolates and cigarettes. Once collected they would be loaded on to several waiting wagons drawn by oxen and camouflaged under piles of hay.

The next phase of the operation was a visit to the cemetery. Borgarelli possessed a family tomb with sixteen places. He had replaced their marble fronts with exquisitely painted cardboard replicas. All night he and five of his most trusted men went back and forth stacking the metal boxes inside the tombs. There was plenty of room. 'At that time only a few of our family were dead. We put them to one side because, well, it gave us the creeps.' However, the problem of what to do with the parachutes remained. They were voluminous and hard to hide. Then someone had a brilliant idea. The church possessed a huge organ in the choir. It was raised to one side and looked over the altar where people took Mass. After obtaining the agreement of the parish priest, Borgarelli rolled the parachutes up tightly and inserted them inside the widest organ pipes. 'Who would ever know they were there?' When the organist started playing at Mass the following Sunday there was a screeching, squawking sound. The priest said, 'That's enough, the organ's broken.' After the war Borgarelli gave the parachutes to local seamstresses who made shirts and underwear from the fine olive-green cloth. These were then distributed round the community.[16]

Discipline was strong in the Garibaldi units. Many comprised officers from the disbanded Italian army who were smarting from the humiliation of being despised by Allies and Germans alike. They wanted to run their unit as a fighting force and prove their worth. Communist leaders such as Cino Moscatelli had trained in Russia and others were veterans of the Spanish Civil War. Recalls Steffè, 'We used to call them the Spaniards. The conflict had been very harsh in Spain and they knew that an iron discipline was necessary.'[17] In these units any breach of discipline was treated seriously and punishment sometimes ran to unwarranted severity. A case of a cook being executed by his own command for stealing chocolate was hotly contested. Two Italian partisans in Steffè's unit in Slovenia were condemned to death for stealing a clock in order to exchange it for a sack of potatoes. It was petty thievery motivated more by hunger than malice, and due to the minimal rations accorded the Italians. Of the five commanders of the battalion, Steffè was one of two against the order. He tried to remonstrate. 'The clock was given back; so in the end nothing was stolen. Why must we shoot two good partisans? We have enough losses fighting the Germans. Why kill each other?' He tried to plead for the men's lives on account of the lack of a unanimous decision. 'And the Commander of the Slovenian Division said, you've been fighting here a year. We've been fighting for four years. We give the orders for your brigade and we order you to execute them.' In the name of setting a good example, the men were shot the next day. Steffè, co-leader of the battalion, suffered a huge crisis over his shared responsibility and his sense of anguish remains to this day.[18]

Luigi Borgarelli commanded a small band affiliated to the Bassa Stella battalion of the Osoppo Friuli Third Division. His band made a conscious decision to remain unarmed and to limit their operations to acts of sabotage. 'I said one thing only to my boys. "We must not kill anyone. If we do something against the Germans they'll put the ten of us against the wall and there'll be reprisals. So we can only protect our families, our women and our homes."'[19] He liaised with and took instructions from a Special Operations agent by the code name of Raoul. Although they worked closely together, Borgarelli never knew if he was English or American. He disappeared after the war, leaving no trace.

Borgarelli believes that it was this decision to not take up arms against the Germans that kept the zone free from reprisals. Like many partisans operating in the Veneto plains, he had a tacit agreement with the German commander of the zone, a Prussian by the name of Colonel Reidel, with whom he had established a respectful friendship.[20] It began one evening when the Colonel and some of his officers were dining in the restaurant owned by Borgarelli's family. They had been plied with wine and were pleasantly drunk. Reidel complimented Borgarelli's mother on her fine cooking then asked his father to step aside with him. Taking off his jacket he said, 'Now I am no longer Colonel Reidel, I am Mr Reidel. Please trust what I am going to ask you. I want you to tell me what you think of our leaders.' Borgarelli's father did not mince words despite his wife's desperate hissing at him to shut up. '*Signor Colonello*, I shall say this whether you are offended or not. I think we are governed by two madmen.' His wife fled sobbing to the kitchen convinced he would be deported. The Colonel remained silent for a while, then, looking over at his officers, murmured in Italian, 'There is probably someone in this room who thinks as you do.' Later Borgarelli himself was approached by the Colonel who wanted to know whether he had the courage to speak his mind like his father. Borgarelli took a deep breath. 'Clearly, I don't agree with your leader, nor mine. I agree with my father that they are both mad. But if I were to go to your home in Germany and say that Germany belongs to Italy, you would rebel. Many of you think we are traitors but this is a war and each side takes up its own position.

'He knew what I meant. He said only one thing. "Mr Borgarelli, we are here not because we wanted to come but because we were sent here. I am an officer of the Wehrmacht and I do not want to be a traitor to my army, nor do I want to be a tyrant. Given that we find ourselves in this situation, let's follow a middle path. You leave us alone and we'll leave you alone."' Reidel was prepared to turn a blind eye to the partisans' activities as long as there were no attacks made against his men. This gentlemanly pact suited Borgarelli who considered himself a patriot and a political moderate.[21]

In fact Borgarelli felt more endangered by the Tito-affiliated Garibaldi group whom he says were the cause of any reprisals taken because of their 'hot-headed' tactics. On one occasion a failed attempt by Garibaldi partisans to ambush two '*repubblichini*' resulted in a roundup. Borgarelli called upon Reidel to intervene to avoid houses in the area being burned to the ground. Cossacks, white Russians recruited into the German troops, formed part of the SS reprisal groups. They were feared more than the Germans.

Borgarelli gave the same advice to a friend who was enrolled in the Fascist forces. 'Do your duty without killing anyone. If you do certain things they'll come and get you.' Unfortunately his friend did not or was unable to comply. He was ambushed by Garibaldi partisans, made to dig his own grave, and shot. Borgarelli himself felt that he was always under surveillance by the Garibaldi units and that they would 'take him out' if they had a chance. He followed his cautious strategy of maintaining contact with them as they wished, but took care to avoid turning up physically at any pre-arranged meeting.

Some hard-liners of the Garibaldi units scorned moderates like Borgarelli who, they felt, were not imbued with the same ideals. Aldo Camponogara's experience as a partisan changed his life. He felt the Osoppo Brigade in Friuli fought under a vague banner of patriotism, but did not advocate a shift of power. Many ex-Fascists or *attendisti*, the waverers who would be on the side of whoever won, collaborated with these groups.[22] Those who fought with the Garibaldi units sincerely wished for social change and believed Communism carried the torch of liberation. In contrast to its claims of being 'non-political' the Osoppo was backed primarily by the Church that saw the spread of Communism as a threat to its power base. Certainly several priests were instrumental in setting up the Osoppo brigades in the Friuli area.[23] One of these was Don Redento Bello (battle name *don Candido*) who was operating in the lower Friuli basin with the blessing of his bishop. Although active in the mountains, he never fired a shot, much to his relief. He emphasises the pluralistic nature of the Osoppo, stating that 'politically, it was founded on respect for the ideas of all the parties. We fought for freedom for everybody.'[24] Socialists, Giellists, Christian Democrats and independents joined the ranks.

In some areas these groups and Garibaldi factions joined forces and fought together against the Germans. But in the Friuli this was never an easy alliance. Garibaldi groups were aligned with Tito's partisans, who made no bones about their intentions to claim back the territory of Venezia Giulia under the banner of a Communist Yugoslavia. This culminated in the massacre at Porzuus where a Garibaldi unit ambushed, disarmed and killed a group of Osoppo partisans. Don Redento Bello escaped being there by pure chance, much to the chagrin of Mario Toffanin or *Giacca*, the perpetrator, who was quoted as looking forward to making Don Candido eat his cassock before killing him. The debate over who masterminded this massacre still rages today.[25]

Bruno Steffè makes a distinction between Garibaldi units fighting for an independent democratic Italy and those affiliated with the Tito-controlled Yugoslav partisans. He was fighting with the latter on 14 September 1944 when Tito expressed his wish to annex Italian territory as far as the Isonzo River in Friuli. This brought about an enormous tension in Italo-Yugoslav relations and alienated all Italians except diehard Communists. Up until now Steffè had fought with his unit under the Italian flag within the Corpus. Now orders were given to erase this separate distinction. At this point he realised he had another choice to make.

Gianfranco Ivancich belongs to an old Venetian family and lives in a villa in the village of San Giorgio di Tagliamento on the Friuli-Veneto border. The family moved in aristocratic and intellectual circles; Ernest Hemingway was a frequent house guest. Ivancich's sister Adriana is said to be the inspiration for Hemingway's novel, *Across the River and into the Trees*, where an American officer has an affair with a Venetian noblewoman many years his junior. Ivancich had fought in North Africa and, wounded, was sent back to Italy where he joined an Osoppo partisan group. His connections and ability to speak English meant that he liaised with the Special Services and took a key role in the spectacular liberation of Venice. This triumph was bittersweet. In the last days of the war Yugoslav partisans captured his father who, as a wealthy landowner, was automatically suspected of being Fascist. They shot him and left his body near a river on his property.[26]

The fighting between the rival political groups could exist even within a single band and could lead to tragic consequences. Giuseppe Crestani, a Communist who had fought as a captain in the Spanish Civil War, joined an early partisan division which contained moderate or 'white' elements. These were supporters of Badoglio, the ex-Fascist general who replaced Mussolini after the Armistice. It was a potent mix with different aims; the Badogliani wanted to await the Allies and only use arms in self-defence. The Communists wanted to form a military unit and provide strong active resistance. Each faction profoundly distrusted the motives, methods and aims of the other. Crestani (*Svizza*) and his three Communist companions were found riddled with bullets at the bottom of a ravine at Conca at the end of December 1943. 'It was us or them,' says a still traumatised survivor today.[27]

Italian-born New Zealander John Crestani, a relative of Giuseppe Crestani, was living in the mountainous Fontanelle district near Bassano del Grappa in the Veneto. His family owned a hotel and tavern, the 'Alpino', that served as a partisan meeting place and refuge for escaped prisoners. Prisoners were hidden in large barrels used to store wine. They would then be assisted to cross into Switzerland. Crestani and his sisters often led them up the mountains on the first stage of their journey. His family, strong anti-Fascists who had suffered dosings of castor oil and beatings for their dissidence, were subjected to imprisonment, beatings and deportation during the roundups of January 1944.[28] Several times their father would disappear for days on end for 'interrogation'. No one knew whether he would return.

Crestani spent from October to May away at a Jesuit school. One night when he was at home during the summer months the 13-year-old woke to a machine-gun pointed at his head. The Germans had discovered his school hat and, suspicious, made him put it on to prove that it fitted. Convinced the family were hiding partisans or escaped prisoners, they had petrol ready to burn the house down if they found them. Despite the family's protestations to the contrary, they ransacked the house. Luckily, prisoners had left their tavern the day before. Spies were always around and young Crestani was vigilant. 'While Dad was listening to his short-wave radio, I had to watch out for anyone moving around. If I saw anything, I would start whistling and that would let him know he had to hide the radio.'

Women and children were the eyes and ears of the Resistance, gleaning information from their daily activities at the markets, the communal washing site, or in the schools. A small number of women fought with the partisans but most women were *staffette* or couriers who took messages to partisans with food or weapons hidden in their baskets. A woman cycling innocently around the countryside would attract less attention and children were even less likely to be noticed.

One *staffetta*, Italian-born New Zealander Ana Tizzoni, was just seventeen and living in Fabriano in the Marches region. Her father, Giovanni Tizzoni, was a leader of the Profili band formed in April 1944 after the assassination of Dr Engles Profili, a prominent leader. Tizzoni also represented the Action Party on the local Committee of National Liberation. His whole family was involved in clandestine action and Ana recalls the fear and uncertainty under which they lived.

She led escaped prisoners at night over the steep mountains surrounding Fabriano. Once she told her father that she was frightened that she would talk if caught by the Germans and tortured. His response was to take off his belt and soundly beat her. 'Your life is just one,' he said. 'But if you talk, hundreds of lives will be lost.' From then on she was given a small tablet of cyanide to keep on her in case she was captured. Ana recounts this incident with a measure of admiration and pride. 'My father was a man of principle.'[29]

Giovanni Tizzoni liaised with the Second New Zealand Division joined to the Allies pushing up the peninsula. Here Ana met New Zealander Gordon Petch, who was working with the ambulance unit. Both Tizzoni and Ana were awarded Gold and Bronze medals respectively by General Freyberg. After her marriage in Wellington, Ana asked Freyberg to allow her parents to join her in New Zealand.

1944 was expected to be the year the war ended. While American and French troops were withdrawn from Italy to invade Southern France, the Germans prepared a major defence known as the Gothic Line that cut across the northern Apennines from La Spezia on the Mediterranean coast to Pesaro on the Adriatic. When the Allied offensive against the Gothic Line failed, General Alexander gave his controversial decree in November 1944 that, as the weather prevented the Allies from advancing further up the peninsula until the following spring, the partisans should return to their homes for the winter and await orders. Ammunition as well as manpower should be conserved as supply drops were to be deployed on other fronts. This was like a death knell to the tens of thousands of partisans still in the mountains and hills who took it as an invitation to disband when they had nowhere to go, leaving them to the tender mercies of the enemy. The political wing believed it was an attempt to destroy their liberation movement. Although Alexander insisted it was a decision made on military grounds alone, it created a wound of bad faith with the Allies that scarred the morale of the partisans and angered the CLN. Ignoring the order, they declared they would intensify their struggle.

As the winter progressed, the partisans became more isolated. Bill Black remembered that food grew scarcer as the drops got more rare and the snow up there was 'shocking'. Some men who set out on treks attempting to join other units were caught in blizzards and perished. It was the snow that saved them in the end, however, as the conditions were too perilous for sustained fighting and German troops were constantly deployed from frontline action to comb through mountain strongholds.[30]

A successful relationship between an escaper and partisan was that of Arch Scott and Gino Panont. Scott had enormous admiration for the partisans who operated in his area. There was reciprocal respect for their different tasks. He kept out of politics. 'I did my job and they did theirs.'[31] Gino Panont, battle name *Treviso*, commanded the Boatto, later renamed Pellegrini, Brigade. A short, slim, fair-haired man, his smiling demeanour belied his tough, uncompromising skills as a commander. He helped place prisoners of the Hare Battalion, provided escorts for them, and reimbursed impoverished sharecropping families, who although feeding prisoners had barely enough food for themselves. Crucially, he alerted Scott to imminent roundups and vetted suspected spies.

One case tormented Scott for years afterwards. He began to suspect that an Italian contact, a very friendly man always eager to help, might be involved in incidents where men were recaptured. He casually voiced these doubts to Panont. The next day the partisan told him not to worry any more as the previous evening the man had been 'taken care of'. Scott was horrified at such a summary execution based on a mere supposition. Before being shot the man had insisted on his mutual friendship with Scott, whom he protested would be upset if anything happened to him. 'The poor bastard. He could have been okay. On the other hand, the partisans might well have known much more about him than I did.'[32] Sixty years later, 90-year-old Panont still remembers Scott's angry distress. However, reliable information confirmed that the man was indeed a spy who regularly visited the SS Command. Hundreds of lives were at risk.[33] Panont is adamant: 'If people were spying we had to eliminate them. And eliminate them we did.' He claims the moral endorsement of the priest, Don Fausto Moschetta. 'He said to us, "Don't you worry. Even if you have to kill them, I absolve you all because those people are wicked."'[34]

On another occasion it was Scott himself who had to make a hard decision. Locals were used to the menacing drone of Allied bombers or *pippo* as the Italians called them, flying over the countryside. But one clear summer day in 1944 Scott gazed into the sky to be greeted by the sight of Sergeant Geoffrey Cheesebrough, a RAF Spitfire pilot, floating down towards the swampy marshlands a few kilometres away. Scott immediately called upon his *staffetta*, Rosetta, to check the area out and learn who picked up the pilot and where he was taken, warning her to be very careful. While Rosetta was heading towards the marshland, Beppi Marson, dedicated partisan and friend of Germans when it suited him, was cycling in the area. Also nearby were some Germans with a motor van. All, like players in a spoof detective film, converged towards the parachutist. Marson, asked directions by the Germans, pointed them towards a maze of dead-end tracks.

The pilot was fortunate to land close to a friendly sharecropper family.

By the time the Germans arrived at the spot, there was no trace of him nor his parachute and no one could shed any light on the matter. However, within a few days a local partisan brought Scott news of a dreadful reprisal. Three youths were taken from each of the families in the locality where the pilot had landed, and an ultimatum was issued. If the pilot was not immediately handed over to the Germans, the young men would be shot. The parents wanted Scott to decide what to do. 'My reply was, "We can't give the airman up . . ." and those poor parents accepted my decision without question.'[35] The next few days were agonising as they awaited the dreaded news. For some unknown reason, the threat was not acted upon and the boys were released.

CHAPTER ELEVEN

The prodigal son of Gemona

Gemona Cemetery, Friuli, July 2001. Margie Gardner stood before a marble tombstone gazing at the photo of a serious-faced young woman with thick dark hair. Her name was Elisabetta Zucchiatti, née Bierti. Born 23 December 1945, she died on 6 June 1976. Margie Gardner placed a small piece of greenstone on the ground in front of the tomb and wept.

Fifty-eight years earlier, one night in October 1943, Gisborne-born Frank Gardner jumped out of a train laden with prisoners bound for Germany. He escaped a few minutes before his friend Jack Lang, but those minutes set them on different journeys, separating them until after the war.

Frank Gardner's memory of his fall from the train was shaky. He remembered the incredible sensation of hurtling through time and space and the rush of air, which, after the cramped, airless conditions of the train wagon, must have seemed like the breath of freedom. He was knocked unconscious and when he came to could hardly move. After what seemed like days, with the assistance of Italians he dragged himself to the door of a two-storeyed farmhouse. Located close to the railway in a village not far from Gemona, it belonged to the Marchetti family who took him in with great hospitality and curiosity. He found his New Zealand nationality was an asset.[1] Although Gardner wrote of breaking his leg in the fall from the train, Guido Marchetti, a young boy at the time, curiously has no recollection of this.[2] What is certain is that Gardner had injured himself to some degree and was suffering from the effects of hunger, stress and exhaustion. Occupying a bedroom on the second floor, he was nursed back to good health by Signora Marchetti and her daughter.[3]

As was often the case, Gardner filled the shoes of a son who was away, a prisoner of the British. He settled in to the simple rhythms of country life and when he was better began to help out with the chores around the house. The Germans were ever present but a survival strategy of many Italians was to form if not sincere friendships, then friendly relations with their invaders. Germans were often guests at meal times where food, wine and family photos were shared. As Arch Scott had once posed as the head of his Italian family, Gardner, by now known as Franco, joined these cordial occasions as the convalescent son of the family. Remaining hidden would have provoked suspicion.

A German soldier called Franz struck up a particularly close friendship with his New Zealand namesake. Both men communicated through their excruciating Italian and Franz was none the wiser. Often the two would walk through the village chatting together, much to the amusement of the locals. Gardner was not enamoured of the association but he liked Franz and his adventurous nature would have relished its element of risk. A dentist by profession, Franz had extracted teeth for locals. When Gardner's teeth were giving him trouble, Franz noticed his swollen face and, suspecting a sore tooth, wanted to look inside his friend's mouth. Emphatically denying there was anything wrong, Gardner manfully chewed on his food with his tender tooth, trying to conceal the agonising pain. He had had extensive dental repairs back in New Zealand and feared that possibly different methods from European dental practices might give him away.[4]

One evening during a celebration with relations, the family were joined by Franz and a German friend. There was much dancing and singing and revelry until well after midnight. When a torrential thunderstorm broke out, the Germans were invited to stay over. That night a chuckling Gardner fell asleep to the tune of the drunken snores of a German stretched out on either side of him. On another occasion he accompanied the Marchetti daughter to a dance after she had baulked at accepting an invitation to go with Franz, whom she disliked. In the interests of keeping on good terms with the German occupiers, they decided that Gardner could go along as chaperone. The role of protective brother was perfectly in keeping with family custom. The next day Franz commented on how unusual it was to see a sister so fond of her brother. 'All the time she was dancing with me she was watching you. It must be nice to have such a sister.'[5]

But enforced idleness did not suit Gardner for long. He met up with a priest who was working with the newly formed partisan forces and agreed to use his friendship with Franz to gain information on German plans and activities. Although he genuinely liked Franz, what had been an amusing pastime now became an active strategy to help the war effort. However, Franz's unofficial protection of Gardner was threatened when the German told him he was due to be transferred. He warned that his replacement would treat him as he would any other fit Italian male. This meant being conscripted to work for the Germans or even being sent to Germany. Ever helpful, Franz insisted he write something across Gardner's non-existent identity papers to arrange special consideration for him. Only a successful ploy to get Franz drunk at his farewell party made him forget this scheme.

After Franz's departure, it was not long before what was common knowledge reached the ears of the new German command. From being an informer for the partisan-priest, Gardner's ill-concealed identity became the target of Fascist informers. One day Fascists searched the Marchetti farm and found Gardner's army greatcoat. Alerted minutes before, Gardner had been able to slip away out a window, but the parents and their daughter, Bella, were arrested and imprisoned. This knowledge was enormously distressing for Gardner, a distress compounded by the fact he could do nothing about it. Although his wife and daughter were released shortly afterwards, Marchetti remained in prison under threat of execution. Fortunately he too was released some months later.[6]

It was too dangerous to remain. With a bounty on his head and in the middle of a bitter winter, Gardner headed for the mountains. But after wading through treacherous snowdrifts in conditions that would test even a suitably clad mountaineer, he returned to the plains. For several weeks he lived rough, enduring hunger and icy cold and hiding where he could. In a hayloft above a cowshed he nourished himself for a couple of days by milking a cow, drawing the contents into a rusty tin. Its owners were mystified why their animal had dried up and argued bitterly, blaming each other. With Germans hunting him and no houses, no matter how rustic, immune from cursory searches, he decided there was no option but to make contact with the partisans.

Through the priest Gardner was guided to Yugoslav partisans operating in the mountains close to the border. He disliked their captain on sight and found their methods haphazard and undisciplined. A woman and her small daughter were brought before the captain and interrogated as suspected spies. Both were bewildered and weeping and Gardner was certain they had nothing to do with the deeds they were accused of. He was horrified and sickened when ten minutes later they were put against a wall and shot. The summary justice of some of these desperate groups verged on indiscriminate brutality. From their perspective, the treacherous voice of one spy could mean death for hundreds. Innocent people, regardless of age and gender, lost their lives rather than run that risk.

Generally partisans did not arm the Allied prisoners in their midst but after the first week, fearful of turning his back on any of his unpredictable companions, Gardner persuaded the captain to give him a pistol. He was also getting tired of the inaction. 'We should be fighting the Germans, not shooting women and children.' They embarked on a successful ambush, killing many Germans and capturing others. However, the Yugoslavs took no prisoners. To Gardner's disgust, some were tortured to death with knives. The Germans then launched a major attack and although the partisans fought back valiantly they were no match for the superior numbers and weapons of their foe and were soon surrounded. Things were looking grim as the Germans began to separate out the officers. Gardner, reckoning he 'may as well die promoted',[7] said he was an officer. This combination of quick thinking and good luck saved him as the men without rank were shot on the spot. The three officers were bundled into a truck, presumably for questioning before meeting the same fate as their hapless companions. Again the tale takes on a fantastic quality as the hairpin bends and the uneven surface of the road caused the truck to bounce and sway dangerously. When the guard stumbled off balance for a moment, Gardner threw himself against him and the two went sprawling off the side of the truck, landing with a sickening thud on the road. The German died instantly, his neck broken.

Free again, he returned to the mountains. But he was at low ebb, wanting nothing more than to get back to his old division and 'do a bit of clean fighting'.[8] He was plagued by 'battle fatigue', the despondent weariness of the hunted, and haunted too by images of the brutalities he had witnessed and the dangers good-hearted Italian folk had suffered on his behalf. His name was now notorious in the district and the Italians were far too scared to give him shelter if he told them who he was. He invented an identity as an American airman, one that to this day is, for some people, still associated with 'Franco'. No, he was a pilot whose plane was shot down, they would say, not a prisoner, even though it was conceded he was a New Zealander.

Gardner spent a few weeks in an empty room above a schoolhouse protected by the teacher, an alarming-looking woman who wore a swastika pinned to her uniform. However, she too was in disguise, having been a marshal in Tito's army who had twice escaped the Germans. Forced to flee again, he shared a dilapidated shack in a field with a sack of potatoes and a swarm of rats. Gardner competed with the rats for the potatoes, which, although they did not agree with him, were the only food available. They also served as ammunition to hurl at the rats when they came too close. The steady gnawing and munching of the rodents, a sound magnified by the black silence, kept him awake at night. 'It was the loneliness I couldn't stick. I might as well not have existed ... and that gives you a funny feeling. Up in the heights it was different. Even though I was really much further away from people, I didn't feel so lonely. The mountains were solid and strong, and, in a way, friendly. But here in the flats ... I never want to feel that way again.'[9] It was not surprising that he felt psychologically at home in the Friuli mountains, given their striking similarity to the rugged, bush-covered Raukumara mountains surrounding the Gardner family's Gisborne farm.

Shortly after this Gardner was sheltered by a farming family whose tall, powerfully built son, Pietro Coppetti, the Big One, was linked to the partisans. But they could not keep him as they were expecting a party of Croats. Gardner could not impose himself on the beleaguered Marchettis again, so new accommodation was urgently needed.

Anna Zanini remembers Frank Gardner as a man of middle height with reddish blond hair, fair skin, full lips and a teasing smile. He was brought to her house one cold night when she was sitting by the fireplace in her kitchen with her neighbours from across the road. 'We heard a knock at the door and this young man – we didn't know if he was English or what he was – said, "I'm hungry. I'm so hungry."'[10] Although finding their dialect hard to understand, Gardner immediately knew he was among friends. He noted that 'the tall, unusual-looking' Zanini was the blondest Italian woman he had ever seen. They felt sorry for the wan-faced young man and plying him with food, bundled him up in blankets in front of the fire. When Zanini was asked if 'Franco' could stay at her house she felt it was too dangerous. 'I have small children and I can't keep them quiet when they go to school. They'll talk to people and the Germans will burn down our house.'[11] However, she agreed to keep him for one night. Beside her was Alice Bierti from the house across the road, who often joined her after dinner to sew and chat. Obviously Gardner had made a favourable impression because she persuaded her husband Pietro to let Gardner stay at their house, saying she was not afraid.

Frank Gardner was to live for fourteen months with the Bierti family in their house on the outskirts of Gemona. Although he was at times away, this was his base and must have seemed like paradise after his recent experience with the Yugoslav partisans. It was an unusual household. The building belonged to two brothers who had married two sisters and they lived with their families in separate quarters with independent entrances. A feud over inheritance matters meant that neither family spoke to the other, a situation that has continued to this day. Gardner with his easy-going, sociable nature had 'no time for this nonsense' and wandered freely between the two households, made to feel welcome in both.

He spent the most time with Pietro and Alice Bierti's family. Bierti was a builder turned small farmer during the war. There were three children, Anna who was nineteen, 18-year-old Luigi, and Aldo who was fourteen. Aldo confirmed that Franco was treated like one of the family. They liked this cheerful New Zealander with his tales of huge sprawling farms with thousands of sheep in *Nuova Zelanda*.[12] For his part, he enjoyed teasing his new friends. Anna Zanini, whom Franco quickly named Blondie, remembers that he used to say that in Friuli they only knew how to eat polenta, nothing else. 'You should come to New Zealand and see how much bread we eat!'[13] He was a great favourite with the children, taking them for rides on the horse and entertaining them with his magician tricks, which he then taught them how to do. Alice and Anna fussed over him, sewing clothes for him and cooking special dishes to feed him up. In the evenings the inside window shutters would be firmly closed, the curtains drawn, and while the two women were sewing, Gardner would listen to the BBC on Radio London, a high point of the day. His bedroom was on a corner with three windows facing in different directions, two of them directly over the road. Above him was the loft with panoramic views of the Friuli countryside. Both rooms provided a perfect look-out.

But Pietro Bierti was nervous. Gardner's Italian, although much improved, was not that of the local dialect, so it was important he kept a low profile. A committed Fascist lived on the other side of the road and although Gardner stayed in his room during the day, a young woman who was about to enter the Fascist's home once noticed him standing at the window. Both Alice and Anna conspired to keep Pietro's nervousness at bay by joining forces with Blondie to concoct a reason for having a strange man in the corner bedroom, divulged to the Fascist household by way of casual chitchat about a workman called to the Bierti household to fix the lights upstairs. After this, to avoid the telltale clomping of his army boots, they made him a pair of slippers from strips of cloth sewn together. Even though they had to be renewed every month, they were ideal for gliding stealthily through the house. These noiseless cloth slippers were invaluable on future partisan sabotage actions. 'Blondie' once lent Gardner her husband's pair when he went to blow up the railway station.

The Italian partisan bands, although fairly haphazard, were already in operation. Gardner was attracted to the idea of building up a force on the outskirts of Gemona and embarking on some mayhem of his own. A friend of Pietro Bierti initially supplied the explosives, and although Gardner was not particularly well acquainted with them, his natural aptitude for tools and machinery meant he was a fast learner. In order to finance this black market supply of explosives, large supplies of tobacco had to be provided to Bierti's contacts. Methods were unorthodox but common enough, although they gave the partisans a bad name. A tobacconist was held up at gunpoint and his shop raided. Gardner justified the 'operation' by explaining that a chit was given to the owner, which could be reclaimed from the government at the end of the war.[14]

With a band comprising about eight members, including Luigi Bierti and two young women, they embarked on a series of some twenty-eight sabotage operations, successfully blowing up cables, railway lines, bridges and roads. The damage to these transport and communication systems caused invaluable delays. They took time to repair and were then instantly targeted again by Gardner and his group, who were also instrumental in damaging a silk factory at Maiano that made parachutes for the German army. The most spectacular feat Gardner's band achieved was the destruction of the main railway bridge over the Orvenco River near Gemona, severing direct rail contact between Italy and Austria after six unsuccessful attacks by the RAF. By this time a bounty of 350,000 lire was on his head and the name Franco became a notorious byword in the community.[15]

When it became too dangerous for Gardner to stay in the house he would hide in an underground bunker used to store arms and ammunition. It was carved by Pietro Bierti out of a small cave opening half-way up the slope behind the Bierti home. This spot was concealed by rows of vines and fresh hay that each day was raked over the opening for safe measure. Once Gardner nearly suffocated from the fumes of the explosives while forced during a particularly intense hunt to remain inside its airless confines. The idea of these individual underground refuges to hide partisans was attributed to Gardner. Giovanni Marzoni wrote of this strategy in his report on Gardner, 'Thanks to his idea, all partisans were ordered to build such bunkers, in secrecy from one to the other, so that each one was secure. It was a relief for all to think that we had a place of security from the Nazi-Fascists.'[16] It also helped protect them from each other and possible revelations under torture.

Gardner relished being able to fight the Germans but his activities were legitimised in November 1944 when he came into contact with the Special Service forces headed by Major Thomas Macpherson. The meeting came shortly after a dispiriting operation to blow up a bridge where the Germans opened fire and two of Gardner's partisans were killed. The entire band was shaken by this experience and it seemed unlikely that more sabotage operations would be carried out. Gardner was then advised to contact the British Mission operating in the mountains. At first sceptical, he was pleasantly surprised when he met Macpherson, a plain-speaking Scotsman around his own age. He wore a kilt much to the embarrassment and mirth of the Italians who thought he was more in danger of dying from the cold than from a German bullet. Although Gardner at this point reports wanting to get back to his own battalion, he was convinced to remain and take his instructions from the British Intelligence Service, a far better move as most escaped prisoners-of-war who returned to their own lines were considered unfit for further service and repatriated. He was given a supply of arms and money, which he knew would raise the spirits of his beleaguered band. Macpherson in his citation of Gardner for the Military Medal and the Distinguished Conduct Medal, wrote, 'In spite of the ever-intensifying German search for Allied personnel in that vital communications area, he voluntarily chose to stay on and work for my Mission.'[17] It was more a loose partnership than a hierarchical relationship; Macpherson would suggest a target but often could not provide the munitions needed to tackle it. Gardner would go about obtaining them in the best way he could.

Although there were occasional RAF drops, munitions were quickly used up by the partisan bands, which then had to set about making their own. On one occasion a special chemical, with which Headquarters were unable to supply them, was required. It was also used in the manufacture of leather and, as luck would have it, a leather factory was located close to Gemona. Gardner and young Luigi Bierti, armed with pistols, paid a visit one evening to 'acquire' the necessary chemical, not a difficult task given that only two terrified employees were in the building.

Macpherson supplied Gardner with his second identity card. His first had given him the name of farmworker Giacomo Londera, a common surname in Gemona, and one borne by a partisan who liaised with Gardner. The second one sported the name of Franco Rossi, a name as common as Smith or Brown in English, born at Buia in the province of Udine thirty-one years previously, occupation tradesman.

According to the partisan commander Giovanni Marzoni, the Germans specifically targeted Gardner. When he was fired upon by a group of Nazi-Fascists, Marzoni told him to save himself and join the Major in the mountains. Enthused Marzoni, 'He replied that he will never leave us and he would have remained even if he knew that he would have died that same evening.'[18]

Bruno Londera, who led an Osoppo partisan band, often participated in sabotage actions with Gardner's group. He too had a reward on his head of 200,000 lire and was lucky to escape capture from the infamous roundups of the Italian Gestapo agent, Palese. He remembers Gardner as an independent spirit, a 'man of nature' who used to give a hand in the countryside. His skill in castrating a pig was much appreciated. Gardner's understanding of the political tensions underlying the area was, however, felt to be limited. It could not be otherwise, given his background as a country boy from the Antipodes. Londera believed Gardner fought for the adventure of it.[19]

Despite his lack of political sophistication, Gardner, like most New Zealanders, had an inbred dislike of injustice and brutality. Giacomo Palese, or 'Squinchi' as he was nicknamed because he was cross-eyed, was an Italian Gestapo agent who terrorised the town of Gemona. His reprisals had caused the deaths of many people and the deportation of others. One of these was the partisan Pietro Coppetti or the Big One as he was known. From his corner room in the Bierti home, Gardner helplessly witnessed his arrest by four Germans with a tommy-gun. For a moment it looked as if Coppetti might take them on but he was surrounded. He was marched away, passing underneath Gardner's window, watched in the distance by his old father.[20] Coppetti was deported to Buchenwald concentration camp. Of the 100 Italians sent with him, he was one of only three who returned. From being a fit, strong man with muscled arms and shoulders, he came home weighing 40 kilograms.

Due to Palese, the Resistance and the British Mission were suffering severe depletion. Macpherson had sent Gardner a note asking if he 'could do something about Squinchi'. By this time the price on Gardner's head had increased to 500,000 lire. Unable to move freely during the day, he depended more than ever on the Biertis and Blondie for information. News arrived on the afternoon of 8 April that Squinchi was travelling in a motorcade along a road that ran parallel to the Orvenco River about 300 metres from the Bierti home. Much to Gardner's frustration, he learned his target was not in uniform and would therefore be difficult to identify. Fortunately Luigi Bierti knew what Squinchi looked like and insisted on accompanying him. Gardner wore his white 'motoring coat' to hide his Sten gun and he and his now 19-year-old companion, who was armed with an Italian tommy-gun, waited on the wall bordering the straight road. Finally the sound of the motorcycle shattered the beautiful windless spring day. As Gardner steadied his Sten and began squeezing the trigger, Bierti screamed out, 'No, Franco, no!' It was the wrong person. Unnerved, Gardner began questioning what he was doing. Before he could make a decision a second motorcade roared into view. Bierti excitedly identified Squinchi and both men shouted at him to halt. Squinchi ordered his driver to accelerate and reached for his pistol.

'He was in my sights. I saw him turn and speak to his driver, and simultaneously reach down for his gun. Wasting no more time I began firing. Suddenly there was a shattering impact as the motorbike and sidecar overturned, throwing its two occupants on the road, stone dead. Luck had run out for Squinchi.'[21] Aldo Bierti gives a slightly different version. Gardner's Sten with its silencer became jammed and Luigi Bierti intercepted the bike with his own firearm. The Biertis worried for the safety of both men when they heard the sound of firing because they knew Gardner's weapon had a silencer attached.[22] Both Gardner and Bierti fled to the mountains and hid in the bunker at the house of Alice Bierti's parents.

Squinchi's death was a major coup for the town, but the fear of reprisals on innocent people as always hung ominously over the inhabitants. Many people, although tacitly supporting the partisans, feared the reprisals that routinely followed their actions. Franco Pischiutti, seven at the time, has vivid memories of that afternoon. He and his father had been visiting the Biertis, old family friends who provided them with food when they ran short of supplies in the town. As they were returning on their bicycles, they passed infuriated Fascist troops and trucks setting off in the direction they had just come from. The next day when his father learned of the slaying of Squinchi, he was angry at not having been warned. 'Those Bierti put us in danger. They knew what Franco was doing. They could have told us to get away earlier so we didn't meet up with the Fascists.'[23] Confirmed Aldo Bierti, 'If you were lucky you were deported to Germany, otherwise you were shot.'

Fortunately there were no reprisals on the town after the killing of Squinchi. These were the final days of the war when German troops were surrendering to the partisans in their thousands and Italian Fascists knew they had to maintain a low profile, their own lives in danger.

It cannot be known exactly when Gardner's relationship with Anna Bierti began. Certainly her immediate family were not aware of it until she became pregnant. Bruno Londera said Gardner never mentioned it, but keeping secrets in a small Italian community is virtually impossible and there were 'murmurings' among the men. A personal memoir of Don Pietro Londera written in Friulan dialect entitled *The Cossacks in Friuli* mentions that during the Germans' retreat they left behind a stockpile of food. People, the majority of them women trying to feed their families, flocked to collect what they could. One day, the story goes, the New Zealand 'airman' Franco and his girlfriend, who was the daughter of Piero 'the dark one', blocked the door to the supplies and prevented people from looting. They were both armed. It was suggested they wanted to take the food to the partisans.[24] Those who knew Anna contest the veracity of this account, saying she would not have accompanied Gardner on such an action and certainly would not have carried arms. There were two young women partisans in Gardner's band who may have taken part, but Anna stayed at home. However inaccurate the tale, it shows that outside of the family circle it was common knowledge that Anna was Franco's girl.

The presence in the house of a foreigner with all the allure of the 'exotic' must have been exciting for Anna. New Zealand men usually treated the daughters of the house with respect and saw them as equals in a way many young Italian women had never experienced. Mothers of families were horrified when their guests would insist on helping with the dishes, an unheard-of task for a male in Italian families, and protesting, would chase them out of the kitchen. Daughters in many rural households were little more than servants and although this was not the case in the Bierti home, Anna would have felt flattered by Gardner's courteous attention and his obvious appreciation of her help. Thrown together by the dramatic and unpredictable tensions of war, it is not surprising that romantic relationships developed in the hothouse emotional proximity of fear and comfort. Anna, like many Italian women who actively assisted the escapers, enjoyed nurturing the attractive young man in her household, who often needed nursing. This attention and mutual dependence combined with courage and loyalty made an impact on many young Allied men. Others however, sensing the pitfalls, did their best to avoid temptation. Roy Johnston affirms, 'One of the keys to survival was not to move in, in any sense of the word, with their womenfolk. Mind you there were pressures! One of the girls, the girlfriend of the partisan guy, did her best to seduce me, subtly! But we were living there on borrowed time and couldn't afford to put a foot wrong.'[25]

For the young and naïve Anna Bierti, Gardner was her first and probably only love. She was no simple peasant girl however. Convent educated, she had reached a level of scholarship that would have enabled her to work as a primary school teacher. Gardner at 28 was worldlier. He may have sincerely loved her, but it was a love born of the vicissitudes of war and the fraught conditions he was living under. His relationship with her may have contributed to his wish to remain with the Special Forces in Italy. In the early months of 1945 the war was coming to an end and with it his life as a partisan. New Zealand was geographically and culturally a world away from the customs of the north-eastern Italian town of Gemona. Although Gardner knew Anna Bierti was pregnant with his child, he must have, uncharacteristically, been at a loss to know what to do. Unable or unwilling to confront the situation, he left abruptly in May shortly after the Liberation without saying goodbye to Anna or her family. This fact still rankles with Aldo Bierti. 'He did not have to say thank you – it was not necessary – but he could have at least said goodbye.'[26] Gardner did go, however, to farewell Anna Zanini. Although in her nineties and speaking a month before her death, Zanini recalled the occasion clearly. 'Ciao Blondie, I'm going away,' he said. 'And Annetta?' asked Zanini, 'Annetta stays here? You're not going to marry her?'

'Oh, Blondie,' replied Gardner, 'you need a lot of love to get married.'[27]

The citizens of Gemona never heard from Franco again. He clearly felt he could not return and must have shut his mind to that episode of his life. He never revealed his secret to anyone in New Zealand and he took it to his grave.

After leaving Italy, Gardner and his brother were sent on furlough to Ireland before being repatriated to New Zealand. They were hosted by author Florence Millar's family and the family were warned that the brother who had been a prisoner-of-war might need to be handled sensitively. Millar found Frank 'friendly and amusing, giving an impression of great reliability' and assumed that the tired, pale Jack was the ex-prisoner-of-war. It was only when Frank began telling his experiences one night in a 'modest, artless way', but with the vivid fluency of a born story-teller in front of a captive audience, that she realised not only was he the prisoner, but his was a remarkable story. Upon Millar's suggestion, they collaborated to piece it together and when it was completed, she sent him the manuscript. Originally published as a boy's adventure story in 1947, it was republished in 1992 as *The 'Signor Kiwi' Saga*, due to the efforts of Arch Scott and Paul Day, who felt that not enough was known about Gardner and his achievements while working with the Italian Resistance. Although the book remains largely indebted to Millar's version, additional material based on research among people who knew him in Italy was added, including an epilogue written by Gardner himself before he died in 1972.

However, some names were changed and details altered, which remain uncorrected to this day. Anna Bierti is mentioned rarely in the book, usually in connection with her mother, and is given the name 'Maria'. She is made to sound younger than she was, as was Luigi Bierti, a partisan in Gardner's group whose part in the execution of Squinchi was reduced to that of a 10-year-old boy. Aldo Bierti shakes his head in sorrow as he recalls those first few months after Gardner's departure. 'At that time it was the old mentality. It was considered shameful. But you have to go on. What do you want to do – go drown yourself with a child inside?'[28] Anna's closest friend, Francesca, supported her as best she could. Every night for months they would pray together that he would return. Even today she insists that Franco was the love of Annetta's life.

Elisabetta Bierti was born at home on 23 December 1945, the same day her father set foot on New Zealand soil. Anna Zanini, the child's godmother, assisted at the birth. 'She was a beautiful baby. Her mother was so good – she didn't cry. She was only 20 years old.' The little girl was named after Frank's mother it was thought, although this was not his mother's name. A freckle-faced child with light brown hair that grew darker as she grew older, Elisabetta or 'Bettet' was much loved and considered a precious jewel by her family. When Anna went to work in Switzerland, Bettet was cared for by her grandparents. Anna later married a man from San Stino di Livenza, some years older than her. Two more children were born, Pierluigi and Nadia. Photos of Elisabetta show a young woman with her mother's thick dark hair, olive skin, her father's full lips and, it appears, the distinctive Gardner nose. Eventually Elisabetta married and had a son, Daniele. The close-knit family owned and operated a laundry business on the ground floor of their apartment in central Gemona. It was here the family returned on a warm afternoon in June 1976 after spending time with friends. Suddenly an earthquake struck, hitting the mountainous north-eastern Friuli area the hardest. Within minutes the town of Gemona lay in ruins, its ancient monuments and precious frescoes destroyed forever. Over 1500 citizens were killed. The building above the laundry collapsed in a pile of rubble: Aldo Bierti lost his sister, Anna, her younger daughter, Nadia, Elisabetta and her husband and little Daniele. In those few devastating minutes the entire Italian branch of Frank Gardner's family perished.

By then Gardner had died at the relatively young age of 56, survived by his wife and six children. It was poignant that such an active risk-taker should succumb to a lingering disease that left him an invalid in the final two years of his life. When he narrated and wrote of his memories of the Resistance, it is impossible to imagine he did not think of Anna and the child he never knew. Despite keeping his secret and disguising some details, he did not change the surname of the Biertis in the papers he left. He thus left open the path that would lead his family to search out and meet the people he lived with and fought alongside, and ultimately, to the discovery of his child.

For the citizens of Gemona, Frank Gardner was an admired hero who fought alongside them against the Germans, but when the war was over, left and never returned. No one heard from him again. Yet he remained vividly alive through his daughter, Elisabetta, widely known as the daughter of Franco. So when fifty years later members of the Gardner family arrived in Gemona searching for the people and places he had known and bringing copies of Frank's book, they sensed, amidst the delight, a watchful curiosity. 'What does he write about us, has he spoken kindly of us?' they would say, but the most commonly asked question (to which the Italians, but not the Gardners at this stage, knew the answer) was 'Why did he never come back and see us?' The response that many men did not wish to dwell on the war years or revisit places that harboured painful memories may have perplexed them.

Although the reason for his failure to return was surmised by the Italians, they said nothing. Language difficulties and a certain delicacy in not wanting to stir up trouble for the Gardner family may have influenced this decision, but inter-family enmity and proprietorship over the Gardner story may have contributed to this reluctance. There was no contact with Aldo Bierti who heard only through others that the Gardners had been in town.

If he had not died prematurely Frank Gardner may have returned one day to receive the honour the city would have undoubtedly bestowed on him. My decision to tell Margie Gardner the truth before she went to Gemona was influenced by a sense that continuing to suppress this major event in her father's story was fanning further the flame of conjecture and innuendo. The tragic nature of the deaths of all the family connected to Gardner has tended to give vent in some quarters to the notion of destiny, or even hint at divine punishment for a liaison that was somehow 'illicit'. The pattern of secrets and silence set in motion nearly 60 years earlier needed to be broken for all concerned, in order to recognise and pay homage to the fact that Elisabetta Bierti, daughter of Frank Gardner, was born, that she lived and that she died. As Margie stood before her sister's tombstone, her act of mourning was also an act of welcome into the hearts and minds of Elisabetta's New Zealand family.

CHAPTER TWELVE

Three men in a cave

Something was going to happen and the dim starlight drifting through the cave entrance made the sensation more eerie.[1]

Jack Lang and Bob Smith became lifelong mates the day they met at the partisan station. It was not surprising that the two should join forces for neither man took kindly to imprisonment and both were serial escapers. Smith had the distinction of escaping five times from his captors and Lang had been at large for 16 months in Greece before giving himself up to the Germans in order to avoid reprisals on the local people. A tenacious, resolute man, his fearless stand against authority had not endeared him to his captors. As Lang put it, 'I spent a bit of time tied up against a barn door.' They had jumped out of the same train but at different points and been directed to a partisan group. Both men gravitated unerringly towards assisting the cook. As Smith observed, 'This close attention of the Allies to the culinary department, while everybody was brandishing weapons was not in the true British tradition of soldiering – or was it?'[2]

The 80-strong partisan group of the Garibaldi Brigade was a mixed bag of all ranks and both sexes. These included 'escapers from reality, domesticity, army and POW life. The head man was a wary, unreliable-looking character, and we had a few idealists and intellectuals to round out our ranks. There was an air of fiesta about the whole set-up.' However, they did note that the women took their place among the men and were given equal consideration.

One of the young women who arrived unexpectedly in their midst was a beautiful platinum blonde from Trieste who had a constant stream of jokes and quips that kept everybody in fits of laughter. A throng of admirers always surrounded her. With up to 100 people for meals there were sacks of potatoes to be peeled and the New Zealanders' assistance was not enough. The cook would delicately bribe Arusca to help, knowing that once she sat down to peel the potatoes, her magnetic qualities were such that in no time she would be surrounded by willing helpers, making swift work of a tedious job.

Everybody piled together into the hayloft to sleep. One morning Smith was astonished to see Arusca wearing the breeches, leggings, bandolier, pistol and holster of the most handsome Italian man there, while he sported her old grey trousers. For some days they continued this intriguing cross-dressing, seeming to assume each other's identities. Arusca swaggered around like a Mediterranean Annie Oakley while the Italian's soldierly bearing, once devoid of his breeches, was not unsurprisingly diminished.

The New Zealanders joined the partisans on patrols and reconnaissance sorties, but at this stage there was no contact with the enemy. It was a pleasant existence in the late Italian summer with trees to provide shade, a stream for washing and enough to eat. However, they were becoming restless. They decided to move on towards Yugoslavia where they had heard an escape route to freedom was in operation. They aimed to travel down to the Dalmatian coast, then take a boat across to southern Italy to reach the Allied lines. Lang felt that they had served their time with the partisans and that if they did not make a move they would be there indefinitely. This plan was not received enthusiastically by the partisans, who tried to put them off.

It was the decisive Jack who made it clear nothing would stop them from going. 'When it came down to brass tacks we were going to do what we wanted to do. And we thought we might be holed up and shot as we turned our backs on them and walked off in what we thought was the appropriate direction.'[3] But the partisans finally co-operated, even agreeing to arrange a courier to escort them from post to post along the escape trail. Their route lay east but to avoid the enemy they could rarely travel along the main roads. Instead they took detours over mountains and out-of-the-way trails. They finally arrived at Caporetto, a picturesque town and site of a celebrated battle where the Italian Army had conquered the Austrian invaders in the First World War. Gun emplacements and barbed wire were still visible in the nearby mountains. Here there was a partisan command headquarters recruiting people from the local population. Support was very strong in this traditionally anti-German zone. Although officially joining the partisans was not part of their escape plan, there was no alternative.

The New Zealanders were interviewed and required to fill in forms, giving their names and addresses. They were issued with rifles and were handed partisan caps with the five-pointed star insignia of the Red Star. They were immediately assigned to the Tolmino Battalion located southeast from Caporetto. As they resumed their march eastwards, they were joined by more and more escaped Allied prisoners-of-war.

The Tolmino Battalion overlooked Santa Lucia, a town situated on a bend of the Isonzo River. Although it was an Italian partisan unit operating on Italian territory, they were controlled by Tito's partisans across the border in Yugoslavia. No contact was at first established with the German troops but they could be seen passing along the road about 300 metres below. Day-to-day life in the 150-strong Tolmino Battalion was similar to any other military unit. The prisoners-of-war, however, did not have much faith in their leader, a former corporal in the Italian Army whose tactics they felt singled them out and put them in danger. During practice manoeuvres, where battle positions were taken up round the countryside, the escapers were systematically being placed out in front, unable to be covered effectively by the rest of the unit. 'It looked as if we were expected to do all the dirty work and . . . that help from our rear wouldn't be effective.'⁴

Lang was unimpressed with the operation they carried out with a demolition squad on the Tolmino Bridge. Their task was to blow up the concrete bridge on the main road from Yugoslavia to Italy. 'We came down from the hills one night and everybody took their positions. We were given the job of crossing over the bridge and protecting the people who were doing the actual job of placing the explosives.' Unfortunately, in the excitement everybody was on the wrong side of the bridge when it blew up. To make matters worse, the bridge remained intact. 'It was so effective we could walk back over the bridge quite safely! A couple of German troopers on patrol came to see what was going on. They were able to cross over the bridge quite successfully too!'

After this Lang decided firstly that they were not going to let themselves be left high and dry and secondly, that he should supervise all future placing of explosives. His father had been involved in goldmining in Thames and Lang as a boy learned a little about how to handle explosives. He trusted his small knowledge over whatever experiences the partisans had.

Rations were obtained from local peasants – food and livestock were taken in return for a signed chit, redeemable after the war. Smith recalled occasions where a cow would be killed after breakfast and the battalion would be eating it, liver and lungs included, by noon. But the meat was too new and tasted like leather. A New Zealander from the West Coast was once so incensed at the way the poor cow was 'murdered' that although not a butcher by trade, he grabbed the axe and dispensed with the animal more efficiently, rather than watch it suffer needlessly.

Ex-prisoners also assisted in the laborious task of carrying rations from neighbouring villages, sometimes trudging many kilometres a day in rugged country. Thirty kilograms was the standard carrying weight of supplies such as potatoes, cornmeal and grains. When the Allied party were given a 30-kilogram wooden box full of munitions to carry 1000 metres up a steep mountain track they baulked. Without any equipment such as leather straps or rope available to secure it, the only way to hold it was by reaching back over one's shoulder in order to prevent it from falling backwards. The ex-prisoners refused point-blank to carry the load a step further and dropped the boxes. It fell to Smith to negotiate before tempers became too frayed. 'There were a lot of trigger-happy irresponsibles among the partisans and looking back, I count this as a dangerous incident.'[5]

Lang recalls having to evacuate a town and return into the mountains in a party of 150 with at least three mules and three horses. 'On the second day up we were crossing a very tricky ravine and one of the horses slipped off the side, packs and all, down into the ravine. They shot the horse, but the situation being as it was, they also butchered it and dished out the horsemeat to all those who wanted it raw. You can bet your life that Bob and I joined the queue and got a good slab of horse meat which we wrapped up carefully and tucked away for further use when we could cook it.'[6] They had not reached the stage where they could eat the meat raw.

A similar fate befell their 'meat on the hoof', a yearling steer which slipped on the treacherous slopes. The sickening thuds of the poor animal as it fell could be heard until it descended out of earshot. This time it was not retrievable and was a tragic loss of food for the partisans.

Mules were used because of their sure-footedness on the mountains but even they were not immune to slipping. Smith recalled a mule losing its footing one night. Gathering speed like a bobsleigh, it hurtled down the steep icy slopes, the attached pots and pans jangling horribly until it thudded against rocks far below.

The winter had by now set in. The mountains were thickly carpeted with snow, often waist-deep. Lang and Smith, the erstwhile cook's assistants, had volunteered to carry the hot box, a large metal box full of provisions it kept hot for a considerable length of time. They put a stout stake right through it so it could be carried on their shoulders but their path was so steep they couldn't use it. 'The hot box kept sliding down the stake. It was a very uncomfortable position for the bloke on the end of it at the bottom.' They both struggled with the box, pushing and pulling it up the mountain to a bleak, windswept range with no snow, only undulating ice. The rest of the journey was undertaken on all fours, manoeuvring the precious hot box between them as they crawled through no-man's land.

The partisans were constantly moving. There were increasing numbers of recruits every day. Lang knew that the overriding danger was being captured by a platoon of well-equipped Germans. But he and Smith were too engrossed in surviving to think much about it. Lang's tactics were, as always, measured and pragmatic. 'Whatever cropped up we would meet when it came.' The small group of Allied escapers tagged along, depending on the partisans yet with their own agenda of making it back to their lines. 'It was advisable to do this because they wanted us with them as we were ... valuable to them in that they could keep contact with the Allied forces and could indicate just how many Allied personnel they were looking after.'[7] As keen as they were to leave the 'polyglot' group of Italian partisans, they did not want to offend their hosts, who said they were doing their best to help them and that they were safer with them. 'It was no good arguing with them. We only discussed it to the point where we knew it was futile arguing with people who were salesmen in their own right, in their own environment. It was their country.'

Crossing the border into Yugoslavia was a desperately risky operation. Many misjudged German positions and were caught. Partisans were shot on the spot while escaped prisoners, if they could prove their identity by producing an army pay book, were transported to prison camps in Germany. The New Zealanders were lucky. A young woman guided them safely into Yugoslavia. Recalled Smith: 'This girl had the sallow, hollow face of the consumptive, but the muscular calves of a rickshaw coolie. We toiled manfully behind her but those legs danced onward and upward ahead of us till at last we had to cry halt. In spite of her wan appearance we couldn't keep up with her pace.' The young woman quietly smiled as they thanked her profusely and swiftly returned in the dusk back down the lengthy trail. She was their unsung heroine.

Yugoslavia was a wild, broken country, zigzagged by borders, some defunct, that had constantly changed over the past fifty years. Jagged mountains rose to heights of 2000 metres and often provided the back trails necessary to avoid the main routes. It was a harsh and arduous existence where the New Zealanders moved from one group of partisans to another. Hunted by the Germans who were better fed, better armed, and better led, they would scatter and then regroup in neighbouring towns. They passed many burned-out skeletons of farmhouses, grim reminders of what happened to people who harboured the partisans, and finally reached Ziri, a prosperous manufacturing town situated on a wide flat plain, which the partisans had reoccupied. People were well dressed, the women even wearing silk stockings. More importantly, there was a large boot factory where a skilled craftsman repaired Lang's leaking boots. He rebuilt them completely, fastening the new soles to the uppers with minute square wooden dowels, as metal nails could not keep out the moisture of new or thawing snow.

The men were placed together in a large house, but despite the luxury of an occasional bath, they could not rid themselves of the lice that flourished in the cramped conditions. The spirit of optimism in Ziri was reflected in a dance held in the town hall and attended by all. Men and women armed to the hilt with rifles slung over their shoulders and assorted cutlery and hardware items hanging around their waists, clomped round the dancefloor. Liquor flowed and there was much backslapping and cries of '*tutti fratelli*', 'we're all brothers', and its Yugoslav equivalent. The arsenal of arms carried on the revellers at all times was in readiness to fight the foe. But according to Smith, the less advertised reason was they risked being stolen if left out of sight.

The continual running from the enemy and the hunger, exhaustion and freezing cold, took their toll on many ex-prisoners. Both John Abel and Jack Lang reported that men were sick of being caught up in a German-versus-partisan battle and felt they had been better off in the prison camp. 'These blokes would just say we're not going any further and they'd swing round and give themselves up to the Germans.'[8] The Germans meanwhile were moving in on them in pincer fashion, gradually compressing the partisan formations into smaller and smaller spaces. When they were mortar-bombed while completing a week-long demolition of the road leading to Ljubljana, things became even more serious. They left Ziri shortly afterwards, but after being shot up by an enemy patrol while trying to cross a main road, they headed straight back towards the town and took refuge in mountains on the opposite side. Ziri was taken over again by the Germans who doubled their efforts to root out the partisans. Sudden waking from sleep in the middle of the night to move deeper into the mountains was common. The enemy was closing in on all sides.

Many of the partisan followers in their groups were simple peasant folk, convinced after a particularly heavy shelling which took several casualties that their last hour had arrived. Smith describes with eloquent poignancy the following scene. 'In an inspired gesture of resignation and courage they sang together "Old Slovenia" and the "Marseillaise". In the involuntary action which causes people to cling together when death is near, hundreds – men and women – joined hands and sang in unison. On a snow-covered crest, high towards the Heavens, the sound of these beautiful Slav voices ringing clear in the night air struck an ethereal note. Never will I forget the tragedy of this soul-stirring scene. It was prophetic. Most of them were killed next day.'[9]

The attack was launched as they were lining up for their cornmeal gruel breakfast the following day. The German tendency to target meal times should have been no surprise. Commented Smith with the wry wisdom of hindsight, 'Greece, Crete, Libya, Mersa Matruh, the Alamein Line, and now here in Yugoslavia. I could set my watch by them – if I had a watch.'[10] Most of the Allied contingent headed for the only escape route possible, westward, but those who rushed back to the head of the pass were killed.

It was at this point that the two decided it was time for a change of tactics. They had been informed that the official escape route was no longer viable and they had had enough of relying on the partisans' shaky tactical abilities. The men decided to head off on their own and retrace their steps north back to Italy. They approached Captain Evan Wilson, the senior New Zealand officer in their group, for permission to do so, although this was a mere courtesy. Their minds were made up. He said he would do the same if he did not have the responsibility of leading men under him. In fact, a few days later, the remainder of the party followed their example and set off in groups, leaving at three-minute intervals. It was every man for himself. Lang and Smith were the only two among 35 Allied men and the remaining partisans who escaped slaughter or recapture.

They took off at right angles across the countryside, picking their way along exposed rocks to avoid leaving telltale traces of their departure in the crunchy snow. The track down the mountain was littered with the bodies of partisans. They found themselves on a trail showing signs of recent footprints. Smith proudly reckoned he was as good as any Aboriginal tracker in deciphering that those footprints had been made only an hour earlier. They led to a forest ranger's hut inhabited by German troops. The two men stayed at a safe distance among the trees and watched, knowing that after a successful military operation the soldiers would head back to more comfortable surroundings. Sure enough, they soon evacuated and the men approached the hut gingerly, uncertain if everyone had left. It was one of their happiest evenings. Food, shelter, warmth, and clothing were theirs for the taking. It seemed an undreamed-of luxury. They blew up the still-warm embers from the fire and soon there was a roaring blaze. Stocks of food in the larder, drawers full of crisp apples in storage – they cooked and ate as much as they could handle and finally stretched out to sleep in front of the fire. Although the bed was inviting, they doubted whether they could sleep comfortably in a bed again.

They knew they could not hang around in their new home longer than that one night. Before leaving early next morning they stocked up on food supplies, bedding and clothing abandoned by the Germans. Lang, hatless for some time, selected a snappy Tyrolean green felt hat that fitted him perfectly. An outsized, belted, woman's raincoat was included, while Smith, rather short on jackets, was unable to resist a heavy grey velour jacket with green lapels. Their satisfaction with their new sartorial elegance was soon interrupted. Making their way down the mountain, they heard the familiar sound of Germans singing as they marched. Their voices carried up into the cool air long before the New Zealanders actually saw them. It was time to head into the back roads again.

The journey back to Italy was fraught with danger. The bitter battles between the Germans and the partisans were at their height. Many people in the towns were initially suspicious of the two men who had no army pay book to prove their identity. They were invariably greeted with a barrage of questions. 'Our best reply to all this, we had found, was the forthright, outspoken attitude of the Australian or New Zealander.

No two German spies or undercover agents could ever have been as brazen as we were, so they always took us at face value.'[11]

One day they set out to cross a long bridge. They were half way across when a sprucely dressed German officer approached them on the other side of the bridge. Sauntering past, they bid him a hearty good morning in Yugoslav. He cordially greeted them back. 'We looked exactly like what we were and that was partisans at the very least. We didn't look like British. We thought that in his position he might do something but alone on the bridge he was probably a lot more scared than we were. He didn't know we were unarmed for a start. We didn't know if he was going to turn around after he passed us and blow us apart. We didn't turn round.'[12] Only when they were out of sight did they start running.

Up in the mountains they passed through partisan units. Again they were unimpressed with their tactics which they felt endangered the lives of everyone. Several Germans had come out for a spot of skiing on the slopes. The partisans opened fire on them, killing two. The reprisal came next day bang on lunchtime when a particularly tasty-smelling mixture of pork, beans and cornmeal was about to be served up. As the shells came screaming over, the partisans scattered but the two Kiwis managed to grab the hot box and head off in a different direction. When they felt it was safe to stop, they feasted on a delicious lunch, chortling grimly.

They returned to Italy via the Tolmino area where they had officially joined the partisans, retracing their steps but on a different route, wading naked across rivers whose bridges they had earlier helped to blow up, holding their belongings high above their heads as the water lapped their shoulders. A Fascist patrol which used the area as a look-out was closing in on them. The two men retreated to a ridge just outside the village and rested against a rock to decide on their next plan of action. They were in plain view of an Italian officer about 20 or 30 metres away who was staring over their heads. He must have thought the two men were a piece of the rock formation for he did not react and they remained frozen. On another occasion they were ordered to stop by a German sentry but, pretending they had not heard, they continued walking. This was psychological warfare conducted on the reckless premise that no guilty person would boldly ignore an enemy command to halt. The guard lowered his rifle, puzzled. Lang was as calm and unperturbed as ever. 'We weren't going to give up after all we had been through.'

By this time they were in familiar country, although they were never quite sure which country it was as they were constantly crossing and re-crossing the ragged borders high above the Lombardy plain. When they came to cross their final border into Italy an Italian platoon blocked the escape routes but they were able to make their way on hands and knees along a deep trench up to the sentry post. As they came level with the post, a thick mist like an all-enveloping skirt descended from the mountain, obliterating everything. This gave the two men the opportunity they needed to stand up and slip across the border. They were well up the valley towards the top ridge before the mist lifted, unveiling a landscape bask-ing under a blue cloudless sky and a dazzling sun. By now they had been seen, but were far enough away to 'put the boot between them and us'.

Instead of going to the mountain village of Masarolis as may have been surmised from their route, the two men broke off at a right angle and headed for Reant, a tiny impoverished hamlet further down the moun-tain. The patrol, as anticipated, went to Masarolis. Shortly afterwards the patrol scoured the neighbouring villages and rounded up every able-bodied man they could find for transport to forced labour camps in Germany. Although the New Zealanders felt themselves to be the sole cause of this, Italians have since confirmed it was unlikely. This was partisan country and reprisals were fierce for the constant hostilities between them and the enemy.

The men had completed a full circle. From the mountains they could look down across the Lombardy plains to their old prison camp at Gruppignano. They had travelled eastwards into Yugoslavia, headed northwards towards the Austrian border, then westwards back into Italy. 'We were back where we had started from and except for still being free, had achieved nothing.' Smith's harsh self-judgement seems unwarranted after what they had been through. Being free was a tribute to their determination, quick-wittedness and a generous amount of luck. Journeying through such a country was virtually impossible. It was time to settle down.

The two men temporarily occupied a charcoal burner's hut on a hill and had roasted chestnuts for their Christmas dinner. They began to explore the area comprising the three villages of Valle, Reant and Masarolis, and found they liked it very much. The villagers gradually came to accept the two New Zealanders, especially when they heard of their exploits. They earned their trust to the extent that a young man from Reant soon led them down a hill, then round a sheer cliff to the 'buca'. It was a cunningly concealed cave in the side of the cliff that could not be seen from any angle. A well-kept secret known only to the locals, it was the stuff of legends and had been used for centuries as a hiding place for revolutionaries, dissidents, bandits, and outcasts – escapers of every sort. It was an honour to be included in such an illustrious line of folk heroes, some glorious, others infamous, fleeing the forces of authoritarianism and oppression. No one had ever been caught there.

Bob Smith describes it as originally a 'soundshell'-shaped indentation extending 8 metres back into the face of the grey stone cliff. The front had gradually filled up with detritus. At its highest point the opening was a metre high and steps formed by falling rock led down to the floor. Inside the cave had the appearance of a large room with a dirt floor and stalactites on the ceiling. The two friends set about making a fireplace. They constructed a chimney by digging a channel up the face of the batter to the entrance. It was covered with sticks and tamped with earth to seal it. The light-grey woodsmoke merged with the whitish rocks framing the background of the cliff and had dissipated by the time it reached the top, so they could light a fire as often as they liked. A pile of hay, some blankets and their overcoats made a comfortable bed. After months of enforced quietness 'we could sing and shout to our hearts' content'.

The villages of Reant and Valle slowly adopted the pair who were given food and clothing and invited into homes. Santina Specogna, who still lives in the now ghost village of Reant, recalls those harsh times. 'People were so hungry in those days. We sometimes had to hide our food.'[13] In order to cement people's trust, the Kiwis invented wives back home so that the men would not suspect them of getting too friendly with the womenfolk and the women would know they were already 'taken'. The pair had heard whispers of an American airman holed up at the priest's house at Masarolis but, as rumours were always flying round, at first they paid little attention.

Don Amelio Pinzano became priest of the impoverished mountain parish of Masarolis, population 810, at the beginning of the war. He defied his bishop who wanted to send him to another parish where his building skills could be put to good use. Nobody ever wanted to go to Masarolis. The departing priest had told him that only a saint or a madman could live there. With the arrival of electricity in October 1942, Don Amelio invested in an ancient Telefunken radio so he could listen to what was happening in the world on Radio London. But after September 1943 the world itself descended on his isolated little mountain town and it became a hotbed for fugitives of diverse nationalities. 'At night from the surrounding mountains, the parsonage was a refuge for the "different" partisans and the various escapers: Italians, English, New Zealanders, Russians, Negroes, Americans: a dangerous mix, with an explosive potential.'[14] It was explosive because below Masarolis at Canalutto was a Fascist garrison, at Torreano were a settlement of Nazi-friendly Cossacks[15] and at Cividale the SS had set up a base. The partisans were active in the mountains and reprisals were common. Neither the doctor nor the mayor came up to Masarolis any more so the stoic priest became, unofficially, the village administrator and doctor.

Don Amelio found himself in a curious situation one cold December night in 1943. The Germans had arrived in the small town and set up their command in the parsonage, leaving their rifles stacked in the hallway. For the following two nights, the commanding officer, a baron from Bavaria, slept in the priest's bed. In an adjoining bedroom, the two bedheads separated by a 12-centimetre partition, lay Colonel Ross Greening, an American airman who was ill with diphtheria. Beside him on a stretcher was the priest.

Recalls the priest, 'I had put my stretcher close to the American to keep him company. He said to me in a shaky voice. "I am afraid for you. If they find me they'll take me to prison. But they'll kill you on the spot!" It was a bad joke. They were trying to round up prisoners and here they were sleeping twelve centimetres away from each other! The locals knew and were afraid for me.'[16] The next day the commander thanked him politely for letting him use his bedroom. The priest's attitude to the dangerous situations he ended up in is gently self-effacing. He attributes the fact that he always seemed to emerge unscathed to 'partly my character, partly thanks to God'.

Colonel Ross Greening had been shot down, captured and was on a train heading for Germany when he escaped in the confusion of a bombing at Bolzano. With false identity papers obtained through partisans, the airman was hiding in Masarolis, protected by the villagers. The hard living, even for a decorated pilot, had taken its toll on his health. As he was recuperating from his illness in the priest's house, cared for by the schoolteacher, the four-man patrol chasing Jack Lang and Bob Smith conducted a room-to-room search of all the houses. When they stormed into the parsonage the schoolteacher had stood firm in front of the bedroom door and said under no circumstances was the priest's sick cousin to be disturbed, on doctor's orders.

As soon as he could, Greening left and lived for a short time under leaves in a tiny cave. One evening he visited the priest's house to listen to Radio London. Suddenly there was a knock at the door. Glimpsing two men in German uniforms, he and his companion escaped to the outhouse. The housekeeper called them back and Ross Greening was introduced to Jack Lang and Bob Smith.

'Their story was fantastic. For two months they had been with the patriot forces and suffered from exposure and hardship. Their appearance gave testimony to their tale. Both were thin and haggard, with unshaven faces. They wore tattered civilian clothes and parts of German uniforms stolen from a patrol cabin in the mountains.'[17] The men liked the look of one another and became firm friends. Greening, who confessed to Lang he was going mad in Masarolis, was invited to share the cave with the New Zealanders.

Greening's initiative and ability to organise projects led the drive to improve their living conditions. They scoured the countryside and found makeshift tools in the surrounding hills – a broken pick blade, a rusty shovel without a handle, bottles, newspapers and boards. They succeeded in carving handles for the pick and shovel with a small machete used for cutting up firewood. Soon they had built a stairway down to the cave, and added chairs, tables, shelves, a large bed, a clothes rack, all the 'mod cons', fashioned from trees and vines. A small platform was constructed in front of the cave from the excess dirt removed to level the cave floor. This provided a flat place to sit or stand outside and was camouflaged with brush and trees. The entry to the cave was excavated then enclosed properly with mud and sticks. A German pup tent served as an awning.

The men revelled in their newfound independence, glad that their friends in the village were spared the risk of hiding them. Although they still relied on the villagers for food, they visited each of the villages on alternating nights in an effort not to be a burden. They had a special mamma in each town who took care of them and they made an effort to be part of the community. Their diet was plain but wholesome, consisting of cornmeal, potatoes, cheese and onions with occasional eggs and milk. The Germans had confiscated so many cows that milk became more and more difficult to come by. There were no green vegetables, coffee, tea, sugar, bread or butter, and salt and olive oil were scarce. Wine, however, was plentiful. They had acquired an old pot which ensured hot meals cooked over the fire when they were snowed in. Water had to be fetched from a spring over the hill in a rusty tin pail and was often spilled on the journey back. They tried to keep themselves and their clothes clean to preserve a modicum of hygiene. Becoming ill was as much feared as being caught by the Germans.

They made their own tobacco from green tobacco leaves which they dried, cut up into pieces, then soaked in water. Once these were sufficiently dry, cigarettes were rolled using newspapers for paper. The brew was so strong the men just about knocked themselves out each time they smoked it.

Their staple was polenta, made from cornmeal that was boiled into a mushy cake. To vary their diet, they would go foraging, usually at night. They would set bird and rabbit traps, borrowing nets from the villagers, but unfortunately they were in competition with other predators, both animal and human, and only a pile of feathers would remain by the next day. Navigating what Greening called the 'frightening cliff' required nerves of steel, especially on moonless nights. In pitch black they had to feel along the trail by foot to reach the ridge, negotiating the bends and rocks in the tracks. They became very skilful at this, amazed at how intimately they got to know the terrain, and how fast and silently they could move, relying on touch alone. They knew exactly how many steps they needed to inch round the cliff.

This made them bolder and they ventured out frequently in daylight, running into some close shaves with German patrols. Once Smith and Lang found themselves unexpectedly trapped. Faced with having to walk past a couple of Germans, they followed their strategy of trying to appear unconcerned. They must have raised suspicion because they were ordered to halt. They broke into a run for their lives down the hill with bullets whistling past their ears. This earned them even greater prestige with their friends.

The three men were particularly fond of the local children and made a big fuss over them. The children had banded together to organise a steady food supply for them and served as an informal information network. 'Go to Pietro's place tonight. They killed a pig yesterday so you will eat well.' Or someone had been to Cividale and brought back eggs and cheese and the children had kept some aside for the men. Some little girls' concern for the cave men bordered on the maternal. They noticed the pitiful state of their socks that were held together with re-patched cloth scraps. They had organised a collection and bought some home-spun wool yarn from a village at the foot of the mountain. Under the eye of the local schoolteacher, Elena Borgnolo, each child had knitted a section. The result was three beautiful thick pairs of woollen socks with patriotic red and blue bands circling the tops. It was a moving scene when the children arrived at the cave and proudly presented their gifts to the men. To receive such a thoughtful present from people who had so little was humbling.

Although they enjoyed seeing them, at one point the men asked the parents to curtail the children's visits because they were afraid the track to the cave would become too beaten down and observed by the German foot or aerial patrols. One day they noticed three small figures about three kilometres away coming towards the base of the cliff. They began to climb the steep and dangerous slope that would test even an experienced mountaineer. Upon closer inspection the men could see they were young girls aged about nine to eleven. Each had a package slung over her shoulder. The men were terrified the girls would fall but they continued on unperturbed, shouting at the men to not try and help them, concerned that *they* might fall! When they arrived at the top they presented the men with eggs and cigarettes in exchange for receiving some drawings earlier. They said they took the precarious route after being told not to use the regular trail round the side of the cliff.

The men worried about their cheerful, brave little companions. The physical condition of all the local children was pitiful. They were thin and malnourished, their bodies covered in sores and rashes, their clothing ragged. Many died before they were five years old. Their well-being was also of concern to the priest who saw them at the catechism hour that he conducted daily at the school. Often he was called in the middle of the night to tend them when they were taken ill. Families lived in little more than hovels with no electricity or water and no heating other than the kitchen fire over which meals were prepared. A bucket in the stable served as a toilet. The children slept in tiny rooms located directly above the stables or above the kitchen. The room was fetid with the choking smoke of the kitchen fire or the stink of the animals below. He would find the sick child shaking and vomiting, its head held by its mother, in a bed shared by numerous brothers and sisters.[18] Lang and Smith could not help comparing their own childhood in New Zealand, which, despite the hardships of the Depression, appeared a paradise of advantage. Many children, working as soon as they could walk, received a couple of years' education at the most and were destined for impoverished, shortened lives. Yet the self-possession, reliability and initiative of these hardy mountain youngsters revealed a wisdom beyond their years.

Greening, an accomplished artist, began making portraits of the children with pen and paper provided by the schoolteacher. Word spread and soon everybody wanted his or her portrait done. Children began arriving at the cave clutching an egg in one hand and a piece of paper in the other. Greening would dutifully complete each portrait and sign his name, Carlo Grini, at the bottom. As the winter set in and it became more difficult to leave the cave, the men felt they were in hibernation.

Sometimes they stayed in bed all day to keep warm. In order to pass the time, Greening made hundreds of sketches of the cave and surrounding countryside. Under his tutelage, the New Zealanders tried their hand at wood sculpting and making model airplanes. Once they even held an exhibition of their work in the cave. Smith, not a keen hobbyist, preferred to write down everything that had happened to him since joining the army in 1939. The men also obtained a first-grade primer to try and improve their Italian, but few people in this border area spoke standard Italian.

Discreetly they became part of the village community life. The inhabitants referred to them as their 'brothers'. All the men felt slightly ashamed when gifts of food or clothing were foisted on them when they knew how little people had to give. They were rarely left alone for too long even when they were snowed in. On one such occasion the schoolteacher's husband ploughed his way to them laden with supplies in case they were hungry.

Once the village of Valle held a three-day dance to herald the official arrival of spring. The men spruced themselves up and used old socks for mittens and rags for scarves. The wine shop was the centre of revelry for the entire district. Its floor was made of rough-hewn logs that yielded up large splinters to inadequately covered feet. The only source of music was a battered accordion and a piccolo which seemed to have a repertoire of two tunes. They were surprised to note that the men danced with each other as much as with the women, and young danced with old. Smith recalled, 'It was an odd sensation to find oneself whisked on to the floor by the arms of some sprightly old gent of eighty odd summers.'[19] Greening confessed to blushing when 'one patriot member with his red scarf grabbed me and swirled me around like I'd never been swirled before. He held me as affectionately as he would a girl.'[20] The men had rehearsed their own item for the occasion, a trio accompanied by a paper-covered comb. Their performance stopped the dancing and they had to do two encores. After three days of continual dancing and drinking, the men were happy to recover in their cave for a week.

There was a bounty on their heads. The sum was 5400 lire, dead or alive, a princely sum for people in those harsh years. Despite hundreds of people knowing where they were, no one claimed the reward. Anselmo Borgnolo confirmed, 'Everyone knew about the hideout but no one betrayed them to the Germans.'[21]

The Germans knew the men were in the area but could not pinpoint their hiding place. From their look-out the men could watch German and Fascist patrols searching in the hills and on the plains below them. At one point they were tracking them with dogs and came quite close. The men raced up the side of a nearby mountain, through scrub so coarse they reckoned dogs would not go through it.

Smith observed, 'It had them puzzled. We rated the honour of having an observation plane set out to look for us. It came over and circled around above us. We could see its occupants quite clearly.'

It is more probable that the planes were scouring the zone for partisans who were causing the real problems for them. Fighting was fierce. Patriots had intercepted two Germans who had been driving in a car about three kilometres from the cave. Both men were killed and their bodies mutilated before being put back in the car and set on fire. This resulted in attack after attack on the villages regardless of whether partisans were hiding there or not. Greening recalls watching a party of partisans blow up a large enemy munitions dump. The shockwaves from the explosion were huge with smoke and debris rising thousands of metres into the air. The dump was re-established after two months as the Germans probably reckoned the partisans would not try to destroy it again. They were wrong. The second blast, greater than the first, rocked the whole countryside. After this the Germans did not try again.

Although the villagers overwhelmingly supported the partisans, reactions to them were mixed. After 8 September, Anselmo Borgnolo had returned to Valle from three years of fighting with the Italian army in Yugoslavia. He was tired of active warfare. 'The partisans wanted me to join them but I said no. No one in Valle joined the partisans.'[22] Like many others he assisted the patriots but trying to stay alive was more important. When the Germans combed through the area he would hide in the woods.

A South African ex-prisoner-of-war dressed in civilian clothes had wanted to join the men in the cave. But the villagers were suspicious of his German-sounding accent and did not want their friends' or their own futures jeopardised. It was not uncommon for Germans to infiltrate the partisans pretending to be escaped prisoners-of-war. They told the men they would sort it out and arranged a meeting for the South African with local partisans. Later they heard he had been shot. Lang was pragmatic about this. 'They couldn't afford the risk. In our eyes he was a South African prisoner-of-war but in their eyes he was a German because of his accent and they may have been quite correct.'[23] He was picked up barely alive with a head wound on a trail below the cave and died in a German hospital at Cividale.

The partisans were not welcome to use the cave because it would become public knowledge and endanger both the men and the villagers. Lang was adamant. 'How did we know they were partisans or infiltrating to find out who we were? We needed proof that they were who they said they were.' They usually agreed to meet up with partisans at Masarolis, about an hour's walk from the cave.

The men had not given up on hope of getting back to their own lines. Yet the news filtering through from the front was grim. The Allied forces were still stuck at Cassino in southern Italy and the hoped-for landing on the Adriatic coast appeared unlikely. A partisan friend had told them that they could get through to Yugoslavia. Although Lang and Smith were initially reluctant, they were persuaded that circumstances were now different. They planned to leave for Yugoslavia within the week.

In the early hours of 23 March 1944, Smith was jolted awake by a strong sense of alarm and anxiety – not unusual after all they had been through. But this time it was different. 'It was a feeling of panic,' he wrote. 'Something was going to happen and the dim starlight drifting through the cave entrance made the sensation more eerie.'[24] Putting it down to an overactive imagination, he drifted back to sleep. He was never to ignore a hunch again.

The three men were still asleep in bed when in the early hours of the morning a fusillade of shots burst into the cave. Holes punctured the groundsheet that covered the cave entrance. The interior filled with smoke and dust and a couple of small rocks fell. Startled awake and frightened out of their wits, they could hear shouting outside in a language that was not Italian. They knew they had had it. Smith instinctively dashed towards the entrance to avoid further damage. An experienced infantryman, he knew that a hand grenade chucked into the cave was the next step. Greening shouted at him to wave something white. Smith grasped a dirty old towel and stuck it out the entrance first. He emerged and was confronted by a man in battle uniform holding a submachine-gun in one hand and a hand grenade in the other.

'Standing there barefoot in the snow, clad in my one article of under-clothing – a short singlet – I must have looked quite ridiculous, certainly cold and just as certainly very scared. I spoke to him and hearing my accent, his tension eased.'[25] He replied in good English, 'So you are the English and the American we have been looking for. We have found you at last. We thought it would be you as no local people would have made a hygienic latrine like you have back along the track, but we weren't taking any chances.' The officer said he was an Austrian doctor and asked if anyone was hurt. It was only later that Smith discovered his hair was matted with blood where a bullet had ricocheted past his scalp. The doctor admired their living quarters and their cosy domestic arrange-ments. He let them eat their food and gave them some cigarettes while his soldiers made a thorough search of the cave for an hour. He said he was looking for patriots but he heard their shouts in English and did not want to kill Americans. He sounded almost sorry he had come upon them but as he was with German soldiers, they were now his prisoners. Despite their circumstances, the men rather liked him. Recalled Lang: 'They didn't treat us roughly at all. They accepted who we were. Like a lot of the Germans they respected the New Zealanders for a start.'[26] On the trek back, the men were allowed to carry as much food, clothing and bedding as they could muster.

At the top of the cliff they joined the main German column and were escorted down the mountain through the nearby village of Valle. It was a tragic scene. The people by now knew what had happened and were clustered together, silently watching, many in a state of shock. Several were in tears. Out of the corner of his eye Lang saw the schoolteacher, Elena Borgnolo, standing back in her doorway, weeping. The villagers were certain the men would be shot. Fearful that reprisals would be carried out on their friends, the men made no sign of recognition and walked past stony-faced, looking straight ahead. It was the last time either New Zealander would see their Italian helpers.

At a junction in the road the procession met up with a Fascist patrol that had been part of the combined operations against them. Among the Fascists was a partisan who had been with the Garibaldi Brigade. He had been a good friend to Lang and guided him to the partisans after his escape from the train. The man looked terrified, but not a flicker of recognition crossed Lang's face. 'He was recruited among the Fascists but he was in reality a partisan spy. If we'd greeted him with open arms, he'd have died on the spot.'

Taken to the German garrison at Cividale, each man was separately questioned. They had agreed before their interrogation to stick to the same story. 'We had never been with the partisans, the locals had never helped us, and we didn't know anybody. While on the run we had lived solely by stealing what we could or could gain by threats.' The Germans tried to trap them into admitting they had been with the partisans, a crime that would have carried an instant death penalty. Fortunately, the verdict was not guilty of being partisans but guilty of escaping. They were sentenced to thirty days solitary confinement.

The men were then taken to prison camp in Germany where they remained until the end of the war, a year later. They later learned that reprisals had been carried out in the area in which several men were shot. Curious to know how their cave had been discovered, they asked their captor. The Austrian doctor told them that they had come upon the footprints by accident while on a training manoeuvre. One of the soldiers was resting on top of the ridge above them and accidentally dropped his rifle. It slipped down the slope and on to the little track. The soldier, wanting to see where the track led, followed it close to the mouth of the cave. He realised that this was probably a hideaway and a surprise dawn attack was planned. Ironically, Greening had got up in the middle of the night and seen the platoon toiling up the slopes far below but thought

All the mod cons. Ross Greening's sketch of part of the interior of the
affectionately named 'Albergo Buco', the Cave Hotel.
(Washington State University Press)

nothing of it as they had watched many such operations from the safety
of their *buca*.

No one had ever been caught in the cave before. The men felt guilty
for spoiling such a fine record and were heartbroken they had let the
villagers down after all the trouble they had taken to protect them.

They may have had a lucky escape. In the roundups of late September
1944 the Nazis carried out a scorched-earth policy to rout out 'sub-
versives'. When they came to burn down Masarolis, Don Amelio swore
there were no partisans in the area. To demonstrate his good faith, he
opened his wallet and presented a document with the signature of the
German Command authorising him to requisition cement to rebuild a
road destroyed by partisans. It worked. A plaque in the main square
commemorates Don Amelio's heroism in saving Masarolis from the
flames. Again he thanked God for his help. In his wallet there was
another document. It was from the Stella Rossa (Red Star) partisan
command requesting help for their sick and wounded.[27]

CHAPTER THIRTEEN

Those bastards are getting bloody personal

That morning a pale sun rose late in the arid sky and a chalky moon dissolved quickly into the frosty blue night, almost as if it could not bear to look. The body of the New Zealand soldier covered by a sack was taken to the cemetery on a wagon drawn by a donkey. And on the icy silent street that flanked the deserted, barred-up houses, the subdued clip-clopping of the hooves of the animal, all skin and bone, resonated solemnly.[1]

The *loggia* of the town hall in the main square of Ponte di Piave, situated on the Piave River fifty kilometres north-east of Venice, bears a gleaming plaque honouring Dave Russell, one of only two New Zealanders to be awarded the George Cross for valour.[2] Just along the road from the square, divided from the street by a high wall, is an elegant seventeenth-century villa. It belongs to an old Venetian family, the Tommaseo, who traditionally use the villa as a summer residence. The garden is rambling with huge leafy trees, hedgerows and well-maintained flowerbeds, a tranquil haven from the noise and bustle of traffic on the streets outside.

Here, inside a basement room of the villa, its tiny barred window visible from outside, Russell spent his last week as a prisoner of the Germans before being marched through the garden to a spot against the iron railings and shot. It was 28 February 1945.

Among the New Zealanders hiding in the Veneto area, Dave Russell was one of the most active of the Hare Battalion. He was restless, daring and confident to the point of cockiness with a thirst for adventure that led him into some tricky situations. His life experience had given him the toughness and mental resourcefulness to survive on his wits. A Scot by nationality, he had moved to New Zealand from Australia in 1931 when the earthquake in Napier created a manpower shortage. He ended up working as an orderly in Napier Hospital. From there he enlisted for service a few days after the declaration of war. Evacuated from Crete, he served in North Africa where he was captured at Ruweisat Ridge. He had not taken kindly to imprisonment and escaped from Camp PG 107, at Torviscosa near Udine, on 8 September, ending up in the flat plains of the Ponte di Piave district where, together with Lofty Hunt, he was among the prisoners helped and housed for a time by the legendary Giacomo Gasparotti, the Italian farm administrator who, finding them in miserable conditions, hid them in his own farm buildings.[3]

From all accounts, Russell was roaming freely from the beginning, liaising with partisans and assisting in planning the evacuation of prisoners in hiding. Arch Scott first heard of Russell through his partisan contacts, but did not meet up with him until October 1944. There is no doubt Russell enjoyed the excitement and uncertainty of this vicarious lifestyle. He would often comment to Scott on the great experiences they would be able to look back on.[4] This sense of invincibility was probably honed from surviving bayonet charges in Crete and being wounded in Ruweisat. He had every intention of returning home and marrying his girlfriend, Nancy Wilson, in Napier.

Riding on his bicycle, he met up with many of the New Zealanders hiding with families in the plains around Caorle, San Donà di Piave, San Stino di Livenza and San Giorgio di Livenza. Among them were John Senior and Bill Black, who admired his humour and his *sang-froid* and marvelled at his independence. Russell's penchant for risk-taking, however, caused a headache for partisan Beppi Marson, his good friend. Barely 19 years old, Marson was the youngest of seven children in a family living at Staffolo about thirty kilometres from Ponte di Piave. A soldier in Naples when the Armistice occurred, he escaped but was captured by Germans near Rome and taken to a camp in Viterbo. Although the Italian soldiers were told they would be sent home, in reality plans were afoot to transport them to Germany. When an Italian officer was shot point blank while giving them instructions, Marson and his companions took advantage of the resulting confusion and fled. A few days later he noticed a bullet hole in his rucksack.[5]

By the time he returned to San Donà di Piave a month and a half later, organised help for escaped prisoners was already under way. His nephew was providing food to prisoners hiding out in the fields. Marson elected to cast his lot with the partisans. The family had always been anti-Fascist: 'The Fascists had caused us some trouble,' was the simple explanation. His family, who by this time had been joined by all his brothers, supported him. 'My mother particularly gave me good advice; she told me to be careful and she always kept her rosary in her hand. It went well for me because I was never caught.'[6]

The New Zealander Russell was one of the first escaped prisoners-of-war Marson met after returning home. 'He was a great person with tremendous courage. Unfortunately Dave got drunk easily. Before he was caught, I had spoken many times to Dave telling him that if he was captured they would make him speak and then they would have caught the lot of us. He told me I was mad.'[7] Marson worried every time he lost contact with Russell. He had told him to call at his house every few days to let them know he was all right. One evening a friend urged him to get to the tavern of the village of Stretti di Eraclea as quickly as possible. Upon arrival, Marson was met with the alarming spectacle of a drunk Russell in company with two Germans, one of whom was an SS officer. 'Dave was singing "Lili Marlene" at the top of his voice, shouting, pretending to be Italian. My friend told me that one of the Germans was a real bastard, he was suspicious and was asking Dave a whole raft of questions.' At one point Russell had begun to argue with his drinking comrades. In the heat of the moment, his Italian, never very good, would desert him, and phrases in English would punctuate his ravings. Marson acted swiftly. Like many Italians actively involved in the Resistance, he had an unofficial pact with a German to keep the peace. But more importantly, 'even though he was aware there were strange comings and goings at my house, he turned a blind eye'.

He went to speak to his German friend and asked him not to take severe measures against what might happen. Then Marson got about ten friends to burst into the bar with him to create a bit of boisterous confusion. 'I got hold of Dave and I gave him a punch in the jaw strong enough to knock him out. I took him outside and I heaved him on to my bicycle. I took him back home with me to keep an eye on him. The next morning I told him everything that happened. He remembered nothing. He asked me who had punched him. I did, I answered, and you're lucky I didn't kill you! Don't you understand that if they catch you and make you talk, they'll take the lot of us!'[8]

It still gives Marson the shudders to think about it. After this episode he decided that Russell should be evacuated with the next group of prisoners. He discussed his concerns with Arch Scott. 'We wanted to get free of him because we considered him a bit dangerous. But all our attempts to get him on the boat failed.' His next move was to put Russell in the underground shelter he had built for him in the middle of a field, ordering him to stay put for a few days. But Russell never did what he was told. The next day he had gone, apparently to visit other prisoners in the area.

Marson remembers Russell with great fondness as generous and altruistic, but his unpredictable, reckless behaviour was exasperating. 'He loved riding his bicycle and often went to San Stino di Livenza, miles away, to meet Arch Scott. More than once he had lunch with families he knew nothing about and when I came to know about this I scolded him.' He was aware of the irony of trying to act as Russell's minder. 'Sometimes I had to reprove him very sharply for his behaviour. I felt sorry afterwards because I was a young boy of twenty and he was more than thirty. More than once I had to tell him that unless he did what he was told no one would help him any more. He was too tall to be a native and his Italian was very poor.'[9]

Russell would have enjoyed the adventure of socialising with the Germans while operating incognito. 'He loved our wine and *grappa* as well. He used to help me making them together with German soldiers who were friends of mine.' Marson's family treated him as a brother, albeit one who needed keeping in line.

Arch Scott concurs with Marson on Russell's thirst for adventure and sense of patriotic duty. Together they had travelled to an Allied military mission at Belluno in the hope of organising an escape route for the prisoners through Yugoslavia. These journeys often failed because, according to Scott, the Special Forces were more interested in defeating the Germans than evacuating prisoners. Scott was always more cautious than Russell, wanting to test out plans before setting out on a dangerous journey, but nothing thrilled Russell more than to be on the move.[10]

Russell went and stayed with Giuseppe Vettorello, a man he had known for some time. The ever-vigilant Marson had not approved. 'I didn't want Dave to go and stay with him because Vettorello was a Fascist who had later changed his mind. He was a good man and Dave trusted him, but I didn't want him to spend too much time with him.'[11] Many people genuinely changed their political allegiance but they were viewed by committed anti-Fascists as opportunists and untrustworthy.

Scott vividly remembers his last meeting with Russell. They had heard that their South African friend had been captured and shot at Torre del Mosto. Although this information was mistaken, the reality of their predicament shook them. 'By hell, Scotty, those bastards are getting bloody personal,' were Russell's last words.[12]

John Senior believes he was the last person to see Russell alive. On 23 February 1945 Senior was hiding in the maize fields when Russell, dressed nattily in a suit and hat, came riding by on his bicycle. He was on his rounds organising for the next group of escaped prisoners to be evacuated. He confirmed that he had arranged for the partisans to send a supply of winter clothing to the prisoners and they chatted a while before Russell resumed his journey. Several days later he heard that Russell had been caught by Fascists and was being held at Ponte di Piave by the Germans.[13] Russell had been captured while resting under a bridge, reportedly betrayed by a woman. He was handed over to the

Germans and because he was found in civilian clothing with a map, treated as a spy.

As soon as Marson heard about Russell's arrest, he confronted Vettorello, suspecting his involvement. 'I threatened him because I wanted to know the truth.' However, a tearful Vettorello swore that he had nothing to do with it. Just a few days before he had noticed strangers, possibly Fascists, snooping around his house. Marson confirmed that in that period his own family had been visited by Fascists. 'My mother gave them a duck to placate them.' He still believes that Vettorello was innocent. 'I never found anybody responsible for his death. At first I wanted to find out more, but then when the war was finished, I decided that it was better to forgive whoever had betrayed him or was somehow responsible. There were so many Fascists in our area that you wouldn't really know whom to start with.'[14]

Russell was taken to the German headquarters in the lovely old Villa Tommaseo at Ponte di Piave. Over the next three or four days he was kept in a basement, chained to a wall, and regularly beaten. He was given no food or water and told that if he did not reveal the names of his helpers he would be executed within a few days. Vettorello was also arrested for having harboured Russell, but was released after Russell repeatedly denied he had ever seen him before.

Marson tried to find out more and went to Ponte di Piave. He met up with a priest involved in helping Allied prisoners-of-war who had advised him to speak with the guard of the villa, a man by the name of Carrer. Marson was appalled to hear that Russell was being tortured. 'Of course I started to worry both for him and for us. If he had spoken . . .' Once Marson caught a glimpse of Russell walking around inside the walled garden. He was wearing a light-coloured shirt with the sleeves rolled up. His face was badly swollen.

The beatings continued, mainly administered by the German, Lieutenant Haupt. Russell was handed over for special treatment to the Italian interpreter, a Fascist by the name of Giuseppe Ardria, who spoke English. They would have wanted to know about the Allied missions in the mountains, the partisan networks in the mountains and on the plains, the families sheltering prisoners-of-war and the names of the people involved in schemes to evacuate the prisoners. Russell remained totally unco-operative, refusing to betray his companions. When threatened with execution, his response, according to an eyewitness, was, 'Let them shoot me.' His courage won him the respect of his torturers.

He was executed by firing squad on a freezing cold morning on 28 February. Arch Scott made inquiries after the Liberation and from eyewitness accounts pieced together Russell's heroic last moments. When his sentence was pronounced David Russell, a New Zealand soldier to the end, stood to attention. He was marched outside and ordered to stand against a wall. He requested a cigarette and smoked part of it before throwing it aside. When asked if he had anything to say, he shook his head, then stood erect. Marson found a concealed spot outside the villa but the high walls prevented him from seeing anything. He could only hear the volley of shots.

Russell was left where he fell until the following morning when a bullock-drawn wagon came and took him to the Ponte di Piave cemetery for burial. Two months later his body was exhumed and re-interred in the British Commonwealth Cemetery in Udine. Beppi Marson was present with a friend who took photos. 'His body hadn't deteriorated. I noticed that Dave was without shoes. The undertaker had stolen them. This made me mad because a friend and I had given those shoes to Dave as a present. I wanted them back!'[15]

Marson's account is a mixture of the deep admiration and intermittent exasperation he felt. 'If Dave had spoken all the people involved with helping Allied POWs would have been arrested and our villages would have been burnt down. A lot of families were involved.' Yet he tells a story which illustrates that his fears were misplaced. 'More than once he asked me, "What would you do if the Germans or Fascists caught you?" I replied that I didn't know. I would only know when it happened. When I asked him the same question he replied that he would not speak because even if he did they would shoot him anyway and he advised his friends to do the same if they were caught.'[16] Fearless to the point of recklessness, he was steadfast and loyal when it came to the crunch. Marson recognised this. 'Dave was a good man. We shared lots of jokes together. He loved his country very much and he believed in the Allied cause. That's why he decided to die for it.' If Russell had stayed put, Marson believes he could have saved himself but he paid the price for not staying put, for being reckless. If he inadvertently put others at risk, he was prepared to die to protect their identities. The news of Dave Russell's execution spread fast. John Senior remembers the fear and agitation it gave rise to in their families and the escapers' own frightening sense of vulnerability. The families established new rules.

'We were ordered to stay clear of roads and the houses at all times. Food was brought out to us at set times, and the *vino* limited to ensure we would always be alert and could leave the area.'[17] The Italians were bombarded with circulars warning them of the penalties for harbouring escapers and deserters. A bounty was on the heads of the Hare Battalion to further entice spies, and the possibility of roundups and executions loomed at the back of everyone's minds. This climate of tension had an understandable impact on the willingness of families to host the escapers on their property. The success of the Allied divisions in pushing up the peninsula meant the Germans were now consolidated in the northern regions and seen more often. Fighting a battle they could not win, German reprisals took on a viciousness born of desperation. As a consequence, people were afraid of hiding people in their houses and asked them to find alternative accommodation.

The Francescon family felt they could no longer permanently keep Dave Taylor in their pumphouse and asked Senior if he could join them in the fields. Ines Martin conferred with her family and reported that the risk was too great. Senior assured her that they always remained alert and would never reveal the family's identity if caught. However, they ended up secretly hiding Taylor in the fields during the day while he crept back to the pumphouse to sleep at night.

When Walter Willis walked into the village of Colleredo di Prato on the outskirts of Udine, he was on his second escape attempt. Recaptured and imprisoned after his initial escape from Camp 107 at Torviscosa, he had jumped off a prison train close to the Austrian border and walked back some 100 kilometres into northern Italy. At Colleredo he was picked up

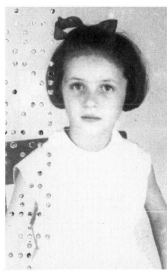

Top left: Frank Gardner (right) with his brother and a friend about to leave Syria.
Above: Elisabetta Bierti, daughter of Frank Gardner.
Left: Frank Bowes with sister Vera, and mother.
Bottom: The wine stands on the site of the 'sump' where Bill Black hid. Don Pietro Buogo is centre. 1970s.

Above: Exhumation of David Russell's body, 1945.
Below: Kiwis enjoying the skiing season, 1944. L–R Doug Dymock, Bill Gyde and George London skiing in Switzerland after their successful escape over the Swiss mountains.

Above left: Maria Pianina and Walter Willis on their wedding day in Wellington, February 1946.
Middle: The Via Spalato prison, Udine, where both Walter Willis and Maria Pianina were interrogated and tortured.
Bottom left: Walter Willis in his guise as Francesco Pianina. He was captured by the Germans near this spot.
Bottom right: Cino Moscatelli – famous partisan captain of the Garibaldi division, 1944.

Top left: Giulia Leder, Pierina's mother, taken June 1945.

Top right Elena Borgnolo, the schoolteacher of Valle in the 1970s.

Middle: Cavemen: L–R Jack Lang, Ros Greening and Bob Smith.

Bottom: John Senio greets his 'big sister' Ines Martin at Caorle after nearly 50 years.

Left: Raimondo (Roy Johnston) (right) with Severino Zoccerato, his partisan contact, during a visit to Jesolo, 1980.
Below left: Beppi Marson, May 2001.
Below right: Sister Giuseppina, the feisty nun of Rivignano, aged 92.
Bottom: Father John Flanagan and a group of New Zealanders in St Peter's Square after the liberation of Rome, June 1944.

Top left: Don Amelio Pinzano, the priest of Masarolis, May 2001.

Middle: From left Gino Panont, Steve Sims (son of Noel Sims), Marilyn Scott (Arch's daughter), Arch Scott and Lucia Antonel in front, 1995, when Scott was awarded citizenship of San Stino di Livenza. Lucia is the daughter of Angelo Antonel. The Antonel family protected Arch Scott and Noel Sims for over a year.

Bottom: Memorial for the seven executed partisans, 'martyrs for the national liberation struggle', at Mosso Santa Maria. Frank Bowes' name is at sixth place.

Above: Arch Scott with members of the Franzin family in 1995. Luciano Franzin is on the right. Their father was Luigi Franzin, the game-keeper of the Piva Estate, who died in Dachau after being arrested for protecting escaped prisoners.

Below: Pierina Leder (daughter of a New Zealand escaped POW), her mother Guilia Leder, and Pierina's husband, May 2001.

Left: Jack Lang, 2000.
Below: Jack's cave today.
Bottom: May 2001, San
Martino Freedom Trail. The
ceremony in Sulmona, Abruzzi,
before the San Martino Freedom
Trail, a four-day walk over
escape routes commemorating
the help given to Allied escaped
servicemen by Italians.

by Paul Pianina's aunt who was driving home in a horse and cart after visiting relatives. Pianina, a young boy at the time, remembers how the New Zealander came to live in their household. His grandfather Pietro said, 'Look, I've got two sons away at war – don't know whether they're dead or alive. We've got plenty of room.'[18] From then on Willis passed off as one of the sons in a family comprising the grandparents, Pianina's father, mother, an uncle who worked at the airfield driving trucks, and two aunts, one of whom was Maria.

Like most of the townsfolk, the Pianina family was anti-Fascist in that they wanted the Germans out. But their feelings towards the partisans were mixed. 'There were a lot of people who didn't want to be committed with either side because if they did, they were right in the middle. So it wasn't so much right or wrong there. It was wrong all the way. If you went with the partisans you were wrong, if you went with the Fascists you were wrong, if you went with the SS you were wrong. So nobody trusted nobody. And if you did anything, you did it with great secrecy.'[19]

The Pianinas had connections with the partisans. But Pianina distinguishes three types of partisans, a distinction fairly common in the highly volatile Friuli region. 'There were the genuine ones against the Germans, there were the Reds, the Communists, and the ones who were there for the spoils, out for themselves. They were the ones causing all the problems.' The family possessed about forty acres of land so were targeted by both partisans and Germans for food supplies. His grandfather had given supplies of wheat to the partisans and when requested a similar amount by the Germans was unable to comply. As a result he was jailed and Pianina's father and uncle had to sell supplies on the black market in order to buy their father's freedom. This caused ill-feeling and fragmented loyalties to the partisan cause.

The area was swarming with Germans. Because he had no identification papers and spoke limited Italian, Willis had to remain under cover. For many months, although he helped out around the house, he never went outside. 'He couldn't do that. No, never. He was a prisoner in our own place really.' Paul Pianina was sworn to secrecy but the new member of the family had been noticed. 'I was told not to tell anybody. I remember there was a lady who used to live close by who asked me,

"Who's that man?" And I'd just say, "My uncle."' This relationship to the family is explained by Willis in his report. 'People start to see me around the backyard and are naturally curious to know who I am so are told I'm the fiancé of Maria Pianina and am from Milan.'[20] True or not at the beginning, it is easy to imagine how his relationship with Maria developed. The hardships of the previous years had taken its toll on Willis's health. For months he was sick with fever, influenza, dysentery and slight ear troubles after banging his head when he leaped from the train. He was often confined to a room where pretty, dark-haired Maria nursed and cared for him, and it was she who persuaded her father to keep him with them indefinitely, despite the dangers.

During these months there were several raids by the Germans but each time Willis received enough warning to reach his hiding place in the hayloft. On one occasion in the summer of 1944 Germans were billeted in the room next to him. When an entire family in a neighbouring village was shot for sheltering a partisan, Willis offered to leave, but the family would not hear of it, knowing he had nowhere to go and risked almost certain capture by the Germans and Fascists. However, one evening towards dusk several German trucks swept into the village and stopped outside the Pianina home. 'The house was quickly surrounded by Germans and this time I had no opportunity to escape, although I did try.' One of the family called out urgently '*Tedeschi, tedeschi!*' and Willis moved swiftly out the back door and down a track through the orchard. He dared not run. The fruit trees, although in bud, were without leaves and there was no cover until the end of the orchard. 'I was about 50 yards from the house when I heard "Alt, alt."[21] I ignored the call and continued walking. Next there was a burst of machine-gun fire and the bullets whistled through the branches above my head. I turned round to see Maria struggling with a big German.' He learned later what happened. When he ignored the order to halt, the German raised his machine-gun to fire and Maria leaped at him and knocked the gun upwards.

The Pianina family and Willis were lined up against the wall facing German machine-guns. The pretext was that they were looking for Russians the family had protected earlier, but Willis believes they were alerted to his presence. There was a roll call from the list of family members every household was required to keep. Willis answered to the name of the son away in Sardinia, Francesco Pianina. But with no identity papers, his decidedly different appearance, and the fact he had tried to escape, the Germans arrested him. A frantic Maria insisted on not being separated from Willis and she went of her own accord in order to cover for him. It was 18 April 1945. Willis's report, written in awkward English two days after his release, is wrought with admiration for her. 'When Maria Pianina heard and saw the intentions of the Jerries, she *volunteered* to come along too, to make it easier as regards interrogation etc. and had the courage to come with me, an English, in their stinking, lousy prisons.'[22]

They were taken together to a large building in Udine and stopped at the doorway to a spacious room. Inside seated at a desk were two Italian civilians. Against the wall in single file were at least twenty Italian partisans. Some were bleeding badly from wounds and were held upright by comrades. The German guards barked some orders and the partisans were cleared away from the desk to make way for Willis and Maria. His arms held firmly by a German on either side, Willis was pushed forward.

'The moment of truth had arrived . . . the two Italian civilians at the desk were to take down particulars of who we were. If they and the Germans were to find out that I was British, at least fifteen people in Maria's home would be shot. Although fluent in Italian, I did have an accent – but the Italians would know that I was not Italian.'[23] It was about seven paces across the room to the desk. As he left the doorway, Willis had no plan whatsoever. 'What could I plan – we were in the hands of the most dreaded, most evil unit of the German Armed Forces – the SS.' But half way across the room Willis remembered being told how well he had stuttered in Italian after he had told an Italian joke. So, in a desperate ruse to hide his identity, he pretended to have a speech impediment. The two Italians at the desk were so preoccupied trying to understand what he was saying that they failed to notice his accent. Embarrassed, they got him to write his details down himself. He had no difficulty doing this as he had taught himself to write through reading the many books in Maria's home, among them such titles as *Gone with the Wind* and *The Stars Look Down* in Italian translation.

He gave his name as Francesco Pianina. He was asked to give his mother's maiden name, which, fortunately, he was able to do. From that first interrogation room they were taken to the jail for political detainees in Via Spalato, Udine, and were confined to different parts of the jail to await interrogation. After two days Willis received a note from Maria lodged inside a piece of bread. In it she stated she would not reveal his identity whatever happened. She was interrogated first. Afterwards he heard what happened to her. He wrote in his report in stilted English, 'She is accused of being a patriot, and that I'm not her brother but a patriot leader who stays in their house, works at night against the Germans, and that I'm the lover of her.'

Maria Pianina was battered, whipped with a leather thong 'as thick as a finger', hung from a ceiling by her wrists which were tied behind her back on and off for three hours, and pulled upwards by her neck. She always insisted Willis was her brother. After this she was placed in a cell adjacent to Willis's for an hour where she was able to communicate to him the nature of the questions. Then it was his turn. At this point Willis was separated from Maria. He was not to see her again until after the German surrender.

It was not the first time he had been in this jail. Recaptured after his escape from the prison camp, he had been held in the underground cells while the Germans checked his identity as an Allied escaped prisoner. His fingerprints had been taken in the big book at the reception desk. He now found himself in front of the same reception desk, the same warden and the same big book. His painful stuttering meant it was some time before all his particulars were taken down. The warden then reached for the carbon pad. Willis's wrist was held firmly and his hand was placed on to the pad, fingers outstretched. His fingertips were dipped in carbon then pressed on to the page of the book. Willis was determined that his fingerprints, already in the book, should not be identified again. So many lives depended on it. 'As the warden forced my hand on to the paper, I gave my hand a slight push forward, enough to smudge the prints.'

He was then taken along numerous dimly lit passageways to a cell door. The prison guard unlocked the door and he was thrust inside. He stood there trying to adjust to the almost total darkness. Suddenly a figure leaped up off the floor and dragged him down, holding him tightly.

'Stay down, stay down,' he hissed. As Willis's eyes became adjusted to the dim light, he could see all the inmates lying around the walls, tightly huddled together. 'The inmate who had dragged me to the floor now took my hand and he pressed it to the wall just above our heads. "Feel the holes," he told me. "Those are bullet holes. The guards outside up on the wallways fire downwards into the cells at the slightest pretext."' All the inmates in the cell squeezed together a bit tighter and made room for him. 'What a wonderful gesture – I was no longer alone – I was with friends. I slept among friends on that bare concrete floor.'[24]

Willis's friends were captured partisans. The treatment meted out to them was always brutal. Seventeen-year-old Vittorino Gaspari of Annone Veneto lost all his teeth in one of the beatings. When there was an attack against a Fascist, random reprisals would be carried out on prisoners. 'They would surround us in a circle and go – "You, you, you, outside." And the next day . . . Six times I went through this!'[25] Usually the men were crammed into small cells with a sprinkling of straw on the floor. They would wait in dread for the sudden clanging of the door and the sharp order to one of their companions. The man would be dragged away and it was the last they would see of him. There was never any warning.

No shots were fired into the cell that night but Willis and his companions all lost blood. The bullet holes in the wall were infested with nocturnal bed bugs, which attacked exposed parts of the body. Although the bite is not felt at the time, a nauseous smell arises during the biting. Later there is a very strong itch and the skin area around the bite turns white.

The next morning a German guard took Willis along several streets to the Gestapo headquarters. Every few paces he received a heavy kick, sometimes on his backside, sometimes down the back of his legs. He was brought into the interrogation room, which was bare except for a long desk. Seated behind the desk were two German officers and two Italian women interpreters. Lying on the ground under the desk Willis could see a cigarette butt. At this point Willis introduced the role not only of stutterer but also of half-wit into his repertoire. He had discovered that people generally treated them as one and the same. He played his part to the utmost, gaining time as the women struggled to gauge his details.

One of the German officers was smoking a cigarette and as he reached forward across the desk to tap the ash into the ashtray, Willis stretched his left hand across the desk to take the cigarette from him. 'My lips were moving, but no sound came forth. The German was completely nonplussed. He had a surprised look on his face – I had a pleading look – thus we stayed for several seconds.' Finally the infuriated German stubbed out the cigarette and moved the ashtray from Willis's reach. The guard who stood behind him knocked down his outstretched arm.

A few minutes later Willis dived for the cigarette butt lying under the desk. He received a heavy kick on the backside, which shot him forward to collide with the legs of the German officer. 'Amidst harsh, guttural commands from the officer, I was grabbed by the feet and pulled out – but I got the cigarette butt, and standing in front of the desk once more proceeded to tuck the butt into my breast pocket, all with a very silly grin on my face.' He was kicked, punched, slapped, his arms pushed upwards in a hammerlock hold behind his back. But the more he was badly treated, the more stupid he became.

The women were then sent out of the room, leaving just the three Germans and Willis. He felt safer because the Germans did not speak Italian. They signalled to him to remove his clothes. He stripped to his waist and stood motionless. The officer then pointed at his trousers and, arm outstretched, made a downward movement with his palm.

'I released my belt and my trousers fell to my ankles. I stood there in my birthday suit with a silly grin still on my face. The officer wrote something down on paper then he reached out with his hand again, but this time with the palm upwards, and signalled an upwards movement. His outstretched hand was level with my testicles. I looked down, put my right hand under my purse and lifted it upwards.

'Germans "do their block" worse than the Italians. The German officer did not "do his block"; he actually blushed. He spoke to the guard behind me and the guard gave my trousers a pull upwards.

'The interrogation was finished and I have no doubt what was written on the record. Half-wit Jew.'[26]

Until the German Occupation, the persecution of the Jewish people was less zealous in Italy than other European countries. Although Mussolini had passed racial laws barring Italian Jews from public office in 1938, there was widespread criticism of this measure from all sectors of Italian society. It was during the German occupation after the 1943 Armistice that Jews were most vulnerable to being rounded up and deported, but there had been reluctance, even from Fascist leaders, to hand over Jews to the Germans. Allied escaped prisoners-of-war often met up with Jews in hiding. However, it is estimated some 6800 Italian Jews lost their lives in concentration camps. Because Italian Jews looked no different physically from Italians, unidentified males were routinely asked to drop their trousers as circumcision was for the Germans undeniable proof of Jewishness. At the time Willis believed they were searching for battle scars.

Walter Willis, like many male New Zealanders of the time, was circumcised. That this common practice, advocated on the grounds of hygiene by the arbiter of New Zealand childcare, the Plunket movement, would have landed him in such a bizarre predicament in enemy territory must have been unimaginable to him and indeed, to any New Zealand soldier.[27]

Fortunately, the interrogation took place during the last two weeks of the war. Both Willis and Maria Pianina were released from the jail by partisans on 30 April before the arrival of the Allied Eighth Army. The Germans did not have time to investigate all the aspects of the story, which, had they done so, could have had devastating consequences. 'I said that I was Francesco Pianina, Maria's brother. Therefore, if I was a Jew, then so were all the family.' However, Willis felt it was better to be considered a Jew, an accident of birth, in that late stage of the war than to be identified as an escaped Allied soldier, actively protected by the Italians. By this time the Germans knew the war was lost and their own survival was at stake. As a result there was no further inquiry into the family's background. As Paul Pianina confirmed, 'Until they discovered who he was they wouldn't do anything. But then again, if the war had still a long way to go, it was a different story.'[28] The Pianinas had a strong suspicion as to who betrayed Willis. The man disappeared in the last days of the war, probably executed by partisans.

The official report states that both Willis and Maria Pianina were subjected to continual ill-treatment and torture. The prison authorities confirmed that Maria Pianina was imprisoned by SS troops on 18 April, but they could not confirm the identity of the man put in prison on the same date, as he would not speak. When an officer from the Allied Repatriation Detachment visited the Pianina family on 5 June 1945 in order to validate Willis's story, he described them as 'a typical honest, hard-working peasant family' with no interest in any politics. Maria was still away in a mountain village recuperating. Soon after his release Willis requested permission to marry her in Italy, but the regulations required that he return to New Zealand. The military authorities viewed proposed marriages to 'enemy aliens' with reluctance, despite the circumstances. 'The question of permitting L/Cpl Willis to marry Pianina Maria has received careful consideration. It is felt that L/Cpl Willis would be well advised not to make a final decision in this matter until after he has returned to New Zealand. This decision has been arrived at after giving full consideration to the great services that were rendered to L/Cpl Willis by his fiancée.' He was permitted to visit her only upon assurance that he would not secretly marry her. Instructions were clear.

'He should therefore proceed to New Zealand and after arrival there, if he still desires to marry the girl, he should make application to Army HQ for the repatriation of his fiancée and this will be arranged as expeditiously as possible.'[29]

They married in Wellington on 11 February 1946 and settled at Otorohanga near Te Kuiti in the North Island King Country. Paul Pianina, together with other members of the Pianina family, joined his aunt in New Zealand in 1957. Neither Willis nor Maria ever spoke of their experiences in the Udine prison to their family or, it seems, to each other.[30] However, her family knew she had suffered barbaric torture and the extent of the damage it inflicted on her. Paul Pianina explains, 'The only thing I know is she could never have children. The SS used to have a whip and they'd poke it right through the vagina. That's why she couldn't have babies.'[31] This detail is omitted in Willis's initial report, probably because he was not aware of it then, or chose not to record it.

Maria's health was often poor. Transition from her Italian village to life in New Zealand was not easy. When she died in 1989, five years before her husband, Willis divided up some personal belongings of his wife to be shared among the five Pianina nieces. He wrote to Paul Pianina's daughter, 'It is understood that the contents of the cartons do not have great monetary value. However, they do have great sentimental value. Each carton contains samples of knitted Viennese lace hand-knitted by your Aunty Maria. The knitting of each pattern required dedication, concentration and intelligence. They are to be treasured. No doubt you all realise that if it were not for your Aunty Maria none of you would be here in New Zealand. In fact you would not have been born at all with your present parentage.'[32]

CHAPTER FOURTEEN

Horace and Fanny: New Zealand priests in the Vatican underground

June 1944. The Reverend John Flanagan of Auckland has gained his doctorate in theology with honours according to information received by his Lordship, Bishop Liston. Father Flanagan, who was ordained in Rome in 1941, has been detained by the war in Italy. Along with Father Owen Snedden, he has been pursuing a course in post-graduate studies.[1]

After the Armistice the number of priests walking through the streets and squares of Rome seemed to double overnight. With their ground-length black soutanes worn over knickerbockers and long socks, round-brimmed hats and flowing outdoor cloaks, they were as familiar a part of the Roman landscape as the imposing sweep of monuments and statues lining every corner of the Eternal City. One cold January day in 1944 a tall, slender young priest from New Zealand, Father Owen Snedden, code name Horace, crossed St Peter's Square and passed through the Vatican gates. He nodded at the German guards stationed outside the gates and walked briskly away. Head bowed, trying to be as inconspicuous as possible, he made his way behind colonnades towards the Via Firenze. This was the most dangerous part of his run because the street bordered the German military headquarters. Here he slowed his pace to a contemplative walk, in keeping with the supposed pastoral nature of his outing. Out of the corner of his eye across the narrow street he noticed two Gestapo agents watching him. As he approached a doorway he heard a hiss from its shadowy interior. Recognising it as a signal of danger, he continued on without faltering. If he had acknowledged the call and stopped he would have given away the safe house of two escaped prisoners who would then have been captured and their Italian hosts executed. The signal meant these billets had been denounced and could no longer be used to hide prisoners. Early in the evening before the 5.30 p.m. curfew, Snedden made another visit to warn his contacts of the betrayal. These contacts would in turn pass the information to their cells, linked to the underground networks of the various groups fighting in the Rome Resistance.

That night he and his friend, Father John Flanagan, code name Fanny, changed the addresses of the escapers on the card index and buried them in the Vatican gardens. This was the official storage place for all records, receipts and documentation. The next day they dug up the biscuit tins and the two priests listed the names of all the New Zealanders on their file. Every Kiwi prisoner known to be hiding in Italy was accounted for.[2]

The priestly soutane was a perfect cover for concealing food, clothing, boots, cigarettes and messages for the thousands of escaped prisoners who were hiding in Rome. It also concealed the identities of prisoners themselves, who for the first and only time in their lives were encouraged to don the cloth by their genuinely religious counterparts in order to be conducted to a secure refuge, or to receive medical or dental treatment. On one such occasion Snedden had to insist an ex-prisoner sacrifice his fulsome moustache, a dead give-away, before he could be accompanied to the dentist. These false clerics became so commonplace that a newspaper cartoon at the time depicted two soldiers saluting a Franciscan friar with the caption: 'You never know. He might be a general.'[3]

Many Romans also found refuge in the Church. In danger of being sent to Germany, lawyer and former aviation lieutenant Francesco Paolo Squillacciotti turned to the Dominican friars for help. He received a new identity card as a priest and was offered shelter in the monastery. When his pregnant wife wanted to discuss family affairs or exchange news with him she would go to the Santa Maria Sopra Minerva church at a pre-arranged time. Here she would head for the confessional where her husband in priest's attire was waiting for her behind the grille. Murmuring softly the couple would converse briefly, then the wife would exit, making the sign of the cross as she did. Once Squillacciotti was crossing the church when a woman stopped him, wanting confession. 'I'm in a hurry,' he replied. 'I'll find you another priest.'[4]

The New Zealand priests Fathers Owen Snedden and John Flanagan were key figures in the Vatican underground which hid over 3000 escaped Allied prisoners-of-war during the nine-month Rome Occupation. The underground was established by the flamboyant Irishman, Monsignor Hugh O'Flaherty, whose patriotic dislike of the English was reputed to be exceeded only by his hatred of Fascism. Attached to the Vatican Secretariat, he mixed in diplomatic circles and enjoyed the company and pursuits of Roman high society. The Pope was said to have turned a blind eye to some of O'Flaherty's more unorthodox methods. An excellent golfer, even if priests were not officially allowed to play golf, his membership of the Rome Golf Club and his frequent attendance at glittering parties provided invaluable contacts for his network. They were an odd assortment of priests, British officers and Italians from all walks of life with a set of code names that were spot on in some cases, wildly bizarre in others. Apart from the New Zealanders Fanny and Horace, there were Golf, Eyerish, Mr Bishop, Sandro, Spike, Emma, Dutchpa, Sailor, Whitebows and Rinso.[5]

When war broke out, Aucklanders Flanagan and Snedden were midway through their doctoral studies in the Vatican, forming part of the international mix of students studying at Urban College. It was a world away from the quiet provincial existence of 1930s New Zealand. By now fluent Italian speakers, they had already witnessed the dramatic sweep of events that would mark that intense, tragic period. These included the death of the outspoken Pope Pius XI, the coronation of the more cautious Pius XII, the public displays of Mussolini who used to inspect his troops while jogging and, during the early war years, visits of Hitler and his high-ranking Nazi officials to Rome. Flanagan was with the crowds in Piazza Venezia on 11 December 1941 when Mussolini in one of his rabble-rousing speeches declared war with America. Already at war with Britain and France, Italy was still clinging to the coat tails of its German ally as they notched up victories in Europe, Crete, Greece and North Africa. Mussolini believed the war would soon be over. His hopes were borne out when Italy became a holding pen for huge numbers of disgruntled captured British and Commonwealth soldiers. The tide had not yet turned.

For anxious families back in New Zealand it was impossible to gain news of husbands, sons and brothers, whose whereabouts were often relayed in a telegram bearing the ominous words, 'Missing in Action'. One evening Catherine Clayton of Wellington, who had received no word of her husband, Captain Colin Clayton, for some time, turned on her radio. 'I was twiddling knobs on my radio when I suddenly heard a resonant New Zealand voice read out names and information about New Zealanders. I took them down and wrote to the families. They all wrote back. Some of them had had no news for two years.'[6]

The rich, deeply sonorous voice with its clear enunciation belonged to Father Owen Snedden, who five times a week would broadcast on Vatican Radio the names of New Zealand prisoners-of-war in Italy. Once a week he also made broadcasts in Italian to Italian prisoners-of-war in Australia. This service was an offshoot of the Vatican Information Bureau set up by Pius XII after the outbreak of war to gather news of prisoners-of-war, refugees and displaced peoples to pass on to anxious relatives all over the world. Although this operated for all, regardless of nationality or religious belief, the initial beneficiaries were the Italians themselves who were the first prisoners to be captured in large numbers. An Italian mother had written to the Pope asking if her missing son could be found. After he was successfully traced, a room was set up to handle further inquiries. The influx of Allied prisoners to Italy after the North African and Greek campaigns meant that the scope of the service now reached mammoth proportions and could not be contained in usual broadcasts to England, where the names of missing men were read out at the end of the news.

In 1941 the International Red Cross reported the first New Zealand and Australian captives. The service was extended, new headquarters arranged and a team of priests from many countries was mobilised to convey information about prisoners to all corners of the world. In Australasia messages for the prisoners were collected at the Apostolic Delegate in Sydney, before being flown in a diplomatic bag to Rome for broadcasting over Vatican Radio. There were over one and a half million requests for information received, on average two thousand a day. Over 50 per cent of all queries were satisfactorily answered. In Italy, chaplains at the prison camps distributed forms to the prisoners and collected them and the messages were read out over Vatican Radio. Only messages in the prisoners' own handwriting or bearing his signature were accepted so that the information was soon respected as being the most authentic and reliable possible. However, with so many different nationalities, deciphering the phonetic and lexical intricacies of an unfamiliar language could be a headache. According to Snedden, 'the greatest difficulty was found with New Zealand place names, and not even after four years of practice could the clerical staff spell "Ngaruawahia" with any degree of confidence.'[7] On the light side he reported having to convey three proposals of marriage from prisoners to sweethearts back home.[8] After the Armistice, based on information in the 'registry' stored in the biscuit tins, Snedden used his weekly broadcasts to convey disguised messages from escaped prisoners to their relatives.[9]

As the war progressed from the south more and more people were forced to leave their homes, and large numbers of refugees, mainly women and children, flocked to Rome. In a month the city's population of around one and a half million had doubled. People were living in underground shelters, schools, tents, caves; even the old Roman ruins in the grounds of the Papal summer villa at Castelgandolfo became temporary accommodation for thousands of homeless families. This put an enormous burden on the city's already scant resources and there was a desperate shortage of food and clothing.[10]

The volatile, transient state of the government and a lack of any functioning central civic authority in Rome meant that the Vatican assumed the responsibility for much relief work. Fleets of Vatican sponsored trucks and lorries regularly dodged Allied bombings to transport food and clothing supplies from northern Italy.

Compounding the flood of Italian refugees were thousands of escaped prisoners reaching Rome on their way down to join their lines. The early arrivals were housed in rooms vacated by students in the Vatican colleges. One guest was Paul Freyberg, the son of General Bernard Freyberg, Commander of the New Zealand forces. He was captured at Anzio but managed to escape to the palatial Castelgandolfo, which, although designated as Vatican extra-territorial property, was surrounded by Germans. He would have been a prize trophy for the Germans, given his connections, so a plan was hatched to transfer him to Rome. He was smuggled into the Vatican after a suffocating 28-kilometre journey in the boot of the official Vatican car after a routine call with supplies. A few days later Freyberg turned twenty-one and the two priests, also young men in their twenties, helped him celebrate in a riotous party held in his honour.[11]

However, soon the quarters were overcrowded and alternative accommodation had to be found for their charges. Fathers Snedden and Flanagan, in close alliance with O'Flaherty, helped arrange for them to be billeted with Italian people who were prepared to take the risk of harbouring them. There was no shortage of safe houses for the prisoners despite the danger, and some 3500 were in hiding. This was despite the Allied bombings of Italian cities, and especially Monte Cassino, when some doors were closed. Angry Italians could not understand why the monastery was bombed with monks still inside, and priests in the underground organisation found themselves in the delicate situation of justifying an ostensibly indefensible action against their faith.

When O'Flaherty came under surveillance and could not leave the Vatican, Snedden, Flanagan and a few other stalwarts in the organisation took over. Sam Derry, a British officer who co-ordinated the underground intelligence network, expressed anxiety about the safety of the priests. 'I was particularly concerned about "Horace" (the New Zealand priest, Father Owen Snedden), for he had the dangerous task of checking up on the flat at Via Firenze.'[12] When Derry visited the flat, Snedden acted as guide, but Derry followed him at some distance so as not to compromise the priest's safety.[13] Via Firenze, located in the political and cultural heart of Rome close to German headquarters, was one of the two holding centres where prisoners were processed before being sent on to billets. Although it seemed absurdly dangerous to be right under the Germans' noses, for this same reason it was an unlikely suspect.

In addition to finding safe houses, they conducted a regular food run, carrying food such as broad beans to prisoners. This was usually obtained on the flourishing black market until funds were made available to them. Later they were able to include clothing for their often ragged protegés. Boots were carried under the voluminous cloaks with the laces tied discreetly around their necks. As the priests became more weighed down by their cargo, they began to transport their growing quantities of supplies in a suitcase. It was not considered unusual because, according to Flanagan, everybody had one. But priests increasingly came under suspicion. It was not uncommon for German spies to be planted as clerics who would then lead unsuspecting escapers to arrest.

Amongst the many refugees protected by the Vatican were Jews hiding from German persecution. When the Germans occupied Rome in September 1943 conditions deteriorated sharply. Within a month the Jewish population of the Trastevere was rounded up and 1800 Jews deported. The role of the Pope in actively opposing the genocide committed by the Nazis has been historically controversial. The main criticism has stemmed from his silence in not formally speaking out against the Nazi persecution and destruction of the Jews that he was aware of from the beginning. Although Pius XII condemned the massacre of all civilian victims no matter which side, he chose not to speak out publicly about the atrocities against the Jews. While his detractors believe that to do so could have saved lives, those who support his stance maintain it could have done just the opposite. It is doubtful that the weight of his moral authority would have deterred the Nazis. His motive was to not antagonise the Germans further and risk the occupation of the Vatican territories (which Hitler had initially wanted) and the annexing of the convents and monasteries which hid and protected so many Jews, anti-Fascists, and escaped prisoners-of-war. It was the lesser of two evils. The Germans had agreed to respect the extra-territorial status of the Vatican and all its property.[14] Although a 24-hour guard was maintained around the outside Vatican walls, no Germans were allowed inside without permission. Keeping the Vatican as a sanctuary for persecuted people, regardless of faith, allowed a strong underground movement to flourish. As a consequence, the work of the two New Zealand priests in the Rome Resistance was made easier by their semblance of protected status. Neither Snedden nor Flanagan ever carried identity cards and not once were they stopped as they hurried through the Roman streets, clutching their heavy suitcases.

However, this was a situation fraught with danger, as the Nazis had no qualms about arresting and executing priests if caught red-handed, especially in the latter stages of the occupation in Rome. The Pensione Iaccarino in Via Tasso was notorious as a place of inhumane torture for political prisoners. Presided over by Gestapo thugs and the cruel Italian torturer Pietro Koch, it specialised in inventive and chilling methods of persuasion. Classical music was played to drown out the screams of the victims. Chopin's Prelude No. 15 in D Flat Major was a favourite. The Maltese priest, Robert Pace, code name Whitebows because of the white bows of the De la Salle Order against his black cassock, was taken here and repeatedly tortured. The two Italians captured with him were shot.[15] Father Anselmo Musters (Dutchpa), dragged from the Sacristy of Santa Maria Maggiore, also suffered brutal interrogation and torture without revealing names or addresses.[16] Both priests survived. Koch was alleged to have said that if he ever got hold of O'Flaherty, he would rip his fingernails off before shooting him.[17]

At one point Flanagan helped officiate every Sunday at a small village church in the Via Appia on the outskirts of Rome when the priest in charge was forced into hiding. The day before the Allies entered Rome the Germans were setting up machine-guns round the church.

Rome assumed the status of 'open city', an uneasy agreement promoted by the Pope to protect the city's priceless treasures from aerial bombings. The Allies did not fully subscribe to the 'open city' policy because German military supplies to both the Anzio and Cassino fronts were passing through Roman roads and rail. Although they avoided the centre, civilian casualties resulted from the bombing of German convoys in the outlying districts.[18] In addition, the Germans imposed a harsh regime on citizens, enforcing the strict curfew of 5.30 p.m. The penalty for small violations was death. Yet, if anything, a sense of outrage as much as fear fuelled people. Rome became a hive of intrigue with several underground movements flourishing concurrently. Although politically diverse, they were united in their aim to defeat the Germans.

An unusual feature of the organised help in Rome for escaped prisoners was that many helpers were from the middle and upper classes, and they included several influential names from the Roman aristocracy. Their contacts with the Vatican and traditional friendships with British aristocrats allowed them to operate under a far more powerful cloak of protection than their counterparts in the countryside who were of much humbler social origins, and thus at far greater risk. [19] Understandably, the Vatican took solace from highborn anti-Fascists who promised a post-war Italy that disturbed the status quo as little as possible. Prince Doria Pamphili, later mayor of Rome, and an 'excellent Catholic', was considered by Snedden and Flanagan as an example of the kind of man Italy should look to.[20]

In March 1944 Communist partisans let off a bomb in Via Rasella in central Rome which killed 32 German soldiers. Kesselring exacted a terrible revenge. He ordered ten Italians killed for every German life lost and threw in some more for good measure. Three hundred and sixty-five political and Jewish prisoners were murdered in a brutal mass slaughter in the Ardeatine Caves on the outskirts of Rome. This climate of fear and intimidation affected the Vatican underground which was beginning to be severely depleted. Five of the organisation's agents, including Umberto Lusena, the radio operator captured during a raid, perished in the slaying. Lusena had provided supplies to escapers in the Umbria and Lazio areas and his radio work had led to the evacuation of others.

When some other safe houses were raided and their occupants captured or killed, Snedden set about organising protection in villages outside the city.

It was through his efforts that two New Zealand officers were hidden with a farming family in the village of Montecelio in the hilly countryside north of Rome. His intermediary or *staffetta* was the village district nurse, Concetta Piazza, code name Midwife, who brought messages from Snedden to the two soldiers, Captain 'Blackie' Burns and Lieutenant Ken Phillips. Burns kept one of Snedden's notes written on the page of a small desk calendar. It read, 'For the moment it's imposs. to gain entrance here, but am working for something almost as good. Will let you know as soon as anything is fixed. Sit tight where you are until then and good luck to you.' False papers were eventually organised for the men who arrived in Rome to a safe house organised by Snedden's network. Another note gives similarly cheerful instructions.

'Dear B and Ph, this gent will take you off to a place of safety. I'll probably be along tomorrow with some grub. He is able to fix things, if it is at all possible, to get back soon, so hang for a few days until something is organised. Good luck and best wishes to the lady, also my sincerest thanks.'[21] The 'lady' was the *staffetta*, Concetta Piazza. She was denounced shortly after and imprisoned in the grim Regina Coeli prison. Protesting her innocence, she wrote a letter to Kesselring (smuggled out to the Vatican which acted as intermediary) detailing her efforts in taking care of the health of all, Germans included, in the face of few trained medical personnel, poor sanitation and the danger of an epidemic. The hygiene-conscious German was persuaded and she was released.[22] Before her arrest she wrote on a piece of paper the names of the men who denounced her and gave it to Burns. Tragically, Concetta Piazza is recorded as one of ten women killed by German and Fascist gunfire in April 1944 when they stormed the Tesei bakehouse, supplier of bread to the Germans, protesting the scarcity of flour. This was one of several spontaneous insurrections at the height of the bread shortages led by angry Roman mothers unable to feed their families.[23]

Father Snedden's 'safe house' turned out to be a German monastery, Santa Maria dell' Anima, where the New Zealanders, virtually imprisoned, whiled away their time in company with other refugees. On Sundays they could watch the notorious Field Marshal Kesselring crossing the courtyard for Mass.

Meanwhile Hilary Evans, holed up in a cave at Vallepietra, north-east of Rome, had become the unofficial overseer of the welfare of about thirty-five prisoners of all nationalities hiding in the area. But they lacked finances to purchase enough food, clothing and above all medical supplies, which could be obtained from the Germans by the local doctor. So Evans wrote a letter to the British Embassy, requesting money. He was unsure of the address but the letter was 'secreted on the person of an Italian who looked for all the world like a brigand'.[24] Within five days the man returned with 40,000 lire from Monsignor O'Flaherty in the Vatican.

Living under such stressful conditions took its toll. Both priests went without themselves in order to help others. Photos show the frightening amount of weight both Snedden and Flanagan lost over their nine-month ordeal. At one point Snedden reportedly weighed just seven stone. Yet those who came into contact with them reported them as being consistently cheerful and helpful.

After the Allies occupied Rome on 5 June 1944 the two Kiwis watched the German retreat from a balcony in the Vatican. Later, when the New Zealand troops were established in the Quirinale Hotel, Snedden and Flanagan arranged Papal audiences for those who wanted them, as well as conducting tours through the Vatican and to the catacombs. Evans met the priests personally when he arrived in Rome shortly after the Liberation. He bought a crucifix and a rosary for his wife and records in his diary that he went to the Vatican to get the Pope to bless both.[25]

The priests also organised and took part in activities like picnics and evenings at the opera. Renamed Flanagan and Allan by the soldiers, they joined in all the festivities as Rome embarked on serious celebration. Colin Clayton recalled that there was a connecting passage between the Quirinale and the Opera House. 'Flanagan and Allan entered the Opera House as priests and exited quasi-soldiers in battledress, to continue the evening.[26] An ex-Tui who married in Rome still had in her possession the priests' wedding present decades later – gambling chips and a set of poker dice.

Both priests were given the chance by General Freyberg to return home as military chaplains on the ship the *General John Grant* in 1945. Flanagan's sister remembers his skeletal frame and his difficulty in eating because his stomach had shrunk so much. They were both awarded the MBE for their services to Allied prisoners during their years in Rome. Snedden went on to become editor of the Catholic newspaper, *Zealandia*, for eighteen years and later Auxiliary Bishop of Wellington 1962–1981 as well as Bishop of New Zealand, Military, while Flanagan, appointed secretary to Archbishop Liston, was made a monsignor in 1969. Both men suffered continuing fragile health. Flanagan died in 1977 and Snedden in 1981.

Neither man ever spoke much about the Vatican Resistance, partly because they were under an oath of secrecy, and partly because of their own reticence. Flanagan expressed gratitude that his beloved nieces and nephews would never know hunger, fear and terror.

CHAPTER FIFTEEN

Escape into Switzerland

We arrived at the top of the mountain about 7.30 that evening, January 18 1944. One of our chaps gave up and returned to the rebels. We then had a hair-raising descent through soft snow, ice, then frozen snow, down this 7000-foot mountain. There was no moon and the starlight's reflection on the snow was not illuminating. Moreover, one could not get perspective of the surface to see if a drop was five, ten or fifty feet. The next four hours were the worst I have ever experienced including battle action.[1]

Faded sepia photos show smiling men on skis, who could be thought to be on vacation. There were tales of skiing lessons, toboggan races, ice skating, excursions round picturesque lakes on bicycles, being billeted in chalets and resort hotels and, above all, wonderful food served on tables carefully set with serviettes. The New Zealanders who escaped over the mountains to neutral Switzerland had not experienced anything like it in four long years. But although the men reached safety more swiftly, they remembered their journey over the mountains as one of the toughest experiences of the war.

Of the three routes available to escaped prisoners-of-war, for the great majority of men in northern Italy climbing over the mountains into Switzerland was the best option. Out of 4900 escapers who flooded across the Swiss borders from Italy, only 108 were New Zealanders. This was because the majority of New Zealanders who were in Camp PG57, close to the Yugoslav border, were transferred to Germany *en masse*. Most of the Kiwis who successfully escaped came from the satellite work camps of Camp PG 106 at Vercelli in north-western Italy. Others were from Camp PG 107 and its offshoots round the Lombardy plains north-east of Venice. The main route for the escapers was over the Apennine Alps whose borders in the early months after the Armistice were not patrolled as rigorously as they were later. There were four main areas where the Swiss border verged upon Italy – near Mount Rosa, near Como, near Tirano and near Bormio.[2]

The men who attacked the mountains soon after the Armistice had the benefit of milder weather. Clarence Peagram and David Jacobs had been interned at Camp 106/2 at Arro in the Vercelli province and were among the first New Zealanders to reach Switzerland. The fine weather enabled them to sleep some nights in the open. After crossing the Turin-Novara highway, they headed north-west following a route that took them close to the town of Biella. Having no desire to encounter the German garrison stationed there, they then headed north across the Salussola River to the farming village of Valdengo. Finding it was unsafe to move in the day wearing telltale battledress, they presented themselves at dusk to a farmer who was sharpening his scythe outside his house.

Although Paolo Berghini thought at first they were Germans, once their identity was established he could not do enough to help them. His son Victor was away fighting with the partisans. Clarence Peagram reports, 'We slept in his hayloft for two nights while he made enquiries round the district as to the whereabouts of any Axis troops. He took our army clothes, giving us old civilian suits in return, saw that we had sufficient food, and presented a 100 lire note to each of us before leaving.'[3] The New Zealanders left their kind hosts in pouring rain. They found that their worn civilian clothes tended to attract more attention than battle uniforms in the small villages they had to pass through en route to the mountains. Fortunately they were not alone as many Italian soldiers, hoping to avoid conscription into the newly formed Fascist army, had donned civilian clothes too. The Italian army valises their friends had provided them with may have helped their disguise because although the pair was frequently stopped and questioned, they were always allowed to continue.

Different factions controlled different parts of the route. When they reached the intersection of two main roads on the summit of a particularly steep hill, they were challenged by a band of 'five rough-looking individuals, armed to the teeth, who dashed out from the bush on the roadside'. Once convinced they were escaped prisoners and thus allies, the partisans were very friendly and let them continue. This interception proved to be a lucky break. An old woman had observed the 'interrogation' and had sent her son on his bicycle to warn them that Germans would be passing soon and advise them to return to her place. The boy gestured frantically in his efforts to persuade them.

The men were in a dilemma. What if it was a trap? Notices were posted in all the towns offering a reward of 2000 lire for escaped prisoners and immediate reprisals against any family caught harbouring POWs. The villages were impoverished; Fascists were appearing again. They accepted the invitation on the flimsy premise that luck had been with them so far and returned with the boy to a cluster of shabby houses perched on the side of the hill below the Biella main road. 'Here we found a real welcome awaiting us – a decent meal, a real bed, friendliness and a pleasant smile. These people, poor though they were, did as much for us as we could expect from our own people, especially when it is remembered they were enemies.'[4]

By now the men realised there was little chance of their joining the Allied troops still stuck south of Naples. Their options were to spend winter in the mountains with the partisans, or reach Switzerland. They were put in touch with an Oxford-educated Italian who made arrangements for them to be taken to Switzerland. The trek to reach their guides was exhausting and involved several stages. Their escort, oblivious to their poor physical condition, 'went at a jog trot all the way of about three miles in darkness'. If it were not for his bald head glistening in the faint moonlight they would have lost sight of him. They soon learned their guides were a group of smugglers who added considerably to their income by taking prisoners over the mountains.

The next leg of the trip was by car to Madonna Europa, a Roman Catholic sanctuary high on the slopes of Mount Mucrone. It had over 1200 rooms and was crowned by an enormous dome. Arriving in bright moonlight at such a magnificent building solemnly dedicated to peace seemed a balm of hope in a war-torn world. From there they climbed to a *rifugio* or mountain refuge about 2000 metres further up where, in the next few days, they were joined by British and Australian prisoners-of-war and Italian deserters. Having heard that the Germans were at the bottom of the valley, the men continued north across the mountain chain until they reached a small village about a couple of kilometres south of Gressoney St Jean in the Val d'Aosta. They were dismayed to learn that the Germans 'were in residence' at Gressoney Trinite, another tourist town further down the valley, close to the foot of Mount Rosa. Located here was the pass they needed to cross to begin the final stage of the climb.

On their way again before dawn, they were able to cross the valley and clamber part of the way up the next ridge of about 3300 metres before patrols learnt of their existence. It was not easy to guide ill-equipped, inexperienced young men. The head guide, Leo Colombo, who had fifteen years' experience as an alpine guide, had brought ice axes and ropes. Under his tutelage after a nine-hour climb they reached the peak and were into Swiss territory.[5] But although they were safe from the Germans the exhausted men, now numbering about ten, had a steep glacier to contend with. The guides were about to leave the men to descend on their own, but were prevailed upon by their panic-stricken charges to accompany them down. When Swiss patrol guards at the bottom met them there was still more terrain to cover before they could rest. By this time they were suffering from snow blindness and could hardly remain upright. 'After nineteen hours of the toughest walk I have ever attempted, the mattress placed on the floor was the acme of comfort.' It was 21 September 1943.

Due to an influx of Germans, Douglas Dymock's stint as a carrier in the village of Salussola was short-lived. Joined by his comrades Bill Gyde and George London, he too began his bid for Switzerland in September, when there was very little snow. Because the men were not particularly fit and had inadequate boots, it was hard climbing. There were three mountains to conquer – Mount Maccagno, the Col Turlo and the soaring Mount Moro. Initially they had no guide and followed a trail marked by patches of painted dots on the rocky terrain.

Dymock took the opportunity to buy picture postcards while passing through the small village of Alagna. Although they had deliberated about taking such an obvious route and being observed by numbers of locals, they had no choice. However, it proved fortuitous. They followed the road along a valley that zigzagged up a mountain. After they had reached a stream near a shrine they sat down to have a wash and something to eat. They had just taken off their boots when a panting figure appeared. 'A chap in a suit arrived, collar and tie on, all dressed up, sweating like a pig. He was running. It might have been a couple of miles up this uphill track. It was not steep but quite steep enough, all the way.' He shouted, '*Presto, presto, via via! Tedeschi. Camion.*'[6] A message had arrived with the village telephone operator to say that a truck loaded with Germans was arriving. Their informant insisted on staying until the men pulled their boots on and set off again down the valley. Dymock still wonders at the enormous risk and effort he took to warn them, knowing that had he not done so, their story may have had a different ending.

Not everyone was so forthcoming. Further down the valley they came to a farmhouse where a mother and her three daughters were harvesting potatoes. The women were most reluctant to have them on the property but the three men, by now starving, sat outside the house. 'Eventually the old lady came out with one of these big coppers and it was full of potatoes, and she told us we could eat them. They were obviously on their way to the pigs. They had been cooked so Gyde and I had a good old feed on them. Poor old George said, "Oh no this is gross. I won't eat those." He was very sorry afterwards when she picked up the dish and took it away.'[7]

Making their way up the bare rocky mountains, they knew they were always visible. Fascists regularly scanned the slopes with their binoculars and if anyone were sighted, would send up patrols with bloodhounds to sniff out their prey.[8] Mountain huts vacated by farmers who used to graze their animals during the summer months provided occasional shelter. Here they could sleep relatively comfortably on sack beds. By now they had collected several other fugitives, and for a small sum were guided by a young boy. Their final climb to freedom was up Mount Moro soaring at 2860 metres which they attacked on an empty stomach.

As the men approached the border they feared that the patrolmen with the peaked hats standing on the rock were Italian soldiers. 'This is lovely. We've run into the Italians right on the border.' The Swiss frontier guard was amused. 'We've been watching you for two hours and we could have picked you off as easy as.' Dymock was sceptical. 'And we laughed because you only had to fire one shot and you wouldn't have seen any of those guys again.'[9]

Although Ian St George and his companions Gordon McLeod and Rex Ryman did not have the right clothing and were not in good physical shape, they were so close to Switzerland near the Tirano border they knew they had to try. Their repaired boots, with new cardboard innersoles, did not bode well for the rocky, snowy conditions. 'We seemed to go on and on forever in and out of crevasses and ridges and eventually came down to the pine tree line. Snow had covered these and the going was tough – one step in the wrong place and down we would go. Clamber out from a great heap of branches on to the surface again, before taking another step.'[10]

The scenery in the Swiss mountains was stunning. Despite the hard climb, the men took time out to admire the panoramic views which were the most beautiful they had seen since leaving the shores of New Zealand. Ian St George wished he had had a camera to record the majestic snow-capped peaks, sweeping valleys and viaducts looming before him. As they climbed the air grew thinner, making it hard to breathe. They were guided part of the way by a young man, possibly a smuggler, who knew the borders intimately. When they parted ways, he left them with a small pick which enabled them to make footholds in the steep icy slopes and thus survive the most dangerous part of their trek. The bottle of wine on St George's back was frozen. At the border a young Swiss patrolman in a green uniform, not unlike that of the Germans, approached them. When they told him in their best Italian who they were the Swiss replied in perfect English: 'You are most welcome.'

For Laurie Read, whose ordeal over Mount Moro occurred at the height of a bitter winter, the descent down the mountain in pitch darkness was pure hell. He describes it as the worst experience of the war, including battle action. The New Zealander had survived bayonet attacks in the North African desert and had been fired at by his own side. He had emerged from the torpedoing of the prisoner transport ship, *Jantzen*, and had experienced various levels of hunger in prison camps, to say nothing of life on the run as an escaped prisoner. Most recently he had fought with a Garibaldi partisan brigade under the redoubtable Moscatelli against the Nazis at their most implacable and brutal. These enemies, however terrifying, were clearly visible and, thus known, could be confronted squarely. As it turned out, however, the invisibility of their mountain route, although psychologically gruelling, was a blessing in disguise. 'If seen by daylight what we were to go through I am sure most of us would not have made it.'[11]

On their trek Read and his companions found themselves sinking into snow that reached their thighs. Walking was extremely difficult and was accomplished by a curious motion, whereby one leg was lifted and put down in the snow before the other leg could be swung round to join it, all the while inching downwards. Negotiating sheets of ice and frozen snow interspersed with pockets of soft snow, they slipped and slid sometimes 10 metres down rock faces, never knowing what they might find at the bottom. 'My personal apprehension was to slip on ice or a rock face, or over a ledge, then to be covered by snow and unable to climb back up an icy face,' wrote Read with customary straightforwardness about the grim prospect of being buried alive.

A man next to him shouted he was slipping and disappeared into the black chasm. He was picked up 'a bundle of nerves' further down the mountain. Total exhaustion and despair overcame another who lay down in the snow and refused to get up. 'We had to kick him repeatedly until he did get up through sheer rage; then one of us on each side assisted him down the mountain to a disused hut.'[12]

On 20 January before dawn they arrived in the town of Borgosesia. Factories worked ceaselessly throughout the night and, as the party crept along the railway line, the lights from the windows threw up their shadows as grotesque shapes against the opposite wall. Their guide, a woman partisan, secured them some bread and meat extract before accompanying them to a stable where they rested under dry leaves for the day. At night it was time to move on and they set out along the railway line, which snaked through a long dark tunnel. Enveloped in a pitch-blackness so thick you could slide a knife through it, the group travelled in silence, 'each holding the chap in front for guidance'. They had just emerged from the tunnel when a train hurtled past. As Read threw himself flat on the ground, he thanked his lucky stars it had not arrived five minutes earlier. They traipsed through valleys and up hills, sleeping in stables, eking out the last of their rations. Their current guide's shoes were falling apart and with every footprint he left a trail of blood. Chewing frozen snow to ward off the aching hunger, they elatedly crossed the border into Switzerland on Sunday 22 January 1944. 'We knew we were in Switzerland by the length of the cigarette ends lying about!'

Paul Day was one of the few lucky ones who made it to Switzerland as late as June 1944 after nine months on the loose. He was unique in that he had no guide and was, on the last leg of the journey alone, armed only with a sketch map and his knowledge of the Italian language.

Day paired up with Ernie Clarke and they set off through the villages then came down the valley to Pieve di Cadore, full of Germans patrolling up and down the borders and therefore to be skirted circumspectly. They passed through another village where the whole population made spectacle lenses. They could not figure out how to get through Predazzo, a ski resort swarming with Germans, and decided that blending in with the locals was the only way. One helper told them that on the outskirts of the town were small allotments where people grew produce and regularly tended their gardens. He gave them a spade and a rake and told them to take off their jackets, hang them over their shoulders and walk through the town as if they were setting off to their *orto*. This they proceeded to do without being noticed.[13]

What worked in one location did not in another. 'You're prisoners, aren't you?' was the greeting of a small man drinking wine in a hostelry to the by now ragged New Zealanders. 'You'll never get across the Valle d'Adige dressed like that.' He told them to wait a few days while he got them some decent clothes. In another small-town tavern they ran into some 'pushy' partisans whom Day believed must have been from a Garibaldi division. Arrayed with knives, tommy-guns and bandoleras, these men invited them in no uncertain terms to join them. 'But we've just left your crowd,' was the response. Things were getting a bit 'sticky' when the formidable Anna Pozza entered the scene and demanded, 'What are these wops trying to do to you boys?' She was one of many English-speaking Italian emigrants encountered by escapers and had returned to Italy from America before the war to take up family land. Others had left to avoid being interned as enemy aliens. In Day's report for the Allied Screening Commission she is listed as having provided him and Clarke with food and lodging for two weeks.[14] She may even have saved their lives. Two prisoners who had passed through a week before had gone up to the partisans and been shot as suspected German spies. Day suspects they were Paul and 'Teddy', the South African and the German deserter, both never heard of again after they left the partisan hideaway. For Day, tall and blue-eyed, his hair bleached white-blond by the alpine sun, it was a very real threat that he too could be taken as a German.

They shared a delicious meal of fried liver with two partisans who had just shot a goat. Then just out of Bormio both men wondered if it was safer to separate and go singly. Soon they were faced with swimming the River Adda. They took off all their clothes and plunged in, holding their garments high above their heads. Somehow they lost each other.

Day looked for Ernie Clarke on the other side but to no avail. He was on his own.

Eventually Day reached a huge amphitheatre, temporary home to a gypsy encampment thronging with women and babies, horses and carts. The gypsies were hostile to the stranger, shooing him away, but not before one man told him he would find a place to stay if he kept on the same path. As Day 'plugged on', exhausted and starving, it started to rain. Darkness fell and through the driving rain he saw a glimmering pinpoint of light emanating from a hut in the distance. A woman who had brought up twelve cows to graze lived there with her five children. She was on the brink of giving birth again. Day cannot forget how she received him, sodden and hungry as he was, asking for shelter.

'I can't describe her manner. It was as if she had been waiting for me. I suppose the answer was that in those areas prisoners were coming and going all the time. So it was not a surprise. The effect on me was absolutely startling.'[15] She gave him food and a bed after turning out one of her children to top and tail with a sibling. The next morning she woke him at 5 a.m. and sent him on his way with a bottle of coffee and a hunk of bread and cheese.

There was one more mountain to scale, Mt Dosdè. 'Treacherous and slippery and rocky. My main fear was that I'd slip and break a leg. It grew misty and I couldn't see a thing.' Day's first glimpse of Switzerland from the top of the mountain was unforgettable. He arrived at a sharp-edged junction between two peaks. 'Just then the mist parted. I saw two lakes beside each other so I thought that's Switzerland!'

Upon reaching Switzerland, several men needed to be hospitalised suffering from bouts of malaria caught in the canal area round Venice. Laurie Read required urgent dental treatment. But life was generally pleasant. Dymock, London and Gyde lived in a disused factory and took walking trips in the summer and skied in the winter. London, Mayor of Petone before the war and a gifted public speaker, gave talks on New Zealand to escaped servicemen. Others had skills that could be utilised. Because he could speak French, Paul Day was sent to Geneva to work on a handbook for the restoration of European universities.

The influx of nearly 5000 Allied escaped prisoners over its borders after 8 September had initially put a strain on Swiss resources. To meet these difficulties Britain allowed sufficient supplies of food and clothing to reach Switzerland and guaranteed some form of authority would be maintained over the escapers who were technically free men. But it was the Italian Resistance which largely undertook the dangerous groundwork of getting the men into Switzerland. It was no accident when Ian St George's group encountered an Italian alerted to their 'English' appearance, who arranged food and accommodation, then pointed them in the right direction. He pulled up some floorboards in his office and showed them a list of escaped prisoners he had helped. Several were New Zealanders.

One of the terms of the Armistice was that the Italian government should give all assistance possible to prisoners-of-war. A special Service of Assistance to Allied POWs was set up by the military wing of the National Committee of Liberation in Milan. Its co-ordinator was a Resistance hero, Ferruccio Parri, leader of the democratic Action Party, who was to become Italy's first post-war Prime Minister. [16] He appointed a Milan engineer, Giuseppe Bacciagaluppi, managing director of the Standard Electric Corporation factory and married to an Englishwoman, as director of the operation. [17] This organisation liaised with local CLN groups, Allied personnel and underground networks. Just about every escaped prisoner who remained at large would, however indirectly, have come under its influence.

Its primary task was to direct the escaped prisoners-of-war into Switzerland as this was the most expedient way of dealing with the welfare of men hidden in houses or at large in the countryside. To achieve this, a network of agents, guides, escorters, interpreters and occasional collaborators were organised, in addition to safe houses, money, transport, false documents, clothing, footwear and supplies. Contacts with the Swiss border were maintained by agents who controlled and paid the guides, organised the false identity cards and discharge forms, and ensured proper attention to the prisoners at the frontier stations. Finding the funds to finance such an operation was the most difficult task in the early months. Yet the organisation ran efficiently until the Germans began to intensify their roundups, applying stricter checks at frontier crossings and occupying garrisons in mountain towns close to the border. As more informants reported helpers of the prisoners to the Fascist authorities, greater losses among the agents were incurred. Bacciagaluppi's arrest in April 1944 was a critical point for the organisation and the numbers of men reaching Switzerland from then on decreased sharply.[18]

Although Bacciagaluppi survived imprisonment, his successors were not so lucky. A liaison agent and guide called Sergio Kasman, an Action Party underground commandant of the Milan Piazza, who replaced Bacciagaluppi as Chief of Service, was killed in an ambush in December 1944, while his assistant chief, Dario Tarantino, who then took over, was shot in January 1945. Many others were wounded, deported or imprisoned. The escaped prisoners could not have achieved their nerve-wracking mountaineering feat without this highly organised network, bravely assisted by countless ordinary people who provided the eyes and the ears, the shelter and food, which sustained and ultimately saved them.

CHAPTER SIXTEEN

Getting out

The truck with two men in it pulled up and they didn't
know whether to shoot us or what the bloody hell to do.
And then we spoke and then they said, where the bloody
hell you bastards been? I said I've been waiting to hear from
you for four years.'

Italy was conquered inch by inch. For those hiding in central Italy, their
ordeal finished in the summer of 1944 after the May breakthrough at
Cassino, which was followed by the liberation of Rome in June and
Florence in July. Maurice Cosgrave was living in the town of Comunanza
sheltered by the Bianchi family when the Allies arrived. Soon afterwards
he bicycled down to the coast from Ascoli on a forage for food and
cigarettes. But his real purpose was to get some medicine for a sick New
Zealander in the hospital at Comunanza as the nuns had run out of
supplies. 'It was a bad situation. There were shells going off – bang, bang,
bang – to the north of us. And I found these bloody Americans working
in an ice-cream factory. So I put it to one and he says, "Say, I'm too busy. I

gotta get this goddamned ice-cream factory going. Our boys can't fight without their ice-cream!'"[2]

He was watching from a hillside as retreating Germans passed by, throwing away their packs and rifles. 'A wonderful sight, a glorious sight.' He caught a lift, passing through Perugia and Rome, then hitchhiked down to Naples to join the New Zealanders. At the reception depot in Naples he wrote a report on his experiences. One evening an Englishman walked in. He was responsible for the execution of the two prisoners witnessed by Cosgrave in the cemetery. 'And the Poms are smart. They put two and two together and then three and three. There was a court-martial in the night and he was shot in the morning. Justice.'

For the New Zealanders north of the Gothic Line, their lives as fugitives lasted as long as the war. Bill Black remained with the partisans until the end. Although it was usual to send men out, those who were viewed as useful stayed. His reunion with his old division was as bizarre as any of his other experiences. It was April 1945 and the Allied troops had made headway north. From a vantage point at the top of a mountain he suddenly noticed 'that the Canadians were underneath us'. He and an English companion walked down to join them and 'got awfully pissed with these blokes'. Among the convoys of trucks heading for Trieste, Black decided to try and find the New Zealanders. To his amazement a Kiwi truck from his old division, the 25th Battalion, approached him as he was walking along the road.

'I thought uh oh, because we were pretty rugged. We had dirty big beards on and red scarves for the Nino Nanetti Division. [We were] partisans with big red scarves and Lugers on our hips and we had all sorts of machine-gun pistols. We were a real rough-looking outfit.' The truck with two men in it pulled up 'and they didn't know whether to shoot us or what the bloody hell to do. And then we spoke and then they said, where the bloody hell you bastards been? I said I've been waiting to hear from you for four years. And the bloke said, who the hell are you? And I said I'm Bill Black. And he said where the hell did you come from? I said from Napier. He said is that right? You wouldn't happen to have a sister called Nola and a sister called Joyce would you? And I said, yeah. And he said, well I used to work with them. He said Joyce has got herself engaged to a bloke called Roy Faulkner and he says Nola has taken her job and I've come over here to look for you. And I said, well, you wouldn't have a smoke, would you?'[3]

A select group of men were successfully evacuated by motor torpedo submarine from beaches south of Caorle on the Veneto plains to the port of Ancona in the Marches. Arch Scott co-ordinated these evacuations, known as the Nelson Expedition, with the assistance of Italian partisans equipped with radio-transmitters, in particular Guido Barbieri, an engineer from Milan who networked with the British missions. Don Fausto Moschetta, the priest of San Giorgio di Livenza, also took an active part in the operation, putting up the partisans in his house.[4] It was a difficult task. Getting even a limited number of men from different directions to the rendezvous at the coast, about sixteen kilometres away across canals, swampy plains and open roads, was extremely dangerous. Although by this time the Allied armies had liberated much of the Italian peninsula, it had the effect of pushing retreating, often embittered German soldiers further north. Martial law was enforced even more severely. For the escapers life was more restricted and their families more frightened as the numbers of Germans concentrated in one area increased at an alarming rate. Such a tricky operation needed to be accomplished with as much stealth as possible at night.[5] As a result, some men, to their distress, had to leave without saying goodbye to their families, a seemingly ungrateful move after nearly eighteen months' protection.

There were four evacuations between March and April of 1945. Of the forty-seven evacuated, twenty-nine were New Zealanders. Several evacuations were aborted at the last moment because of unexpected movements of Germans or poor weather conditions which prevented the motor torpedo boat from arriving. The third evacuation was the most difficult because the men came from further afield. John Senior and his companions Toby Pearce, Roy Ryan and Dave Taylor came out on this trip. Their first attempt was aborted because the gusting wind made the sea too rough for the craft to land. Also, Allied planes were roaring overhead, dropping flares that lit up the whole area and sent the men diving for cover until they burned out. At first they thought they were German searchlights. A few days later on 10 April they tried again. Partisans were always present, often in disguise. As they were walking in single file along a road, Senior recalls a tall Italian man in a mule-driven cart heading in the opposite direction. Later they were told that he was there to protect them. Hidden in the cart were stacks of machine-guns.[6]

The men lay waiting on the beach as Guido Barbieri flashed the torch. Eventually a reply signal came and two groups of British seamen appeared from the gloom towing a line of inflatable rubber dinghies laden with equipment. The partisans unloaded their cargo of machine-guns, ammunition and radio equipment. Then it was time to leave. Each boat could take only three men at a time. Ryan rowed while Senior directed him through choppy seas to the side of the motor torpedo boat.

Roy Johnston came out with the fourth and last batch on Friday 13 April. In this case there was no secrecy and he had time to say goodbye to his beloved family. They insisted on holding a public bathing ceremony where he and Giacomo were required to strip and wash themselves. The big copper vat was taken out only on ceremonial occasions such as killing the pig. 'We were surprised. The other guys who went aboard before us must have smelt pretty badly!'[7] However, this ablution ceremony was more a symbolic handing over of their charges as well turned out as possible to reflect favourably on the family's care of them. Then, guided by their partisan contact, Severino Zoccerato, they left at dusk on a devious route where they crossed a number of canals and aqueducts, even creeping past German barracks full of noisy troops. Someone flicked a lamp, giving a pre-arranged signal, and again inflatable rubber boats were towed in to the beach. Johnston recalls the derisive anger of some of his companions when a British major stepped out of one of the rubber boats dressed in full livery. A barrage of abuse greeted him. ' "What do you think you are doing, you silly bastard! Do you think you're in Piccadilly? This place is alive. You can't wear a uniform here." The poor old major must have thought New Zealanders were very rude!'[8]

The boats drifted out with the men paddling aimlessly. However, as Johnston soon realised, precision was unnecessary as the torpedo boat was steering towards them, using radar to pick up their position. The commander of the torpedo boat, 'an Aussie redheaded skipper naturally called Blue', was horrified at roll call to find that among the newcomers on board was a deserter from the German Army. 'Willy', an Austrian sergeant major, had been living with two South African evaders in an Italian family. Although harmless, he knew too much about the clandestine operations to be left behind; the partisans would not hear of it. 'The commander said this was a top security scheme and the navy's going to have kittens. And we said yes, yes, we realised that and we'd leave that to the shore men to deal with.' Roy Johnston had befriended the German who spoke no English. They communicated in their common language, the Venetian dialect. When a beautiful breakfast of New Zealand biscuits, butter and cheese was laid out for their consumption at Ancona, he was convinced it was all propaganda. 'He still believed Nazi brainwashing that the Allies were all starving.'[9]

Johnston wanted assurances that Willy would receive good treatment. If put in a camp with other German prisoners he may have been roughed up. 'The reaction of these base wallahs to us marching in with a German sergeant major was too much. They phoned desperately for the military police to come so we insisted on getting him a good supply of cigarettes.'

The change from being an Italian peasant to the form and structure of the Allied military was at first disorienting. The men spoke broken English and had to consciously 'unlearn' mannerisms such as hand gestures that were by now second nature to them. When Roy Johnston had to give a speech thanking the pursers, he began speaking in English and then lapsed into Italian. 'It was embarrassing. You'd suddenly flip to the other side. I finished what I was saying with *arrivederci, addio*.'[10]

John Senior was threatened with arrest for insubordination when he asked a woman Royal Air Force officer walking towards him in Ancona if she spoke English. He apologised, attributing his indiscretion to not having heard a woman speak in English for four years. When he tried to impress some Italians with his command of their language, the response was hostile. 'The antisocial locals didn't want a bar of us, as their proud city had been bombed and left in tatters.'[11] For a time they felt as if they did not fit in anywhere.

At the repatriation centre they were relieved of their clothes, showered, deloused, given medical attention if warranted, issued with uniforms, some money, and interviewed. According to Johnston, 'We were debriefed – as it were. I don't know if anyone took that very seriously. However, we did settle into some serious drinking.'

The policy of the Repatriation Unit stationed at Resina (now called Ercolano) near Naples was to transfer the ex-prisoners-of-war back to New Zealand as quickly as possible. Only in a handful of cases were they allowed to stay. First they were sent to England where they were billeted with families. Then they were put on a ship bound for New Zealand. Many of the men who successfully escaped out of Italy were back in New Zealand before the end of 1944.

The encounter with military authority was exasperating for the escapers. The men had been making their own decisions and surviving on their wits for too long to be impressed with expectations of deference to rank or regulations that for them had no meaning. Inevitably, the ex-prisoners disliked having their welfare organised by people they felt had no understanding of what they had been through. The interrogation services had little information on what had been happening behind the lines as much of it was still top-secret. As a consequence, they did not always believe what they heard until they received corroborating information. This questioning of the authenticity of their experiences caused misunderstanding and resentment and some ex-prisoners were scathing of the service.[12]

In their turn, staff at the Repatriation Unit were exasperated by the unruly and hard-case behaviour of some of the men. Entertainment and relaxation were the order of the day and a few exploits got out of hand. Although it was acknowledged that these men had been under considerable strain, there were none of the facilities to deal with the effects of prolonged stress that are available today.[13] Wally Willis, fresh from his award-winning performance before the SS in the Udine jail, was given a clean bill of health and sent on his way:

Report on Walter Willis 25 May 1945:
1. Good physical condition although slightly underweight.
2. Mental condition. He is frank, reasonable and consistent in his statements and did not show any unusual or exaggerated emotional reaction. He shows no dangerous tendency such as suicidal intent or persecution fears. In my opinion he remains Grade A.[14]

The effect of their experiences did not register until later. Tony Jacobs in a letter to a nephew twenty-five years on writes, 'I spent four months [in England] before going back to New Zealand none the worse for my experience, not then anyhow.'[15]

Many men wished to return to their Italian families in the north to ensure they received credit for having looked after them. They wanted to thank them properly and let them know they had reached safety. John Senior and his comrades, worried about what had happened to their families, seriously considered returning to San Giorgio di Livenza. His concern was justified. Shortly after he left, a German SS officer harshly interrogated Ines Martin for several hours on their whereabouts. She could not reveal what she did not know and says she would have refused to anyway.[16] Senior also wanted to help secure the release of Gastardo Borin from the prison in Portogruaro. Information on his activities had been passed on to the German command and he had been arrested. Men like Borin were in danger from both Fascist and partisan reprisals. Senior was persuaded to remain, but for others the urge to return was strong, and they absented themselves without permission.

For the Italian families, saying goodbye to young men who had lived in their homes for over a year was heart-breaking. Most of the men promised to return when they could. Some even left an item of personal worth such as a wristwatch as proof of their good intentions. Many hoped to recompense their families by leaving chits detailing the help given. Few Italian families professed to care about monetary payment as they said they did it out of the goodness of their hearts for another human being. However, many did receive a small amount of compensation from the Allied Screening Commission, a body set up to reimburse Italians for the assistance given to the escaped prisoners when they could ill afford it. For most, receiving the Alexander Certificate, a personal written acknowledgement by General Alexander, commander of the Allied Troops, of the assistance given to prisoners was thanks enough.[17] Issued in English and Italian, it is a treasured memento for many families, handed down to each new generation.

But some ex-prisoners were never heard of again and their Italian helpers felt hurt that they could not find the time to let them know if they had arrived safely. This was the case where prisoners had remained with families for some weeks or months. Men deliberately did not carry the addresses of their families for fear of compromising them if they were caught. Postcards and letters were exchanged but some went unanswered because people had moved, or for the simple fact they did not understand each other's language. Luciano Franzin recalls, 'My mother used to say, "I have never known whether my husband died for something or if he died for nothing." This is because afterwards we never saw any of the men my father helped. And she was sad when she thought of this because it was unthinkable that he had died in vain.'[18] However, they found out later that several men had tried to contact his mother but were unable to trace her, as the family had long since moved from the area. The emotional meeting with Arch Scott in 1995 laid to rest Franzin's doubts. Scott told him he had always thought of his father in gratitude and prayed for him.

Angelo Antonel would speak for the majority of helpers when he said they did not expect it to go on for as long as it did, but they had the satisfaction of a job well done. 'It was very hard for us because we were very poor. But we succeeded in sending both our prisoners back safe and sound to New Zealand.' Scott promised to send him a rugby ball when he returned home. After some months the ball arrived. 'It was the most

This certificate is awarded to

Dio Attilio

as a token of gratitude for and
appreciation of the help given to the
Sailors, Soldiers and Airmen of the
British Commonwealth of Nations,
which enabled them to escape from, or
evade capture by the enemy.

H. R. Alexander

Field-Marshal,
Supreme Allied Commander,
Mediterranean Theatre

1939-1945

A copy of the Alexander Certificate awarded to helpers. Italian and
English versions were on the one copy.

wonderful present he could have given me. Every evening we used to have a game of rugby.'[19]

Throughout 1944 the New Zealand military had been keeping track of some of the escaped prisoners by means of fragmented reports from the field. They were alarmed at the more unorthodox experiences. The greatest irritant seemed to be that some of these soldiers while roaming the countryside had committed the unpardonable sin of jumping rank. One such report dryly comments: 'TRR Natusch Roy Spencer suspected of using the rank of captain while escaping. (He was captured in Greece.) He admits to being a sapper. "Captain" Natusch said he used the rank for purposes while escaping.'[20] This was considered cheek of the highest order. Colonel Ross Greening, the American airman who shared the cave in the mountains with New Zealanders Jack Lang and Bob Smith, writes of his first meeting with them.

'I liked these fellows the moment I set eyes on them. Both were enlisted men, but one was passing himself off as a major and the other as a captain, because they received better treatment if people thought they were officers. Actually, Bob was a sergeant major and Jack a private.'[21]

This was extremely common. Many of the men who distinguished themselves during their time in Italy were of lowly rank. Being at large in enemy territory required skills of quick-wittedness, flexibility and endurance. Assuming an officer's rank was thus a strategy for survival rather than a deliberate impertinence to the military. People were more trusting of those who ostensibly held military rank and, if caught, they were likely to be treated better. Declaring himself an officer saved Private Frank Gardner's life. Men in those conditions were a world away from the concerns of military propriety.

In the partisan formations soldiers of lowly rank were reported as having jumped to the status of major or captain. But within an independent newly formed fighting force the rules had changed, and partisans assumed positions according to leadership and ability. To have any trained soldier on board was a plus when there were youngsters who had never held a gun before.

Those men who, having reached Switzerland, wished to stay and put some of the knowledge and skills they had acquired to good use, were rebuffed from the outset. The application for an ex-prisoner to remain employed in the Embassy in Switzerland was received frostily: 'Unless it can be stated that the work on which Signalman Higgins is employed is of vital importance, he should be repatriated at the first opportunity. Experience has shown that unless in a few cases, it is in the best interests of the ex-PW to repatriate him as quickly as possible and it is the policy of this HQ to refuse all applications from ex-PW to serve again in this theatre.'[22] Ex-prisoners were considered to be suffering from 'POW-itis', a condition involving being nervous, highly strung and unpredictable. This was not surprising given the enormous stress prisoners were under for such long periods of time. A lack of respect for authority was evident too after months, sometimes years, of acting independently and living side by side with others on equitable terms. One gunner was reported absent without leave from an Allied ex-PW repatriation camp after he turned up at a New Zealand VD treatment centre on 5 September 1944. He handed in a document which said, 'Tell the sergeant that this is the last he will see of me.'[23]

Fighting with the partisans was also regarded with a jaundiced eye, not least because corporals were reported fighting under the rank of captain. One document from a wing commander is eloquent in its testy demand for clarification.

Information has been received from the field that:
48004 Signaller S. B. Macfarlane, 25 Bn NZ EF is fighting with the Garibaldi Brigade.
???????????[24]

Men who stayed to fight were suspected of having ulterior motives. On 20 June 1945 a report in response to two ex-prisoners working with the Ferret Mission stationed at Biella stated: 'It is highly desirable that these men be evacuated to repatriation camps in southern Italy at the earliest possible moment. The retention of them in their present occupations can only lead to further complications and we have already had the case of New Zealanders marrying enemy aliens after the cessation of hostilities.'[25]

Of course this was the biggest headache for the army – what their boys might be up to with the enemy. Not unnaturally, liaisons occurred when men were taken into families with daughters and all the Italian men away.

The escaped prisoners-of-war who were not recovered were thought to belong to two categories. The first category was being employed with a British Unit liaising or fighting with the partisans, and the second was perceived as having no desire to come out. Those in the first category were to be sent to a repatriation unit as soon as possible, while those in the second were faced with necessary 'drastic action' such as being arrested, charged and having their army pay docked. The reasons why some POWs did not want to return were given as, 'Women mainly, lack of transport and being reasonably treated.'[26] There was some truth in this. Six New Zealanders at large in Italy who remained unaccounted for are recorded as 'fate unknown'.[27] A small but significant number of men from all Allied countries simply disappeared and were never heard of again. Some may have died but others are suspected to have permanently assumed their Italian identities, married Italian girls and stayed.[28] The warmth and sense of belonging they experienced in their rural Italian families surpassed anything they had ever known in their own countries.

The army, however, was very reluctant to grant men permission to marry Italian women. In Walter Willis's file the observation is typical: 'Experience over the past 12 months has taught us that men who desire to remain behind in enemy territory invariably wish to do so for some private and personal reason. In the majority of cases the reason is a woman.'[29] Certainly there were a flood of requests. Some soldiers got married anyway while at large. One Kiwi explains why to a no doubt livid military after they caught up with him some three months after the end of the war. 'When I was short of food she gave [it] to me and she also gave us the BBC News every night. When the war was over she kept me in food and clothing until 28 July. On 9 July she told me she was pregnant, and I was married on 21 July.'[30]

These relationships begun in clandestine conditions were a natural consequence of young people thrown together in charged, dramatic conditions. The young men from a foreign country who were given shelter in barns, haystacks or makeshift huts and caves were hungry, tired and dependent on the people around them. In those early months after the Armistice, most Italian men were away fighting with the partisans or the Fascist *repubblichini* or alternatively, they were in hiding to avoid both. All the men noticed how hard the women worked in the fields and in the home. They observed that women would eat in another room after serving the men, generally playing a subservient role. The men were grateful for every kindness shown them and particularly for the food that was regularly brought to them. Women washed, darned, sewed and cooked for them. After years in male company such female nurturing was a balm for tightrope emotions. Men like Frank Gardner and Walter Willis lived for many months in the houses of these families and it was not surprising that genuine love affairs would flourish in these circumstances.

Yet they were aware of the pitfalls. Maria Cusin considered Arch Scott and Noel Sims true gentlemen towards the girls. 'They would often say that the girls of San Stino were very beautiful and when I asked them why they wouldn't marry one after the war, they replied that they couldn't because they would have to take them back to New Zealand. It would mean tearing them away from their families to go to a distant country and they would have most certainly suffered homesickness.'[31] Jack Lang and Bob Smith invented wives back home as a way of maintaining trust and not raising hopes. They knew that they could not afford to trample on the sensibilities of those whose help ensured their survival.

Giulia Leder is a beautiful, dignified woman of ninety. Her daughter Pierina is the daughter too of a New Zealand escaper, who lived in the Leder household at Annone Veneto for fourteen months. He fully intended to marry Giulia Leder, aged thirty-four at the time, having converted to Roman Catholicism and gained the permission of the Italian government. He was reluctant to leave but after the Liberation all prisoners-of-war were expected to report to the Repatriation Centre. He delayed until July when the military sent a car to collect him and he left promising to return to marry her. A report of his interview conducted on 13 July 1945 at the New Zealand Repatriation Centre at Resina near

Naples confirms the seriousness of his intentions. '[He] states that he is very keen to marry the girl and that he is expecting a family in approximately six months time and wants to marry before this event. He also states that he is determined to proceed further with his application on arriving in the UK, and seems to be genuine in his case. According to his own statement he is forty-two years of age and seems to be of a steady consistent nature.'[32] Permission was never granted, even in a case as deserving as Walter Willis's. Men were sent to England, then shipped back to New Zealand where, if they were still keen, they could apply as civilians. Although he continued to write from England, letters only arrived much later due to poor communication services. Leder could not trace him. Soon there was silence and Giulia Leder never heard from her lover again, nor tried to contact him. She named her daughter Pierina, which is the feminine version of 'little Peter' in Italian. After some years she destroyed all the photos. She lives with her brother in the same house at Annone Veneto. She never married nor had another relationship.[33]

Despite the tolerance shown to the thousands of illegitimate children born in any war (known as *figli della guerra*, or war children), Pierina observes, 'It has not been easy for me to be an illegitimate child growing up in the Italy of more than fifty years ago. In the same way it was difficult for my mother. These feelings have always been kept secret, reserved. The figure of an unknown father, who lived far away, accompanied many fantasies of my childhood and adolescence. Finding a sense of balance and detachment has been a difficult struggle.'[34]

The bureaucratic logistics of obtaining permission to marry 'an enemy alien' obviously defeated some men in the end. Furthermore, the impact of their former way of life may have convinced them that they could not share such a different culture with their Italian sweethearts. Their lives in rural wartime Italy must have receded into the semblance of a dream as they faced the challenges of 'normal life'.

CHAPTER SEVENTEEN

Liberation

*I have been told that **PW** are demobilised as soon as they get home. If possible I would remain here as a civilian then pay my own way home.*[1]

Arch Scott came out, albeit reluctantly, in the fourth evacuation. All his 'cobbers' of the Hare Battalion had gone and he felt he had done his duty by them. After two years of running away from the enemy and practising non-violence so as not to bring retribution to Italian friends, he was itching to get back into what he called real action and was delighted to be seconded to the American Office of Strategic Services (OSS) where plans were made to drop him behind the lines to fight with the partisans. However, after three unsuccessful attempts, much to his disappointment this was abandoned. Scott then drove up north with the advancing Allied army in a small easily manoeuvrable Jeep that overtook the lumbering tanks. In no time at all they made it back to San Stino di Livenza where he was able to reunite with the Antonel family and explain his hasty departure.

Spurred on by the Allied victories, the partisans had regrouped in massive numbers after a difficult winter and set about capturing towns and villages from their German occupiers. By the time the troops of the Fifth and Eighth Armies arrived, they had freed just about every major northern city and some 40,000 German prisoners were handed over. Genoa and Venice had been captured in fierce fighting and the German commanders had formally surrendered to the partisans. Both Frank Gardner and Walter Willis assisted partisans in takeovers in their towns. Under the direction of the CLN, democratic administration services were set up and were already effectively operating by the time the Allies entered the scene. Partisans were also largely responsible for preventing the Germans carrying out a scorched earth policy as they retreated by sabotaging ports, bridges, electric power plants, dams and industries, many of which had already been mined. Bruno Bisioli felt sorry for the departing Germans, anxious to be taken prisoner by the Allies rather than fall into partisan hands. On 28 April, Mussolini fled disguised as a German soldier. He was intercepted by partisans, given a summary trial and executed with his mistress Clara Petacci.[2]

Under the terms of the agreement with the Allies signed in December 1944, the CLN ordered that Italian partisans disband and surrender their arms. Control of the cities was handed over to the Allied Military Government in Occupied Territory (AMGOT) in order to oversee the return to civilian life. Due to his language skills and his reputation among the people, Arch Scott became acting military governor of Portogruaro and of the nearby town of San Donà di Piave. When Harold Lavendar, the official military governor, took over, Scott remained for three months as assistant and interpreter. One of their tasks was to preside over an informal court in the municipal halls where people could bring their problems and be helped or referred to another body. Each day there was a long line of Italians waiting.

The more militant partisans were reluctant to surrender their arms. There were scores to be settled. Ian St George heard that the postman suspected of betraying escapers from Camp 107/4 was 'dealt to' by peasants. Thousands of reprisals were carried out on Fascists, some of which amounted to lynchings. Novella Bigotto saw a man hanged from a tree.

At the first attempt the rope broke and the man fell, still alive. A woman, a mother of ten, went to her shed and got a thick rope used to tether the cow. 'This will do the job better,' she said.[3] For these crimes some partisans were brought to trial and received lengthy prison sentences.

After the Liberation, Ciprian, the mechanic of Prati Nuovi who rescued Paul Day and Martin Hodge, was arrested by partisans and imprisoned at Portogruaro. According to his sons he would have been executed by a summary tribunal but for the arrival of Hodge after his adventures in Yugoslavia.[4] However, Bruno Bisioli testifies that it was his partisan father, the overseer, who accompanied 'Martino' to the prison in Portogruaro, and while the New Zealander used his influence with the Allied command, Bisioli negotiated with the partisans for Ciprian's release. Such arbitrary arrests were common in the heady climate immediately following the Liberation. These were often meted out to known Blackshirts involved in hit squads which used to attack anti-Fascists, beating them up and administering doses of castor oil. The hit men would descend on people in towns outside of their zone. Carrying out 'actions' on strangers spared them from beating up their friends and co-workers. In several homes Arch Scott had pointed out to him a prominently displayed bottle of what appeared to be old sauce preserved for several years. The story was the same. 'They made us drink oil; when they ran out of castor oil it was engine oil. That's what it made me do.' They kept the contents so that one day they could return the favour – to a Fascist.[5]

When the leaders of the Fascist Black Brigade at San Stino di Livenza were arrested and put on trial, Gino Panont testified in their favour. 'We had a pact with them that we would not bother each other' – an agreement cemented over a meal during the height of the conflict. Even if the Fascists were trying to ensure their salvation later, they had kept to their side of the bargain, on occasion providing useful information to the partisans.[6]

By 1947 the Cold War atmosphere had quenched Left hopes of a revolution. Many partisans aligned with the Communists found themselves subjected to what Querino Bullian calls 'the partisan witch-hunt'. He states that partisans were discriminated against in his zone and the majority were forced to emigrate to find work. Not one man in his brigade stayed in Italy. Called as a witness in a trial at one point he asked the judge, 'Am I on trial because I was a partisan or a delinquent? Why don't you put on trial the people who sent me to fight the partisans in Yugoslavia? That's where it all started.'[7] He spent five years in France before returning to Italy, but others such as Vittorino Gaspari spent over thirty years away.

Bruno Steffè counts himself lucky to be a native of Trieste and living in the zone controlled until 1954 by the Allied military government. He benefited from a law it passed which established that all businesses in the state sectors with more than fifty employees must employ a percentage of ex-partisans. This law was not enforced in other areas.[8]

Luigi Borgarelli shunned any recognition for his activities. He felt he had done his duty as a patriot and just wanted to finish his medical studies and get on with his life.

For partisans who had fought in the Resistance in a sincere hope for a new Italy, it was galling to see Fascists who had happily socialised with the Germans now holding glittering functions for the Allies. Arch Scott was disgusted at the first and last such reception he attended where British and Italian officers resplendently decked out in uniform mingled with arrays of beautiful women. Although many well-to-do people had genuinely supported his network, Scott noted that the people who emerged at these occasions were 'the winning team supporters, the good-time Charlies, the fawning sycophants'.[9] No partisan leaders were present. He became concerned that the sight of former Fascists throwing dances and parties for the Allies would destroy the almost unanimous support the Italian people had shown for the Allies. They knew that these people would be making a fortune working alongside the Allies as they had previously with the Germans. 'How little the aftermath of war depended upon the men who fought and how much on the machinations of people at receptions such as this.'[10]

For Scott staying in Italy was desperately important. After two months of Allied occupation people were facing unemployment, lower wages, increased prices and a thriving black market. Distressed by the hardships, he dearly wished to remain both to repay the Italian people and contribute to their well-being. He spoke their language, had earned their respect and friendship, and had liaised with partisans and civilians to successfully organise the evacuation of up to fifty Allied escapers. He felt he still had a lot to offer and had earned the right to remain. After he heard that all New Zealand soldiers were to be repatriated to England, he made a number of attempts to stay in Italy. Scott's letter dated Portogruaro, 28 June 1945, demonstrates the extent of his passionate determination.

'I have intimate friends from the poorest *contadini* to the richest landowners. I get a lot of information not available to anyone else. Working with me is a group of Italians who helped our chaps get out by sea including the man who was in charge of the radio transmitting set we had in the area. Must we break up just when we seem to be getting somewhere?

'I have been told that PW are demobilised as soon as they get home. If possible I would remain here as a civilian then pay my own way home.

'The forms people have helped PW fill in all have to be checked and I am the only one left here who knows whether the claims are just or not. I have already had requests from all the *Sindaci* concerned to help them out with this but so far I have not had time to do so. I regret having been obliged to write all this to justify my remaining here as I would not like you to think I have an exaggerated sense of my own importance – I haven't.'

There was a postscript: 'All this may not seem very important to you but it is to me and to the Italian people concerned.'[11] Despite his request being supported by those with whom he worked, permission was refused.

The Resistance gave Italians a sense of pride and identity, and established the groundwork for an anti-Fascist democracy. Although there was disagreement on the form it would take, some crucial changes were made. In 1946 women were granted the vote and in 1947 Italians voted in a referendum to become a Republic. The monarch and his family, compromised by Fascism, were sent into exile. Many Resistance leaders played a role in post-war political life. For the Communists who had fought valiantly against the Nazi-Fascists, the Resistance gave them a prestige and respectability that enabled them to enter the mainstream of Italian political life as a party with strong support, powerful in local government and trade union organisations.[12] In the words of the Supreme Commander of the Allied Forces, General Alexander, 'Italy had worked her passage.'[13] Although the Allies would have undoubtedly won the war without the partisans it would have been more costly in time and manpower. They had provided vital intelligence networks and carried out essential sabotage operations that facilitated the Allied attack and ultimately saved the lives of its soldiers. As Italy, in the words of Giorgio Bocca, 'paid its return ticket to democracy'[14] at a price of 45,000 partisans and civilians dead and over 20,000 wounded, the New Zealanders who had lived and fought alongside them returned quietly home.

The returned soldiers had witnessed the devastation of Europe. They had seen cities and towns razed to the ground, leaving jagged carcasses of blackened, burned-out buildings. Exploding shells and landmines had ripped apart the intensely cultivated countryside and left it strewn with barbed wire, wrecked aircraft, tanks and trucks. Whole villages had been destroyed. Shocked, dazed and hungry people searched for scraps amongst the rubble. It made a huge impression on Paul Day. 'I really became slightly disoriented. It seemed there couldn't be any place in the world that was whole.' When he arrived in Cairo on his journey homeward, he bought up lengths of shirt material to take to his mother fearing that New Zealand, like everywhere else, must be suffering shortages.

But unlike the civilians of Italy, New Zealanders had not experienced a war fought in their streets and mountains. People seemed cut off and were calmly going about their normal business. Day recalls the anguish of being in Auckland on VE Day, unable to fit in with what was happening. 'Here was everyone with their fancy hats, here were the gutters of Queen Street filled with smashed bottles and broken glass, everybody dancing and going mad with joy. I walked around like a ghost. You go through the motions but things were out of synch. Everything was like a charade.'[15]

Maurice Cosgrave was back in New Zealand by November 1944. He wanted to get back into the army but this was not allowed for ex-prisoners. 'I didn't want to come back to New Zealand. I wanted to carry on with what I knew. You build up a sort of comradeship. You move from one regiment to another. You don't have any friends there but it is sort of a brotherhood. It's hard to explain . . . In those days [New Zealand was] a pretty corny sort of place. There was no sophistication. It was a vast concentration camp with a hell of a lot of nice people in it.'[16]

Most men returned to New Zealand nervy and unsettled after their experiences. In varying degrees they jumped at loud noises – 'hit the ground running' as Arch Scott put it, had nightmares and struggled to deal with a 'normality' that seemed complacent after years of dealing with the extremes of human experience. Many men, thankful it was all over, wanted to put the war behind them for a family, a mortgage, a steady job and a quiet life in the suburbs or on the farm. The mutual support gained from their comrades continued through ex-prisoners-of-war associations, and lasted all their lives. A minority found adjustment too difficult and sought refuge in the alcohol that had soothed taut nerves while at large.

Above all they returned with a deep appreciation of the simple things in life, never taking for granted basic necessities. Few initially talked openly of their experiences. When Frank Bowes wrote a detailed account of his battle experiences to his wife he did so in order to lay them to rest as 'in retrospect they appear part of a nightmare'. He never wanted to recall them again. An underlying factor common to most men is a sense of fair play. They had all witnessed injustice and brutality. They detested the Fascists. Despite misgivings about partisan tactics, they knew they were on the right side. The much-touted New Zealand soldier's independence, self-reliance and scorn of 'grandstanding' did not spare anyone. Mussolini, unused to such insubordination, was not far wrong when he detected a larrikin element in the New Zealand prisoners he encountered. Being at large in enemy territory required qualities that were not learned on a military training field. Survival was uppermost for all the men; learning a language, adapting to unfamiliar practices and respect were what stood them in good stead.

Living, working and fighting alongside their former enemies encouraged men to broaden their outlook and value a common humanity. One ex-prisoner sums up the sense of identification he now shared with Italians. 'I had been in enough tight corners with Italian partisans to have the greatest faith in their courage, irrespective of the understandably large number of Italians who had surrendered so easily in North Africa. After all, we also surrendered there – when we were ballsed up by command and communication.'[17]

Many of the veterans have made visits back to see their Italian friends. For those who returned after fifty years the change was startling. Italy is a fast-paced modern democracy, where crippling social divisions, if not entirely overcome, have been addressed. Grandchildren of illiterate peasants are educated professionals. The rural tenements with their stables and barns lie in ruins, abandoned for the city. The veterans of the Hare Battalion had witnessed the last vestiges of the old life, of the peasant civilisation that after the war disappeared for good. Although there is little nostalgia for the hardship of being yoked to the land and whim of the *padrone*, a sense of community is often missed.

The two countries share a public holiday of remembrance for their war dead. April 25 in New Zealand is marked by Anzac Day while Italy solemnly observes Liberation Day. On this day in 1995 in a ceremony attended by hundreds in the main square, Arch Scott was made an honorary citizen of San Stino di Livenza.

John Senior was to hug his 'big sister' Ines Martin again after nearly fifty years in 1994. As the train pulled into Caorle the national anthems of both New Zealand and Italy were played, followed by a formal welcome, attended by former partisans in red and green scarves.

Paul Day revisited Prati Nuovi and played a part in championing the survival of his old prison headquarters. For some years Prati Nuovi's deserted buildings had been under threat to make way for commercial development. Vigorous opposition to this was eventually successful on the grounds that they should be preserved as part of the zone's historic and cultural heritage.

David Russell and Frank Bowes are heroes of the Resistance, considered sons of the nation they gave their lives for.

Roy Johnston and Pat Moncur never lost touch with their families. Johnston's grandchildren are regular visitors, while in the last year of his life Moncur was still receiving Easter goodies from the people who looked after him.

Although many men never went back to Italy, the warmth and esteem in which they were held has been transferred down through the generations. Isacco Zanella wrote to Bill Black, 'We have not forgotten you. Even my children know you from hearing talk of you so often and they regard you as a hero.' Black died in 1999. He received several gongs but never the Italian Star, the one he felt he really deserved.

Black would have concurred with the sentiments of Wally Willis who successfully applied for the same medal. He wrote, 'I am proud of my participation in the Greece Campaign. I am proud of my participation in the Western Desert – very much so as I was a machine-gunner at Sidi Rezegh. However, I am equally proud of my private campaign, as you might call it, in Italy.'[18]

The debt of gratitude felt for the unsung heroism and sacrifice of ordinary Italians lasted all their lives. Although many men felt they could never pay the Italians back for literally saving their lives, Hilary Evans tried to do so in 1959 when he brought out to New Zealand two sons of the Rotondi family who assisted him at Vallepietra.

In 1989 the Monte San Martino Trust was set up by former British escaped prisoners-of-war in recognition of the courage and generosity of Italians, what Churchill called 'a great spontaneous gesture of humanity', towards Allied servicemen. The Trust awards bursaries to young Italians to travel to England to improve their language skills. It provides funding for a one-month course at an English language school and lodging with a family during the course. Precedence is given to students who can prove to be descendants of families who gave help to escaped prisoners-of-war, and secondly, to those who come from areas where substantial assistance was known to have been given by the local population. New Zealander Stephen Sims, son of Noel Sims, is a trustee, while Lucia Antonel, daughter of Angelo and granddaughter of Pietro Antonel, the family who sheltered Arch Scott and Sims, was the first recipient of the award. In 2001 the first San Martino Freedom Trail took place, a four-day walk through an escape route in the mountains round Sulmona in the Abruzzi region in recognition of the sacrifice of Italians. Over 200 people, Italians, and descendants of families from many nations, took part.

For some the legacy is more complex. Since 1952 Giovanni Nicolli has made only two trips back to Italy. He considers himself a Kiwi and feels that Italy brought him only heartache. He suffers from nightmares where he dreams the Germans have captured him.

For Pierina Leder there is an aching silence. 'As a little girl I used to dream that one day towards sunset a train would stop and a gentleman would get off. He would be searching for . . . me. But that man never alighted from any train. And after many sunsets came many nights and many other days. At a certain point I stopped waiting for anything.'[19]

The 'cave men' shared a lifelong friendship. When Bob Smith arrived to spend Christmas 1994 with the Langs he suffered a heart attack in the taxi and died in his friend's arms. Although he never went back to Italy, Lang kept in touch with the Borgnolo family of Valle. A sense of regret lingered over their discovery in the legendary cave.

The true story emerged on my visit back. The locals and the priest confirmed that the men had been betrayed to the Germans by a ten-year-old boy from the neighbouring village of Pedrosa. One of the ragged children who brought food to the cave, he had sold them in return for a packet of cigarettes. Jack Lang died in May 2001, a few days before he could learn about the little boy. I pressed the flower from the cave mouth into his cold hand and told him everything.

Acknowledgements

There are many people whose participation and generosity in this project have been invaluable.

Firstly, I would like to thank all the New Zealand veterans who shared their experiences of being escaped prisoners-of-war in Italy. Sadly, several will not see the finished book. Their stories, friendship and zest for living are an inspiration. Thanks are also due to the families of veterans no longer alive for allowing me to use their fathers' memoirs and for illuminating conversations on their fathers' post-war lives. Many provided me, too, with the contacts to begin my research in Italy.

In Italy the past is not a distant country but alive, debated and cherished. The presence of a researcher from afar is a spur for collaboration and dialogue. In this way the experiences of veterans can be placed in context, the details of which are found in archives in small towns, among surviving witnesses and memoirs.

To the ex-partisans and many families of helpers I met in Italy I owe a strong debt. So many people willingly gave me their time. My research became a journey in itself through crowded bars, a home for retired nuns, a crumbling villa where Hemingway spent his summers and deserted mountain villages. Like the New Zealanders sixty years ago, I was humbled by the hospitality to a stranger and I learned to relish polenta.

Five people in particular have been magnificent in assisting my research in Italy and making so much possible. They are Lucia Antonel, Francesco Frattolin, Giorgio Nascimbene, Ugo Perissinotto and Franco Pischiutti. Their generosity, time and enthusiasm in sharing their work, ideas and providing me with direct access to so many contacts has added to and enriched this project. Eugenio and the late Cecilia Pesarini gave support and friendship. *Vi ringrazio di cuore.*

Other acknowledgements are due. I thank AIS St Helens for allowing me leave to complete the project. I also pay affectionate tribute to my eternally supportive friend Belinda Kusabs who kept me on task, and not least my lovely family, daughters Sara, Rebecca, Grace, and Alice, and my partner Ric who give me so much love and encouragement and put up with my distraction.

Endnotes

The author is responsible for the English translation of all Italian material.

Chapter One

1 Ferruccio Lupis, *La diga. Pettegolezzi umani e diplomatici. Memorie. 1880–1959.* Ferrara: Art Word Media, 1990, pp. 331–333.
2 John Senior, interview with Susan Jacobs, Auckland, 16 March 2001. Also Senior, *The Price of Freedom*, p. 65.
3 Galeazzo Ciano, *Diaries 1937–1943*, edited by Renzo De Felice. Milan: Rizzoli, 2000, p. 637. The English version is from the abridged *Ciano's Diary 1939–1943*. London: Heinemann, 1947, p. 489.
4 This was probably derived from paintings of tattooed Maori performing the haka in early New Zealand.
5 In the Libyan battles of November–December 1941, 2042 New Zealanders were captured, cited in Mason, p. vi.
6 Laurie Read, *My Interesting Four Years, 1940–1944*, p. 12.
7 Johnston, *The First 85 Years*, p. 49.
8 A New Zealand beer, famous in the South Island.
9 Johnston, p. 53.
10 Ian St George, *Out the Main Entrance*, 1993, p. 20.
11 Douglas Dymock, interview with Susan Jacobs, 23 March 2001.
12 Scott, *Dark of the Moon*, p. 37.
13 Wynne Mason, *Prisoners-of-war*, p. v. In the Second World War over 9000 New Zealanders became prisoners-of-war, as compared to less than 500 in the First World War. Wynne Mason, *Prisoners-of-war, Official History of New Zealand in the Second World War 1939–1945*, p. v.
14 Bill Black, interview with Lawrence Lowe, 1997.
15 Scott, p. 42.
16 Read, p. 13.
17 Read, *My Interesting Four Years 1940–1944*, pp. 15–16.
18 Bill Black, interview.
19 Ian St George, p. 22, Arch Scott, p. 47.
20 Scott, p. 49.
21 St George, p. 23.
22 Read, p. 18.
23 Jack Lang, interview with Susan Jacobs, 7 April 2000.
24 Galeazzo Ciano, *Diaries 1937–43*, p. 268.
25 Galeazzo Ciano, *Diaries 1937–43*, 24 August 1939, p. 133.
26 See note 3.
27 This resulted in the unification and self-determination of Italy, which had been until then a series of disparate states and kingdoms largely under foreign domination.
28 Mussolini's anti-Communism and strong-man tactics ensured approval from the prevalent he-made-the-trains-run-on-time school of opinion.

Chapter Two

1 Mario Testa, head horseman at Camp 146, who came from an anti-

Fascist family. In Laurie Read, *My Interesting Four Years 1940–44*, p. 33.

2 Lucia Antonel, *Friends in War: Allied Prisoners-of-war and Contadini in German-Occupied Northern Italy, 1943–1945 – A Page of Forgotten History*. Thesis, Università degli Studi di Venezia Ca'Foscari, Facoltà di Lingue e Letterature Straniere. 1992–93, p. 21.

3 Wynne Mason, p. 217.

4 ibid., p. 217.

5 Barnett, p .5.

6 John Senior, interview with Susan Jacobs, 23 September 2000.

7 Read, p. 25.

8 Johnston, *The First 85 Years*, p. 57.

9 Read, pp. 26–7.

10 John Senior, interview, 16 March 2001.

11 Mason, p. 216.

12 Scott, pp. 70–1.

13 Angelo Antonel, written testimony, May 2001.

14 Sergio Rigola, interview with Luigi Moranini, *L'Impegno*, April 1989.

15 St George, p. 28.

16 Read, p. 31.

17 Sergio Rigola, interview.

18 Read, pp. 31–2.

19 Ian Millar, *A Long Walk*, p. 9.

20 St George, p. 28.

21 Doug Dymock, interview with Susan Jacobs, 23 March 2001.

22 Millar, pp. 9–10.

23 Scott, p. 72.

24 Scott, p. 74.

25 ibid., pp. 74–5.

26 St George, p. 28.

27 Johnston, p. 59.

28 ibid., p. 61.

29 Paul Day, interview with Susan Jacobs, 18 August 2000.

30 Doug Johnston, letter to Paul Day, 2001.

31 Bruno Blasigh, interview with Susan Jacobs, 23 April 2001.

32 Gino Fraulin, Roberto Perosa, interview with Susan Jacobs, 27 April 2001.

33 Bruno Bisioli, interview with Susan Jacobs, 4 May 2001.

34 Millar, p. 8.

35 Day, interview.

36 St George, p. 28.

Chapter Three

1 Doug Dymock, interview with Susan Jacobs, 23 March 2001.

2 Wynne Mason, *Prisoners-of-war: Official History of New Zealand in the Second World War*, p. 278.

3 Arch Scott, *Dark of the Moon*, p. 78.

4 Cliff Manson, interview with Susan Jacobs, 18 August 2000.

5 Ian St George, *Out the Main Gate*, p. 28.

6 John Senior, interview with Susan Jacobs, 16 March 2001.

7 Laurie Read, *My Interesting Four Years*, pp. 34–5.

8 Dymock, interview with Susan Jacobs, 23 March 2001.

9 John Abel, interview with Susan Jacobs, 17 November 2001.

10 Paul Day, interview with Susan Jacobs, 18 August 2001.

11 Benito Ciprian, interview with Susan Jacobs, 27 April 2001.

12 Franco Ghirardelli, interview with Susan Jacobs, 28 April 2001.

13 Day, interview.

14 Bruno Blasigh, interview and Benito Ciprian, interview.

15 Costantino Visentin, interview with Susan Jacobs 27 April 2001.

16 ibid.

17 Gino Fraulin, interview with Susan Jacobs, 27 April 2001.

18 Ghirardelli, interview.

19 His POW report at the time confirms this. WO 208/1247 1909, Public Records Office, Kew, London.

20 Maurice Cosgrave, interview with Susan Jacobs, 12 November 2000.

21 Wynne Mason, p. 282.

22 Jack Lang, interview with Susan Jacobs, 7 April 2000.

23 Wynne Mason, p. 289.

24 Bill Black, interview with Lawrence Lowe.

25 Wynne Mason, p. 281.

26 ibid., p. 281.

27 ibid., p. 301.

Chapter Four

1 Cited in Lamb, p. 100. Mussolini's fiery speech to the San Marco troops on 24 April 1944 was inspirational and heralded his first foray into the public arena since he was deposed in 1943. This division was in Bavaria training to join the newly formed Republican Army which was, alongside the Germans, optimistically to take on the joint Allied forces.

2 Lucia Antonel, p. 56.

3 Some anti-Fascists fought with the International Brigade in the Spanish Civil War and put their skills to use in the partisan formations after 8 September. Antonio Gramsci, a founder of the Italian Communist Party arrested in 1926, died after many years in prison, while Togliatti, the leader of the party, had sought political refuge in Russia. Intellectuals such as Cesare Pavese were sent to isolated villages under police guard.

4 Imelde Rosa Pellegrini. *Storie di ebrei: Transiti, asilo e deportazioni nel Veneto Orientale*. Portogruaro: Ediciclo Editore, 2001, p. 179.

5 The survival rate of Italian Jews at 85 per cent is, along with Danish Jews, the highest in Europe. They were a very small minority of the population (less than 1 per cent), physically resembled Italians, and there was no virulent anti-Semitic tradition, which fuelled denunciations *en masse*. Italian Jews are represented across the spectrum of political parties, many supporting Mussolini in the early years, although they are disproportionately represented among the ranks of prominent anti-Fascists. For an excellent discussion, see Susan Zuccotti, *The Italians and the Holocaust*, pp. 272–87.

6 The passage to Ecuador was organised by Oreffice's wife through the intervention of Galeazzo Ciano, Mussolini's son-in-law, executed with other members of the Fascist Grand Council in October 1944 for plotting to overthrow him in July 1943.

7 Philip Cooke, ed. *The Italian Resistance: An Anthology*, p. 2.

8 Aldo Camponogara, interview with Susan Jacobs, Portugraro, Italy, 26 April 2001.

9 Italo Ziggiotti, interview with Susan Jacobs, Meolo, Italy, 29 April 2001.

10 Luigi Borgarelli, interview with Susan Jacobs, Latisana, Italy, 1 May 2001.

11 Bruno Londera, interview with Susan Jacobs, 2 May 2001.

12 Bruno Steffè, interview with Susan Jacobs, 7 May 2001.

13 Bullian, interview.

14 Panont, interview with Susan Jacobs, San Stino di Livenza, 9 May 2001.

15 Giovanni Nicolli, interview with Susan Jacobs, 2 September 2001.

16 Claudio Pavone, *Una guerra civile: saggio storico sulla moralità nella Resistenza.* Torino: Bollati Boringhieri, 1994, p. 199.

Chapter Five

1 Scott, *Dark of the Moon,* p. 77.
2 Cliff Manson, interview with Susan Jacobs, 18 August 2000.
3 Laurie Read, *My Interesting Four Years,* p. 36.
4 Ian Millar, *The Long Walk,* p. 13.
5 ibid., p. 15.
6 Hilary Evans, wartime diary.
7 Bill Black, interview with Lawrence Lowe, 1997.
8 Roy Johnston, interview with Susan Jacobs, 23 August 2000. Also *The First 85 Years.*
9 The Left Book Club was an organisation dedicated to the development of informed political and social debate from the Left perspective. From 1937–1940, twenty-six branches were established throughout New Zealand. Affiliated to the London-based club founded in 1936 by the socialist publisher Victor Gollancz, it produced a series of books bound in trademark orange cloth on political, social and economic topics. Fascism, the threat of war, poverty and unemployment were the main focus of the discussion groups and cultural activities that sprang up from the readership. See Rachel Barrowman, 'The Left Book Club' in *A Popular Vision: The Arts and the Left in New Zealand, 1930–1950.* Wellington: Victoria University Press, 1991.
10 Jim Locke is the brother of Jack Locke, a prominent member of the early New Zealand Communist Party, so would also have been familiar with the aspirations of the European left.
11 Luigi and Gianni Toniutto, interview with Susan Jacobs, 12 May 2001.
12 Maurice Cosgrave, interview with Susan Jacobs, 12 November 2000.
13 Angelo Antonel, written testimony, May 2001.
14 Maria Cusin, interview with Lucia Antonel, 26 August 1993.
15 ibid.
16 Rosetta Gobbo, interview with Susan Jacobs, 10 May 2001.
17 Rossana Rossetti, interview with Susan Jacobs, 30 April 2001.
18 Laurie Read, p. 35.
19 ibid., p. 37.
20 ibid., p. 38.
21 Millar, p. 22.
22 Roger Absalom, *A Strange Alliance: Aspects of Escape and Survival in Italy 1943–45,* p. 39.
23 Millar, p. 30.

Chapter Six

1 Italico Formentin, interview with Susan Jacobs, Marano Lagunare, 7 May 2001. He was a Fascist sympathiser who referred to the Allies as 'our so-called liberators'.
2 Lucia Antonel, *Friends in War: Allied Prisoners-of-war and Contadini in German-Occupied Northern Italy, 1943–1945 – A Page of Forgotten History,* p. 245.
3 Luigi Borgarelli, interview with Susan Jacobs, 1 May 2001.
4 I have relied on the testimonies of Bruno Rossetto, Italico Formentin and Salvatore Dri, interviewed 7 May 2001. Also Bruno 'Doria' Rossetto, *Se pudissi parlà le mure: Aneddoti e vicende della comunità Maranese.* Udine: La Bassa, 1999, p. 70 gives a detailed account. An

abbreviated version with some alterations can be found in Roger Absalom, *A Strange Alliance: Aspects of Escape and Survival in Italy 1943–45*. Firenze: Leo Olschki Editore, 1991, p. 262.

5 Men such as 'Sandòn' were usually attached to the clandestine missions that sent them in to organise the escape routes for the prisoners. The first such agency was an Anglo-American organisation known as the 'A' Force. However, the number of prisoners who got out through the organisation was disappointing. It has been suggested that some of the agents were poorly trained and knew little of the area. Antonel, p. 63.

6 Luciano Franzin, interview with Susan Jacobs, 30 April 2001.

7 Hilary Evans, diary.

8 Tony Jacobs, letter, 27 June 1969.

9 Ian St George, *Out the Main Entrance*, p. 33.

10 ibid., p. 39.

11 ibid., p. 41.

12 Walter Willis, see letter to Alwyn Hewitt, 16 June 1985 for all citations.

13 Waii 1 DA/322/15/2, Ref.p 9/197, New Zealand National Archives, Wellington.

14 ibid.

15 This was pointed out to me by an historian in the Vercelli district, Giorgio Nascimbene, after investigating the matter.

16 Ian Millar, p. 20.

17 This was confirmed by Giorgio Nascimbene A similar incident is recorded of six escapers being killed by GNR troops in Val Sessera on 5 May after a reported 'exchange of fire' which independent eyewitnesses have testified was an execution of unarmed men.

18. Waii 1 DA/322/15/2, Ref.p9/194.

19 Scott, p. 103.

Chapter Seven

1 Bianca Sguazzin, interview with Susan Jacobs, 3 May 2001.

2 Patriarchal families were so called because the sons of the family remained in their parents' home with their wives and children. This was an economic necessity because a shortage of farm tools and equipment meant more hands were needed to work on the land.

3 Roy Johnston, interview with Susan Jacobs, 23 August 2000. Also Johnston, *The First 85 Years*, and his fictionalised memoir, *To Find a Way: A New Zealand Narrative* for vivid accounts of his experiences.

4 Johnston, interview.

5 ibid.

6 ibid.

7 Maurice Cosgrave, interview with Susan Jacobs, 12 November 2000.

8 Ines Martin, interview with Lucia Antonel, 30 August 1994.

9 ibid.

10 Roger Absalom used this term in his extensively researched book, *A Strange Alliance: Aspects of Escape and Survival in Italy 1943–45*. Firenze: Leo Olschki Editore, 1991. It can probably be attributed to Sir Noel Charles, the British Ambassador to Rome, who stated 'the majority of the Italian people formed a strange alliance with the prisoners, and they worked together against the Germans and the Republican Fascists', cited in Foot and Langley, *M19: Escape and Evasion 1939–1945*, p. 235.

11 Johnston, *The First 85 Years*, p. 63.

12 Novella Bogotto, interview with Susan Jacobs, 28 April 2001.

13 Churchill called this 'communism of the stomach'.

14 I have extended Absalom's theory of the 'moral economy' to include a maternal economy functioning as mutual nurturance. Absalom has described how a 'moral economy' operated in relation to the prisoners with an implicit system of exchanges based on mutual respect and support instead of an economic exchange. In 'Per una storia di sopravvivenze: contadini italiani e prigionieri evasi britannici'. In *Italia contemporanea*, n. 140, Settembre 1980, pp. 106–122. Also discussed in Antonel, *Friends in War: Allied Prisoners-of-war and Contadini in German-Occupied Northern Italy, 1943–1945 – A Page of Forgotten History*, p. 86.

15 Ian Millar, *A Long Walk*, p. 14.

16 Lucia Antonel observes, 'When the peasants perceived that they had become the main or, in some cases, the only protectors of those men whose social status was [usually] higher than their own, they realised that they had been given a new role and were exercising a power they had never experienced before. These new roles could be further steps towards the realisation of that human identity which up to that moment nobody had ever recognised.' *Friends in War*, p. 137.

17 Allan Yeoman, *The Long Road to Freedom*, p. 89.

18 Millar, pp. 22–3.

19 Maurice Cosgrave, interview with Susan Jacobs, 12 November 2000.

20 Bill Black, interview with Lawrence Lowe.

21 Clelia Furlanetto, interview with Lucia Antonel, Torre di Mosto, 29 August 1994. Also John Senior, *The Price of Freedom*, p. 113–4.

22 Ines Martin, interview with Lucia Antonel at San Biagio di Callalta, 30 August 1994.

23 Arch Scott, *Dark of the Moon*, pp. 123–4.

24 Maria Varaschin, interview with Susan Jacobs, 10 May 2001.

25 Black, interview.

26 Johnston, *The First 85 Years*, p. 63; *To Find a Way*, p. 96.

Chapter Eight

1 Bill Black, interview with Lawrence Lowe.

2 Ian Millar, *A Long Walk*, p. 27.

3 ibid., p. 27.

4 John Senior, interview, June 22, 2001.

5 Cosgrave's chosen Italian name derived from his middle name, Peter, before he realised that 'Maurice' had an Italian equivalent, Maurizio.

6 Maurice Cosgrave, interview, November 12, 2002.

7 Scott, *Dark of the Moon*, p. 117.

8 ibid.

9 Millar, p. 33.

10 ibid., p. 40.

11 Scott, pp. 105–6.

12 ibid., p. 99.

13 Millar, p. 29.

14 Millar, *A Long Walk*, p. 42. Ian Millar was to successfully escape through Yugoslavia.

15 Cosgrave, interview, 12 November 2000.

16 Roy Johnston, *The First 85 Years*, p. 65.

17 Bill Black, interview with Lawrence Lowe.

18 Senior, *The Price of Freedom*, p. 132.

19 Senior, ibid., pp. 130–1. Also interview with Susan Jacobs, 16 March 2001.

20 Paul Day, interview with Susan Jacobs, 18 August 2000.

21 Terenzio Baldoni, *La resistenza nel Fabrianese: vicende e protagonisti*, p. 163. Also *Movimento operaio e Resistenza a Fabriano 1884–1944*, pp. 50–3.

22 Senior, p. 118.

23 ibid.

24 Some of these Germans liked the area so much they bought holiday homes in the vicinity after the war.

25 Bruno Bisioli, interview with Susan Jacobs, 4 May 2001.

26 Costantin Visentin, interview with Susan Jacobs, 27 April 2001.

27 Bisioli, interview.

28 Day, interview.

29 Tony Williams, *Cassino: New Zealand Soldiers in the Battle for Italy*, New Zealand: Penguin, 2002, p. 232.

30 John Senior, interview with Susan Jacobs, 22 June 2001.

31 Lucia Antonel, *Friends in War: Allied Prisoners-of-war and Contadini in German-Occupied Northern Italy, 1943–1945 – A Page of Forgotten History*, p. 254. Don Pietro Buogo of Cessalto who helped Bill Black and other New Zealanders is one such example.

32 John Senior, interview.

33 Arch Scott, *Dark of the Moon*, pp. 86–7.

34 Roger Absalom, *A Strange Alliance: Aspects of Escape and Survival in Italy 1943–45*, p. 251.

35 Sister Giuseppina, interview with Susan Jacobs, 28 April 2001. This incident is described by Roger Absalom, *A Strange Alliance*, pp. 251–2. Details of Private Swainson supplied in 'Documenti della guerra di liberazione', fascicolo N.20, cartella N.4, Biblioteca comunale, Udine.

36 Sister Giuseppina, interview with Susan Jacobs.

37 Maurice Cosgrave, interview.

Chapter Nine

1 Bill Black, interview with Lawrence Lowe.

2 Paul Day, interview with Susan Jacobs, 18 August 2000.

3 Ian Millar, *A Long Walk*, p. 31.

4 Giorgio Bocca, *Storia dell'Italia partigiana*, p. 82.

5 Lucia Antonel, pp. 228–9.

6 Bocca, p. 82.

7 Querino Bullian, interview with Susan Jacobs, 7 May 2001.

8 Gino Panont, interview with Susan Jacobs, 9 May 2001.

9 Pat Moncur, interview with Susan Jacobs, 14 April 2000.

10 Ian Millar, pp. 31–2.

11 Moncur, interview.

12 Maurice Cosgrave, interview with Susan Jacobs.

13 Laurie Read, *My Interesting Four Years*, p. 39.

14 ibid., p. 39.

15 Jocumsen, known as Frank l'Australiano, received the Medaglia d'oro, Italy's highest award for valour. Probably because of his association with a high profile Communist leader, even though he himself was not Communist, he received no recognition from his own country. Absalom, pp. 62–3.

16 Read, p. 40. Moscatelli's strong Communist sympathies alienated him from non-Communist groups which in other areas collaborated closely. He did not receive drops from the Allies and is alleged to have taken over a drop destined for the Action Party group.

17 ibid., p. 42.

18 ibid., p. 42.

19 Read, pp. 40–1.

20 ibid., p. 41.

21 ibid., p. 42.

22 These battles are described in many Italian publications which focus on the struggle of the partisans in a particular zone. I have been able to construct the names and dates of battles and protagonists through the help of Vercelli historian Giorgio Nascimbene who has carefully checked the references in Read's account and corrected any inaccuracies.

23 Read, p. 43.

24 ibid., p. 43.

25 Cino Moscatelli, cited in Cesare Bermani, *Pagine di guerriglia: L'esperienza dei garibaldini della Valsesia*, volume 1, tomo 1, undated, p. 63.

26 Read, p. 44.

27 Allan Yeoman, *The Long Road to Freedom*, p. 157.

28 Several other New Zealanders died while fighting with the partisans. Corporal Lawrence Roderick was shot and killed in a Fascist ambush at Sasso d'Ombrone near Grosseto while leading a band of rebels. He was buried in bush near the village of Monte Merano approximately 30 kilometres north-west of Viterbo. The Italians of the zone consider him a hero. Also a Major Reed in command of a band of rebels was reported killed about 1 June 1944 and is reportedly buried at Laterina.Waii I DA 322/15/2, New Zealand National Archives.

29 Frank Bowes, letter to Rhona Bowes, 1942. All other quotes derive from the same source.

30 Mason, p. 192.

31 Bowes, letter, Camp 57, Udine, January 1943.

32 Bowes, letter, Camp 106, Vercelli, probably May–July 1943.

33 ibid.

34 I am indebted to phone conversations with Bowes' son, John Bowes. Similar sentiments are expressed by Frank Gardner. Also, 'A New Zealander, Private Grainger of the 26 Battalion who was reported to be leading a band of partisans in the Tagliamento district wished to stay as he considered them very stupid.' This indictment may have owed as much to the soldier's justification in military terms for staying on. A Private Pullen reported encountering Bill Duigan of Wellington at partisan headquarters. 'He gave few details about the activities of Duigan except to say that his strongest impression was of the great admiration the Kiwi had for the Italian partisan leader, whom he regarded as one of the bravest men he had ever met.' Waii 1 DA 447. 28/45.

35 At the end of November 1943 a major strike, organised by Communist and Socialist underground leaders in Turin, had paralysed industrial production.

36 The German platoon ascended from the west and arrived at Bocchetto di Sessera in the evening, setting fire to the hotel there. Despite this the Germans and Fascists sustained many losses and most of the partisans units managed to escape.

37 These events are described in Luigi Moranino, *Il primo inverno dei partigiani biellesi*, pp. 36–44; Anello Poma-Gianni Perona, *La*

Resistenza nel Biellese, pp. 135–9;
Edgardo Sogno, *Guerra Senza
Bandiera*, pp. 114–9. I am also
indebted to conversations between
Girolamo Crestani and Giorgio
Nascimbene reported to me by the
latter.

38 Giorgio Nascimbene, based on
testimonies by Girolamo Crestani
and others.

39 Testimony of Girolamo Crestani to
Giorgio Nascimbene.

40 Moranino, pp. 36–7; Poma, Perona,
p. 134.

41 Poma, Perona, p. 138.

42 Letter from Adriano Motta, priest
of Mosso Santa Maria, to Rhona
Bowes, 10 August 1946.

43 Delzell, *Mussolini's Enemies: The
Italian Anti-Fascist Resistance*,
pp. 360–1.

Chapter Ten

1 Ref. ACC/507/4.PAT Appendix
XII to Report on Patriot Activities
in Region XII. General Report on
City of Belluno *c.* July–August
1944. London, Public Records
Office.

2 Bill Black, interview.

3 Charles Delzell, pp. 302, 362, 420.

4 Geoffrey Cox, *Race to Trieste*, p. 126.

5 John Senior, conversation with
Susan Jacobs, 23 September 2000.
Senior did not believe the claim.

6 Black, interview.

7 ibid.

8 ibid.

9 Bruno Steffè, interview with Susan
Jacobs, 9 May 2001.

10 Read, *My Interesting Four Years*,
p. 40.

11 Black, interview.

12 Cosgrave, interview.

13 Aldo Camponogara, interview with
Susan Jacobs, 26 April 2001.

14 Black, interview.

15 Delzell, p. 368.

16 Luigi Borgarelli, interview with
Susan Jacobs, 1 May 2001.

17 Bruno Steffè, interview.

18 ibid.

19 Borgarelli, interview.

20 ibid.

21 Mussolini was aware of this 'modus
vivendi' between local German
commanders and partisans and
feared it increased the strength and
prestige of the partisans. Cited in
Lamb, p. 219. Several partisans
interviewed described similar
relationships.

22 Camponogara, interview.

23 The prime organiser of the Osoppo
was Don Aldo Moretti (Don Lino)
who wanted to counteract
Communist totalitarianism. A
conference attended by about 50
clergy was held at the seminary in
Udine to discuss the spiritual
ramifications of supporting the
armed resistance. Bocca, p. 171.

24 Don Redento Bello, p. 66.

25 The Communist leaders of the
Udine CLN, under pressure from
the Yugoslav Command, are
believed to have ordered the
massacre.

26 Gianfranco Ivancich, interview with
Susan Jacobs, 30 April 2001.

27 Gios, *Controversie sulla resistenza
ad Asiago e in Altopiano*, p. 13.

28 John Crestani, discussion with
Susan Jacobs; also testimony of his
brother, Giordano Crestani, in
Gios, p. 30.

29 Feliciana Petch, conversation with
Susan Jacobs, February 2001.

30 Delzell, p. 549.

31 Arch Scott, interview with Susan
Jacobs, March 2000.

32 Scott, *Dark of the Moon*, p. 121.

33 Gino Panont, interview.
34 ibid.
35 Scott, p. 123.

Chapter Eleven

1 The events described can be found in *The 'Signor Kiwi' Saga*, edited by Paul Day, 55 Hill Road, Manurewa, 1993. It is based on the manuscript, *Signor Kiwi* by F. N. Millar, as narrated to her by Frank Gardner and published as a boys' adventure book, *The Lone Kiwi*, in Dublin, 1947. The edited version is based on further research by Lucia Antonel in Italy with appendices added. Of special interest is Appendix C, 'The Shooting of Squinchi', written by Frank Gardner shortly before his death in 1972. My work, although indebted to this text, is based on my own research and interviews with people intimately connected to the Frank Gardner story.
2 Guido Marchetti in conversation with Margie Gardner, July 2001.
3 *The 'Signor Kiwi' Saga*, pp. 16–17.
4 ibid., pp. 22–3.
5 ibid., p. 22.
6 ibid., pp. 24–31.
7 ibid., p. 39.
8 ibid., p. 40.
9 ibid., p. 56.
10 Anna Zanini, interview with Susan Jacobs, 2 May 2001. Italians considered Gardner's light brown hair 'blond'.
11 ibid.
12 Aldo Bierti, interview with Susan Jacobs, 2 May 2001.
13 Anna Zanini, interview with Susan Jacobs.
14 Partisan bands, especially at the beginning, were without a steady supply of funds and descending on factories and shops to appropriate them was common. These tactics did not endear them to many but when the population was on side, as in Pat Moncur's experience, they received active assistance.
15 Giovanni Marzoni, Commander 1st Company Sabatoeurs, 3rd Division Osoppo Friuli. Appendix A, *The 'Signor Kiwi' Saga*, pp. 135–8.
16 ibid., p. 136.
17 Major Thomas Macpherson, Appendix B, *The 'Signor Kiwi' Saga*, p. 140.
18 Marzoni, Appendix A, *The 'Signor Kiwi' Saga*, p. 136.
19 Bruno Londera, interview with Susan Jacobs, 2 May 2001.
20 *The 'Signor Kiwi' Saga*, p. 120.
21 Frank Gardner, Appendix C, 'The Shooting of Squinchi', *The 'Signor Kiwi' Saga*, p. 147.
22 Aldo Bierti, interview. However, Gardner has been generally credited with the elimination of Palese.
23 Franco Pischiutti, interview with Susan Jacobs, 2 May 2001.
24 Don Pietro Londera, *I Cosacs in Friul: ricuarz personai di Pieri Picul*, p. 67. This is a collection of personal recollections previously published in various issues (1969–1971) of *Int Furlane*, a Friulan dialect magazine.
25 Roy Johnston, *The First 85 Years*, p. 67.
26 Aldo Bierti, interview.
27 Anna Zanini, interview.
28 Aldo Bierti, interview.

Chapter Twelve

1 Bob Smith, 'Wartime Experiences', serialised in *New Zealand RSA Review*, September 1955. Jack Lang assisted him with this account.
2 Smith, 'Wartime Experiences'.

3 Jack Lang, interview with Susan Jacobs, 7 April 2000.
4 ibid.
5 Smith, 'Wartime Experiences'.
6 Lang, interview.
7 ibid.
8 John Abel, interview with Susan Jacobs, 17 November 2001.
9 Smith, 'Wartime Experiences'.
10 ibid.
11 ibid.
12 Lang, interview.
13 Santina Specogna, interview with Susan Jacobs, 5 May 2001.
14 Don Amelio Pinzano, *Ancora Memorie Vive*, Masarolis: Chiandetti, 1996, p. 32.
15 The Cossacks were anti-Communist Russians who joined forces with the Germans when Hitler's armies invaded the Ukraine and Cossack regions of the Don, Kubak and Terek on their push towards Stalingrad. There was tension when Germans resettled communities of dispossessed Cossacks in the Friuli area, ejecting Italians from their homes and land. The Cossack Army was used to fight partisans in Carnia and block Tito's army from pushing into north-eastern Italy and was renowned for its brutality.
16 Don Amelio Pinzano, interview with Susan Jacobs, 5 May 2000. Also see *Ancora memorie vive*, pp. 34–5.
17 C. Ross Greening, *Not as Briefed: From the Doolittle Raid to a German Stalag*. Compiled and edited by Dorothy Greening and Karen Morgan Driscoll. Washington: Washington State University Press, 2001, p. 152.
18 Don Amelio Pinzano, *Ancora memorie vive*, p. 43.

19 Smith, 'Wartime Experiences'.
20 C. Ross Greening, *Not as Briefed*, p. 155.
21 Anselmo Borgnolo, interview with Susan Jacobs, 5 May 2001.
22 ibid.
23 Lang, interview.
24 Smith, 'Wartime Experiences'.
25 ibid.
26 Lang, interview.
27 Don Amelio Pinzano, pp. 37–8. Also interview. Masarolis is erroneously recorded as having been destroyed in Lamb, p. 242.

Chapter Thirteen

1 Tommaso Tommaseo, *La carrozza del nonno*, Treviso: Editrice Santi Quaranta, 2000, p. 24.
2 Phillip O'Shea, *An Unknown Few*, Wellington: Government Printer, 1981, pp. 28–31.
3 Antonio Puppo, *Giacomo Gasparotti e i prigionieri di guerra alleati*, Venezia: Stamperia editrice, Gia Zanetti, 1946, p. 123.
4 Arch Scott, *Dark of the Moon*, p. 128.
5 Beppi (Giuseppe) Marson, interview with Susan Jacobs, 10 May 2001.
6 ibid.
7 ibid.
8 ibid.
9 Marson, interview with Lucia Antonel, 27 February 1997.
10 Scott, *Dark of the Moon*, p. 137. Also Wynne Mason, p. 474.
11 Marson, interview with Lucia Antonel.
12 Scott, p. 142.
13 Senior, interview with Susan Jacobs, 16 March 2001.
14 Marson, interview with Lucia Antonel.
15 ibid. Events have been pieced

together from several eyewitness
accounts.

16 ibid.

17 Senior. *The Price of Freedom*, p. 127.

18 Paul Pianina, interview with Susan
Jacobs, 29 August 2001.

19 ibid. All comments from Paul
Pianina come from the above
interview.

20 The Statement of Walter Willis,
Interrogation Report on Walter
Willis, May 2. 1945. Waii 1 Da
323/15/2, National Archives,
Wellington, New Zealand.

21 Letter to Alwyn Hewitt, 16 June
1985. Also events described in
statement of Walter Willis, see
above.

22 Walter Willis, report.

23 Willis, letter.

24 ibid.

25 Vittorino Gaspari, interview with
Susan Jacobs, Anone Veneto, 9 May
2001.

26 Willis, letter.

27 Letter. 'Although my father was not
circumcised, for some reason or
other both my brother and I were.
He was never to know the
predicament that it put me into so
many years later.' The New Zealand
Plunket Society was influential in
increasing the rate of circumcised
males in the first half of the 20th
century.

28 Paul Pianina, interview.

29 Report on Walter Willis.

30 Walter Willis, letter, 16 June 1985.
'I can sit here and write about it. I
could not talk about it. Maria and I
have never talked about it – we just
cannot. We have discussed what the
Germans did to the Jews. We have
discussed "The Holocaust". We
have experienced the brutality of
the Germans.'

31 Paul Pianina, interview.

32 Willis, letter to Simonette Pianina,
1 January 1990.

Chapter Fourteen

1 *Zealandia*, 8 June 1944, p. 11.

2 I am indebted to the material in an
article by Rosemary Conway,
'Dodging the Gestapo in Rome'.
New Zealand Tablet, June 3, 1981,
pp. 10–11. Also Sam Derry, '*The
Rome Escape Line*' and Roger
Absalom, 'Escape to Rome', in *A
Strange Alliance*, pp. 277–303.

3 'The priest who was part of the
Vatican underground', *Zealandia*,
6 May 1971, p. 13.

4 Cecilia Squillacciotti Pesarini,
interview with Susan Jacobs, Passo
Corese, 9 April 2001.

5 Derry, *The Rome Escape Line. The
Story of the British Organisation in
Rome for assisting Escaped
Prisoners-of-War 1943–44.*
London: George G. Harrap & Co.
Ltd, 1960, pp. 90, 199.

6 Conway, p. 10.

7 Owen Snedden, 'The Vatican and
Prisoners-of-war', *The Catholic
Review,* May 1945, Vol. 1, No. 1,
p. 82.

8 See 'New Zealand Priests Tell Story
of Wartime Italy', *Zealandia*, 18
January 1945, p. 5.

9 Roger Absalom, *A Strange Alliance*,
p. 279, p. 282. See also 'A New
Zealand Prisoner-of-war tells his
own Story', *Zealandia*, 5 October
1944, p. 8.

10 'New Zealand Priests Tell Story of
Wartime Italy', *Zealandia*, 18
January 1945, p. 5.

11 An account of this incident is given
in Derry, *The Rome Escape Line*,
pp. 145–6.

12 Derry, p. 104.

13 ibid., p. 57.
14 Richard Lamb, p. 39.
15 Derry, pp. 171–2.
16 ibid., pp. 207–9.
17 Eric Morris, p. 252.
18 Lamb, p. 56.
19 Absalom, p. 290–1. Among them were Luchino Visconti, the Communist film director, and Princess Barberini.
20 'New Zealand Priests Tell Story of Wartime Italy', *Zealandia*, 18 January 1945, p. 5. 'Fathers Snedden and Flanagan say the hope for future Italy lies in this type of man.' A member of an old Roman family who spent two years in a concentration camp for his beliefs, Doria is an unusual example of his class, who were generally compromised by their close association with Fascism.
21 Conway, p. 11.
22 Derry, p. 90.
23 Alessandro Portelli, *L'Ordine è già stato eseguito: Roma, le Fosse Ardeatine, la memoria*. Roma: Donzelli editore, 2001, p. 409, note 112. The previous day Caterina Martinelli, mother of seven, was gunned down in front of a bakery in the Tiburtina district. She was the inspiration for the woman played by Anna Magnani in Roberto Rossellini's famous Neorealist film, *Rome Open City*.
24 'A New Zealand Prisoner-of-war tells his own Story', *Zealandia*, 5 October 1944, p. 8.
25 Evans, diary, entry of 15 June 1944.
26 Conway, p. 11.

Chapter Fifteen
1 Laurie Read, *My Interesting Four Years*, p. 44.
2 Wynne Mason, pp. 301–3.

3 Clarence Peagram, transcript for 3ZB radio talk, given in mid-1945. Also newspaper article on David Jacobs' story in *Christchurch Press*, 1991.
4 Peagram also refers to this woman in his report. 'She was of utmost value and was warned by Fascists against us. However, she kept us in her home from 13–16 September.' Report of Clarence Peagram, WO 208/465 PW/Ex/ Switzerland, Public Records Office, London.
5 Leo Colombo, responsible for guiding hundreds of escapers over the mountains, was a partisan, renowned for never firing a shot despite carrying a pistol at all times. He was in contact with the partisans, Allied Command, and the Italian Embassy in Switzerland and besides ex-prisoners transported secret documents. He operated closely with the commander of the Garibaldi Division, Moscatelli. Costantino Burla, *Novelle alpine*, Borgosesia (VC): Palmiro Corradini, 1980, p. 152.
6 Doug Dymock, interview with Susan Jacobs, 23 March 2001.
7 ibid.
8 Mason, p. 305.
9 Doug Dymock, interview.
10 Ian St George, *Out the Main Entrance*, p. 42.
11 Laurie Read, *My Interesting Four Years*, p. 44.
12 ibid., p. 44.
13 Paul Day, interview with Susan Jacobs, 18 August 2000.
14 Report of L/Cpl Paul Day of the 24th New Zealand Battalion, in WO 208/1247 1909, Public Records Office, London.
15 Paul Day, interview.

16 Lucia Antonel, *Friends in War:
    Allied Prisoners-of-war and
    Contadini in German-Occupied
    Northern Italy, 1943–1945 –
    A Page of Forgotten History,*
    p. 66.
17 Richard Lamb, *War in Italy
    1943–1945: A Brutal Story,* p. 165.
18 For a comprehensive report in
    Italian Giuseppe Bacciagaluppi,
    'Rapporto finale sull'attività svolta
    dal CLN Alta Italia in favore di ex
    prigionieri di guerra alleati', in *Il
    Movimento di liberazione in Italia,*
    novembre 1954, n. 33, pp. 3–31. In
    English, see Antonel.

Chapter Sixteen
1 Bill Black, interview.
2 Maurice Cosgrave, interview, Susan
   Jacobs, 12 November 2000.
3 Bill Black, interview.
4 Lucia Antonel, *Friends in War,*
   p. 250.
5 It was also a method used by
   Germans and Italians to recapture
   escapers. A woman or man in
   civilian clothes would make contact
   with prisoners and claim to be an
   agent for a scheme for evacuating
   escaped prisoners. They would
   arrange a rendezvous and the
   prisoners would be arrested. A
   whole boatload of prisoners was
   caught this way near Venice. Mason,
   p. 419.
6 John Senior, *The Price of Freedom,*
   p. 60.
7 Roy Johnston, interview with Susan
   Jacobs, 23 August 2000.
8 Johnston, *The First 85 Years,* p. 66.
9 Johnston, interview. 'Willy,
   Austrian', is mentioned in the list of
   men evacuated on 13 April; cited in
   Scott, p. 186.
10 Johnston, interview.

11 Senior, p. 61.
12 Wynne Mason, p. 433.
13 ibid., p. 432.
14 Report on Walter Willis, Waii 1
   DA/322/15/2 Ref 9/18, NZ
   Archives, Wellington.
15 Tony Jacobs, letter to Nigel
   Macfarlane, 27 June 1969.
16 Ines Martin, interview with Lucia
   Antonel, 30 August 1994.
17 A surprising number of Italians
   refused any monetary
   compensation, Absalom, p. 114.
18 Luciano Franzin, interview with
   Susan Jacobs, 30 April 2001.
19 Angelo Antonel, written testimony,
   May 2001.
20 3882 Signalman Higgins D
   HQ2NZEF A 36/10, National
   Archives, Wellington, New
   Zealand.
21 Colonel C. Ross Greening, *Not as
   Briefed: From the Doolittle Raid to
   a German Stalag.* Compiled and
   edited by Dorothy Greening and
   Karen Morgan Driscoll.
   Washington: Washington State
   University Press, 2001, pp. 150–1.
22 Waii i 322/15/2 38822 Signalman
   Higgins D HQ2NZEF A 36/10,
   National Archives, Wellington,
   New Zealand.
23 Waii 1 Ref 2/1/61 01, 21128,
   DA322/15/2, National Archives,
   Wellington, New Zealand.
24 Ref 150/411, Waii DA322/15/2,
   National Archives.
25 Waii 1 DA322/15/2 A36/2,
   National Archives.
26 Waii 1 DA322/15/2, National
   Archives.
27 Wynne Mason, p. 281.
28 'In mid-July 1944, N section's
   emissaries remarked how difficult it
   sometimes was to winkle ex-
   prisoners out of village

communities in which they had become settled and accepted members. Quite a few of these people merged quietly into the local population, were missed by N section and everybody else, and have never bothered to surface. Others declared their identity when eventually the battle caught up with them, in 1944 or 1945, returned to Britain or New Zealand or wherever, and ceased to try to pass as Italians.' Foot, p. 236. Absalom puts the number at 'a few hundred', p. 314.

29 Report on Walter Willis, Waii I DA322/15/2, 63, National Archives, Wellington, New Zealand.

30 Waii I DA 322/15/2, National Archives.

31 Maria Cusin, interview with Lucia Antonel, San Stino di Livenza, 1994.

32 Applications to Marry, Waii 1 DA/ 322/15/2, Ref. 1/9/36.

33 Giulia and Pierina Leder, interview with Susan Jacobs, 24 April 2001.

34 Pierina Leder, letter to Susan Jacobs, 31 October 2002.

Chapter Seventeen

1 Arch Scott, letter dated Portogruaro, 28 June 1945. Waii 322/15/2, 62457, National Archives, Wellington, New Zealand.

2 In one of the more shameful incidents in the immediate post-war, his body was hung by its heels in Piazza Loreto, Milan, in front of a baying crowd.

3 Novella Bigotto, interview with Susan Jacobs, 28 April 2001.

4 Costantin Visentin, interview with Susan Jacobs, April 2001.

5 Scott, pp. 124–5.

6 Gino Panont, interview with Susan Jacobs, 10 May 2001.

7 Querino Bullian, interview with Susan Jacobs, Sequals, 7 May 2001.

8 Bruno Steffè, interview, 7 May 2001.

9 Scott, *Dark of the Moon*, p. 172.

10 ibid.

11 Scott, letter, Waii 322/15/2, 62457, National Archives, Wellington, New Zealand.

12 Communist leader Palmiro Togliatti was credited with renouncing the Stalinist totalitarian model as unsuitable for Italians and inserting his party within the democratic framework of post-war Italy.

13 Delzell, *Mussolini's Enemies*, p. 550.

14 Bocca, p. 528.

15 Paul Day, interview with Susan Jacobs, Hamilton, 18 August 2000.

16 Maurice Cosgrave, interview.

17 Scott, p. 169.

18 Willis, letter to Army Headquarters, 15 September 1969.

19 Pierina Leder, letter, 20 November 2002.

Bibliography

Absalom, Roger. *A Strange Alliance: Aspects of Escape and Survival in Italy 1943–45*. Florence: Leo Olschki Editore, 1991.

Absalom, Roger. Per una storia di sopravvivenze: contadini italiani e prigionieri evasi britannici. In *Italia contemporanea*, n.140, Settembre 1980, pp. 106–122.

Antonel, Lucia. *Friends in War: Allied Prisoners-of-war and Contadini in German-Occupied Northern Italy, 1943–1945 – A Page of Forgotten History*. Tesi di Laurea. Università degli Studi di Venezia Ca'Foscari, Facoltà di Lingue e Letterature Straniere. (Anno accademico 1992–93.).

Antonel, Lucia. *I silenzi della guerra: prigionieri alleati e contadini nel Veneto Orientale 1943–1945*. Portogruaro: Nuova Dimensione, 1995.

Bacciagaluppi, Giuseppe. Rapporto finale sull'attività svolta dal CLN Alta Italia in favore di ex prigionieri di guerra alleati, in *Il Movimento di liberazione in Italia*, Novembre 1954, n. 33, pp. 3–31.

Baldoni, Terenzio. *La Resistenza nel Fabrianese: Vicende e protagonisti*. Ancona: il Lavoro editoriale, 2002.

Barnett, Alex. *Hitler's Digger Slaves: Caught in the Web of Axis Labour Camps*. Australia: Australian Military History Publications, 2001.

Barrowman, Rachel. *A Popular Vision: The Arts and the Left in New Zealand 1930–1950*. Wellington: Victoria University Press, 1991.

Battaglia, Roberto. *Storia della resistenza italiana*. Turin: Einaudi, 1965.

Bello, Redento. *Scusate ... mi racconto*. Friuli Venezia Giulia: Editrice Leonardo, 2001.

Bermani, Cesare. *Pagine di guerriglia: L'esperienza dei garibaldini della Valsesia*, volume 1, tomo 1. Vercelli: Istituto per la storia della Resistenza e della società contemporanea nelle provincie di Biella e Vercelli 'Cino Moscatelli'.

Bocca, Giorgio. *Storia dell'Italia partigiana: settembre 1943–maggio 1945*. Milan: Mondadori, 1995.

Burla, Costantino. *Novelle alpine*. Borgosesia (VC): Palmiro Corradini, 1980.

Ciano, Galeazzo. *Diario 1937–1943*, 6th edition, curato da Renzo De Felice. Milan: Rizzoli, 2000.

Ciano, Galeazzo. *Ciano's Diary 1939–1943*. London: Heinemann, 1947.

Colombo, Enzo, a cura di. *Matrimonio in Brigata: Le opere e i giorni di Renata Viganò e Antonio Meluschi*. Bologna: Grafis Edizioni, 1995.

Conway, Rosaleen. 'Dodging the Gestapo in Rome'. In *New Zealand Tablet*, June 3 1981, pp. 10–11.

Cooke, Philip, ed. *The Italian Resistance: An Anthology*. Manchester: Manchester University Press, 1997.

Cox, Geoffrey. *The Road to Trieste*. Auckland: Whitcoulls, 1947.

Davidson, Alistair and Steve Wright eds. *'Never Give In'. The Italian Resistance and Politics*. New York: Peter Lang Publishing, 1998.

Davidson, Basil. *Special Operations Europe: Scenes from the Anti-Nazi War*. London: Victor Gollancz, 1980.

Dear, Ian. *Escape and Evasion: Prisoner-of-war Breakouts and the Routes to Safety in World War 2*. London: Arms and Armour Press, 1997.

Delzell, Charles. *Mussolini's Enemies: The Italian Anti-Fascist Resistance*. Princeton: Princeton University Press, 1961.

Derry, Sam. *The Rome Escape Line. The Story of the British Organisation in Rome for assisting Escaped Prisoners-of-War 1943–44*. London: George G. Harrap & Co. Ltd, 1960.

Ellwood, David W. *Italy 1943–1945*. New York: Holmes & Meier, 1985.

Evans, Hilary. Diary. September 8 1943–June 28 1944. Unpublished manuscript.

Foot, M. R. D. and Langley, J.M. *M19: Escape and Evasion 1939-1945*. London: The Bodley Head, 1979.

Gios, Pierantonio. *Controversie sulla resistenza ad Asiago e in Altopiano*. Asiago: 1999.

Greening, Colonel C. Ross. *Not as Briefed: From the Doolittle Raid to a German Stalag*. Compiled and edited by Dorothy Greening and Karen Morgan Driscoll. Washington: Washington State University Press, 2001.

Johnston, Roy. *The First 85 Years*. Unpublished manuscript recorded at Raumati Beach, May 2000.

Johnston, Roy. *To Find a Way: A New Zealand Narrative*. Unpublished manuscript.

Lamb, Richard. *War in Italy 1943–1945: A Brutal Story*. London: John Murray, 1993.

Luppis, Ferruccio. *La Diga. Pettegolezze umani e diplomatici. Memorie 1880–1959*. Introduzione di Vittorio Sgarbi. Biografia di Lucio Scardino, Ferrara: Art Word Media, 1990.

Bibliography

McGill, David. *P.O.W.: The Untold Stories of New Zealanders as Prisoners-of-war.* Lower Hutt: Mills Publications, 1987.

Mason, Wynne. *Prisoners-of-war. Official History of New Zealand in the Second World War 1939–1945.* War History Branch. Wellington: Department of Internal Affairs, 1954.

Millar, Florence and Day, Paul. *The 'Signor Kiwi' Saga.* ('Signor Kiwi' by F. Millar, edited by Paul Day). Auckland: 55 Hill Rd, Manurewa, 1993.

Millar Ian. *A Long Walk.* Unpublished manuscript, 1996.

Moranino, Luigi. *Il primo inverno dei partigiani Biellesi.* Vercelli: Istituto per la storia della Resistenza e della società contemporanea in Provincia di Vercelli.

Mori Aldo. *La Resistenza nel mondo contadino. La lotta di liberazione nel Portogruarese,* Udine, De Bianco editore, 1977.

Morris, Eric. *Circles of Hell: The War in Italy 1943–1945.* London: Hutchinson, 1993.

Movimento operaio e Resistenza a Fabriano 1884–1944. Studi sulla Resistenza. Urbino: Agalìa editore, 1977.

Origo, Iris. *War in Val d'Orcia.* London: Murray, 1984.

Pascutto, Romano, *Uno dei mille paesi.* Portogruaro: Nuova Dimensione, 1986, p. 16.

Passerini, Luisa. Trans. Robert Lumley and Jude Bloomfield. *Fascism in Popular Memory: The Cultural Experience of the Turin Working Class.* Cambridge: Cambridge University Press, 1987.

Pavone, Claudio. *Una guerra civile: saggio storico sulla moralità nella Resistenza.* Torino: Bollati Boringhieri, 1994.

Pellegrini, Imelde Rosa. *Storie di ebrei: Transiti, asilo e deportazioni nel Veneto Orientale.* Portugruaro: Ediciclo Editore, 2001.

Pinzano, Don Amelio. *Ancora memorie vive.* Masarolis: Chiandetti, 1996.

Pomà, Annello, e Gianni Perona. *La Resistenza nel Biellese.* Biella: Istituto storico della Resistenza nel Biellese: 1978.

Portelli, Alessandro. *The Death of Luigi Trastulli and Other Stories: Form and Memory in Oral History.* New York: State University of New York Press, 1991.

Portelli, Alessandro. *L'Ordine è gia stato eseguito: Roma, Fosse Ardeatine, la memoria.* Rome: Donizelli editore, 2001.

Puppo, Antonio. *Giacomo Gasparotto e i prigionieri di guerra alleati.* Venice: Stamperia Editrice già Zanetti, 1946.

Read, Laurie. *My Interesting Four Years 1941–1945.* Unpublished manuscript.

Rossetto, Bruno 'Doria'. *Se pudissi parlà le mure: Aneddoti e vicende della comunità Maranese*. Udine: La Bassa, 1999.

Rusconi, Gian Enrico. *Resistenza e Post-Fascismo*. Bologna: Società editrice il Mulino, 1995.

Scott, Arch. *Dark of the Moon: The Unusual Story of One Kiwi's War*. Auckland: Cresset Books, 1985.

Senior, John. *The Price of Freedom*. Unpublished manuscript, 2001.

Slaughter, Jane. *Women and the Italian Resistance 1943–1945*. Colorado: Arden Press, 1997.

Smith, Bob. 'War time Experiences' in *New Zealand RSA Review*, September 1955.

Steffè, Bruno. *La guerra di liberazione nel territorio della provincia di Pordenone 1943–1945*. Seconda edizione riveduta e integrata. Pordenone: Edizioni Ets.

St George, Ian. *Out the Main Gate*. Unpublished manuscript, 1993.

Tommaseo, Tommaso. *La carrozza del nonno*. Treviso: Editrice Santi Quaranta, 2000.

Wilhelm, Maria de Blasio. *The Other Italy: The Italian Resistance in World War II*. New York: Norton, 1988.

Yeoman, Allan. *The Long Road to Freedom*. Auckland: Random Century NZ Ltd., 1991.

Zuccotti, Susan. *The Italians and the Holocaust: Persecution, Rescue and Survival*. New York: Basic Books, 1987.

I am indebted to interviews and conversations with the following veterans:

New Zealand
John Abel, Bill Black (recorded by Laurence Lowe), Maurice Cosgrave, Paul Day, Douglas Dymock, Roy Johnston, Jack Lang, Cliff Manson, Pat Moncur, Roy Natusch, Arch Scott, John Senior, Allan Wilson.

I have used manuscripts, letters, diaries, videos regarding the following: Frank Bowes, Laurie Read, Hilary Evans, Tony Jacobs, Ian St George, Ian Millar, Bob Smith, David Jacobs, Frank Gardner, Walter Willis, Clarence Peagram, Stewart Stevenson, David Russell, George London.

Also family members have been most helpful. Among them are: Bob Anderson, John Bowes, Claire Brickell, Owen Craddock, John Crestani, Felicity Day, Catherine Day, Karen Driscoll, Malcolm Evans, Margie Gardner, Judy Gardner, Noreen Jacobs, Karen Holyoake, Beryl Lang, Paul London, Patricia McHugh, Grant Millar, Joan Molloy, Paul (Velio) and Jewel Pianina,

Colin Read, Stephen Sims and Jan von Pein. Thanks also to Marian Nee of the Catholic Church Archives, Auckland, and Jeffery Plowman-Holmes.

Italy
I am grateful for interviews with the following ex-partisans and *staffette*: Luigi Borgarelli, Querino Bullian, Aldo Camponogara, Vittorino Gaspari, Rosetta Gobbo, Gianfranco Ivancich, Bruno Londera, Beppi Marson, Giovanni Nicolli, Gino Panont, Feliciana Petch (née Tizzoni), Bruno Steffè, Italo Ziggiotti.

Many people, among them local historians, surviving helpers and family members, were unfailingly generous with their time and assistance. In particular I thank: Lucia Antonel, Angelo Antonel, Aldo Bierti, Giona Bigotto, Druillio Bigotto, Novella Bigotto, Bruno Bisioli, Nino Bisioli, Bruno Blasigh, Anselmo Borgnolo, Ario Cargnelutti, Benito Ciprian, Severino Dreon, Salvatore Dri, Italico Formentin, Luciano Franzin, Francesco Frattolin, Gino Fraulin, Dario Ghirardelli, Franco Ghirardelli, Suora Giuseppina, Daniele Guglielmi, Giulia Leder, Pierina Leder, Roberto Lucioli, Guido Marchetti, Cav. Secondo Libero Martinis, Giorgio Nascimbene, Gianfranco Parcorigh, Piero Paron, Imelde Rosa Pellegrini, Ugo Perissinotto, Roberto Perosa, Eugenio Pesarini, Cecilia Squillacciotti Pesarini, Don Amelio Pinzano, Franco Pischiutti, Graziano Pizzolitto, Bruno Rossetto, Rossana Rossetto, Flavia Schiff, Bianca Sguazzin, Santina Specogna, Gianni Toniutto, Luigi Toniutto, Maria Varaschin, Costantino Visentin, Anna Zanini.

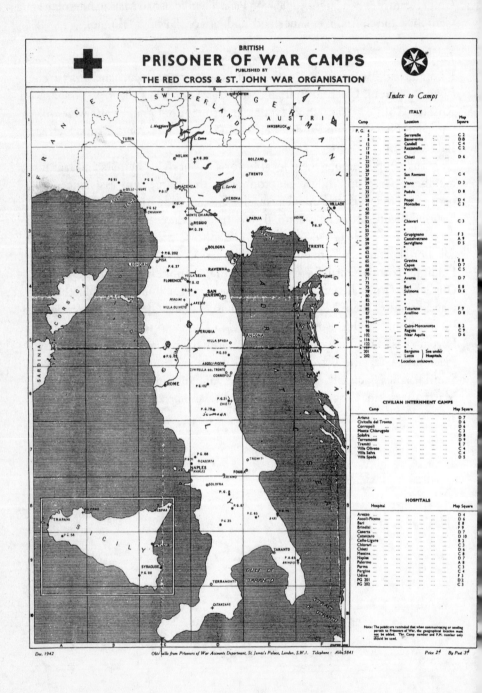

BRITISH
PRISONER OF WAR CAMPS
PUBLISHED BY
THE RED CROSS & ST. JOHN WAR ORGANISATION

Index to Camps

ITALY

Camp	Location	Map Square
P.G. 4	*	
5	Serravalle	C 2
8	Benevento	D 8
12	Candell	C 4
17	Rezzanello	C 2
19	*	
21	Chieti	D 6
22	*	
26	*	
27	San Romano	C 4
28	*	
29	Viano	D 3
33	Pedula	D 8
35	*	
37	*	
38	Poppi	D 4
41	Montalbo	C 3
50	*	
51	*	
54	Chiavari	C 3
55	*	
53	Gruppignano	F 3
58	Castelvetrano	A 9
59	Servigliano	D 5
60	*	
62	*	
65	Gravina	E 8
66	Capua	D 5
68	Vetralli	C 5
70	*	
71	Aversa	D 7
73	*	
75	Bari	E 8
78	Sulmona	D 6
80	*	
82	*	
85	Tuturano	F 9
87	Avellino	D 8
89	*	
95	Cairo-Montenotte	B 2
98	Ragusa	C 9
102	Near Aquila	D 6
116	*	
122	*	
201	Bergamo } See under	
202	Lucca } Hospitals.	
	* Location unknown.	

CIVILIAN INTERNMENT CAMPS

Camp	Map Square
Ariano	D 7
Civitella del Tronto	D 6
Corropoli	D 6
Monte Chiarugolo	C 3
Solofra	D 8
Terramonti	D 9
Tremiti	E 7
Villa Oliveto	C 4
Villa Selva	C 4
Villa Spada	D 5

HOSPITALS

Hospital	Map Square
Arezzo	D 4
Ascoli-Piceno	D 6
Bari	E 8
Brindisi	F 9
Caserta	D 7
Catanzaro	D 10
Celle-Ligure	B 2
Chiavari	C 3
Chieti	D 6
Messina	D 8
Naples	D 7
Palermo	C 8
Parma	C 3
Pergine	C 4
Udine	F 3
PG 201	D 2
PG 202	C 3

Note: The public are reminded that when communicating or sending parcels to Prisoners of War, the geographical location must not be added. The Camp number and P.M. number only should be used.